Hands-on Pipeline as Code with Jenkins

CI/CD Implementation for Mobile, Web, and Hybrid Applications Using Declarative Pipeline in Jenkins

Ankita Patil

Mitesh Soni

www.bpbonline.com

FIRST EDITION 2021

Copyright © BPB Publications, India

ISBN: 978-93-89898-606

Distributors:

BPB PUBLICATIONS
20, Ansari Road, Darya Ganj
New Delhi-110002
Ph: 23254990/23254991

DECCAN AGENCIES
4-3-329, Bank Street,
Hyderabad-500195
Ph: 24756967/24756400

MICRO MEDIA
Shop No. 5, Mahendra Chambers,
150 DN Rd. Next to Capital Cinema,
V.T. (C.S.T.) Station, MUMBAI-400 001
Ph: 22078296/22078297

BPB BOOK CENTRE
376 Old Lajpat Rai Market,
Delhi-110006
Ph: 23861747

To View Complete
BPB Publications Catalogue
Scan the QR Code:

Published by Manish Jain for BPB Publications, 20 Ansari Road, Darya Ganj, New Delhi-110002 and Printed by him at Repro India Ltd, Mumbai

Foreword

Siddharth is currently the Vice President of a consulting leading a DevOps Centre of Excellence practice for a European bank. He is a digital evangelist known for DevOps and cloud transformation primarily for the banking and finance industries. He's an enterprise agile and lean coach focused on improving functional and financial results through the adoption of cultural mindset change. He is also on the board of the expert panel for the Cloud Credential Council (CCC) and the world's first individual to be certified across the complete portfolio of CCC. He has co-authored a whitepaper on global digital skills and writes on multiple topics, in particular about Cloud, DevOps, Agile, Lean, and ITSM. He's a regular industry speaker at global and regional events and conferences. He is also the Global Ambassador for DevOps Institute and DASA Influencer for DevOps and Agile Skill association.

DevOps practices implementation is getting very popular in organizations. Many organizations have realized the benefits of Automation and Culture transformation to gain speed and quality in Agile development. Jenkins is one of the most popular tools to implement DevOps practices using Pipeline as Code and its integration with many tools available in the market. Everything as a Code is a new normal in the Industry and Pipeline as Code is one of the most important pillars of it.

It's a comprehensive book on Jenkins that covers the perspective of the developers and is not limited to any specific technologies; hence, it's useful for Python dev, mobile (both iOS and Android), Flutter, Ionic Cordova, Angular and NodeJS apps, and the traditionally popular Java and .Net ones. The cherry on the cake is the Blue Ocean version of Jenkins and the underlying best practices for any user. The value addition that this book brings in today's world is that it covers the aspect that most of the software engineers missed out on earlier with hands-on exercises. The pictorial diagrams for most of the steps executed by the authors themselves make learning easier for even a novice developer.

'Practice makes a man perfect' is a famous proverb which has been implemented here very nicely by having exercises at the end of each chapter, thus allowing the readers of this book to do recap and do hands-on exercises that have been taught in the given chapter. If the key theme across the book needs to call out it's interesting to see how the Quality aspect is been addressed throughout, which is generally missed out or not emphasized by the dev. Unit testing as a practice or in my words as a habit plays a key role in this book.

As a DevOps consultant myself, it's nice to see the focus of the book on CI/CD for SMEs on various programming languages and not covering more than what can be chewed by the developer community. Rather than being broad, an in-depth knowledge on the skill-sets covered in this book would help the workforce to be ready in the industry.

Though the complete book is useful; however, the chapters that should not be missed out by any reader are *Chapter 1* which talks about the mindset, people, processes, and tools, *Chapter 2* which discusses Blue Ocean as mentioned earlier and *Chapter 11* which discusses how effectively you can work on Jenkins.

I would like to congratulate Mitesh Soni and Ankita Patil for identifying what the individuals want, and at the same time, the business needs, thereby bridging this gap with their knowledge. I am sure the reader will have a good time.

Best Wishes !

—Siddharth Pareek

DevOps has been my passion for years. My interest in DevOps has helped me contribute to various companies' progress by making them understand the role of DevOps in digital transformation thus, driving businesses forward through the adoption of best practices and changing needs. Being a DevOps Thought Leader, Coach, and with over 18 years of industry experience, I have had the opportunity to train the tech leaders on strategic initiatives to evangelize DevOps, shift-left security practices, and cultivate a culture of continuous deliveries, process assurance, and quality.

DevOps combines cultural philosophies, practices, and tools that enhance an organization's ability to deliver applications and services at high velocity. DevOps enables organizations to serve their customers and compete more effectively in the market. Companies in today's world must transform how they build and deliver software to succeed in today's digital landscape.

Digital transformation is gaining momentum, and organizations are continuously chasing excellence for the delivery pipelines as it is a vital part of the pragmatic DevOps practices. Such delivery pipelines are treated as a foundation practice to enable the DevOps journey. Several OTS tools in the market get this done with minimal disruption, but the buck doesn't stop here. It is equally vital to ensure we enable the right set of tools that provide value to the team in the long term, not something full of fancy features that teams may not even use. One of such humble open-source automation servers is Jenkins. It helps automate various dimensions in the SDLC and, at times, it is a preferred choice by open-source enthusiasts. If you are thinking about beginning your DevOps journey and pondering over a CI/CD solution, then Jenkins may be the right choice for you.

This book 'Hands-on Pipeline as Code with Jenkins' covers a good overview of what DevOps is for any relevant stakeholder. It starts with a general introduction to DevOps, which is an excellent insight into the philosophy, giving you an overview of why a company needs DevOps, the benefits, various value streams, and how DevOps creates a delivery continuum via a structured CI/CD pipeline. The authors have done an excellent job identifying several crucial factors on Jenkins as solutions, starting with a nice and crisp overview of the open-source server and an overview requiring a bare minimum knowledge of the solution. The details are specified in a step-by-step approach, which is friendly for most of the target audience. The best part I like about the book is how the various pipelines are covered extensively and crisply, including pipelines for Blue Ocean, Java Apps, Android, iOS, Angular, Node, .NET, Python, Hybrid – you name it! The objectives, easy-to-follow steps, and examples are clearly illustrated, which is undoubtedly a useful read for several readers who always get lost in translation with the overabundance of resources available across the internet like blogs, videos, and tutorials. It gives the reader a holistic perspective on the solution and an opportunity to evaluate various implementations against a series of such identified best practices. The use of real but straightforward examples with screenshots, screen outputs, and logs is commendable.

As a reader, I have experienced my fair share of articles, books, and tutorials. And I must say that sometimes such reads are either written with intricate details or the described examples are not in line with the tune of such reads. This book justifies the title and provides adequate information on Jenkins with clear objectives and a step-by-step approach to enhance your knowledge and provide you with a good source of information.

— *Anshul Lalit (anshul.me)*

Dedicated to

Mummy-Dad, Ayush, Anurag, and Mummy-Papa
—Ankita

Dada, Dadi, Shreyu, Mummy-Papa, Jigi-Nitesh, Priyanka,
Ruby and Mummy-Papa, Mayur, and Vinay Kher
—Mitesh

About the Authors

- **Ankita** is a DevOps evangelist. She is passionate learner and practitioner of Agile and DevOps. As a change agent, she always tries to bring change in an organization to get maximum benefits of DevOps. So, she wants to share her knowledge and make sure IT professionals are trained and empowered to make those changes.

  Ankita has worked on multiple projects and tools for automating the entire software development life. Her approach has always been to develop a solution using different DevOps tools, which would make the development to deployment cycle shorter to deliver software as fast as possible to market. She also has knowledge of the development of Java web applications and also has a lot of experience in Hybrid mobile app development. Her tools/technologies stacks are Jenkins, Azure DevOps, GitHub, Bitbucket, Rundeck, AWS Developer tools, and many more.

  Ankita is a great lover of art and craft. She likes to paint and sketch during her free time while listening to silent old Bollywood music. She likes to watch movies and series.

- **Mitesh** is a DevOps engineer. He is in love with the DevOps culture and concept. Continuous improvement is his motto in life with existing imperfection. Mitesh has worked on multiple DevOps practices implementation initiatives. His primary focus is on the improvement of the existing culture of an organization or a project using Continuous Integration and Continuous Delivery. He believes that attitude and dedication are one of the biggest virtues that can improve the professional as well as personal life! He has good experience in DevOps consulting, and he enjoys talking about DevOps and CULTURE transformation using existing practices and improving them with open source or commercial tools.

  Mitesh always believes that DevOps is a cultural transformation, and it is facilitated by people, processes, and tools. DevOps transformation is a tools agnostic approach. He loves to impart training and share knowledge with the community. He has knowledge of programming, and he is aware of different languages/frameworks/platforms such as Java, Android, iOS, NodeJS, and

Angular. His main objective is to get enough information related to the project in such a way that it helps create an end-to-end automation pipeline.

In his leisure time, he likes to walk in the garden, click photographs, and do cycling. He prefers to spend time in peaceful places. His favourite tools/ services for DevOps practices implementation is Azure DevOps and Jenkins in commercial and open sources categories, respectively.

Mitesh has authored the following books with BPB:
1. **Hands-on Azure DevOps**
2. **Agile, Devops and Cloud Computing with Microsoft Azure**

About the Reviewers

◆ **Vlad Silverman** resides in Silicon Valley and has more than 100 repositories, listed on his GitHub site, showing his use of DevOps tools, like Bash, Jenkins, Git, Docker and others. He had automated build, test, integration and deployment processes for companies, like FICO, Cisco, BofA, Guidewire. Vlad is currently contributing to the Jenkins project.

◆ **Dr. Mark Peters** works for Technica Corporation as Lead Information Assurance/Security Engineer on a US Air Force cyber weapon system program in San Antonio, TX emphasizing DevOps during an Agile transition. During a full US Air Force intelligence career, he worked with various units to integrate and automate intelligence with operational delivery. A cybersecurity expert, he holds multiple industry certifications including a CISSP. The author of the book, "Cashing in on Cyberpower" to analyze 10 years of cyber-attacks from an economic perspective. In his spare time, he reads, thinks, writes, and then speaks and is also a Judo black belt. A DevOps Institute ambassador, he enjoys working with individuals to implement DevSecOps. He remains excited by the potential to incorporate DevOps across multiple industries.

◆ **Palash Purohit** has 5 years of experience in DevOps implementation on various technologies and enterprise scale projects. He worked extensively on CICD process setup and improvements using various processes, technologies and various version control tools, Continuous Integration and Deployment tool suites and Artifact management system. Palash pursued B.E from Medicaps Institute of Technology and Management, Indore. Currently he is working as part of the core DevOps Team for an enterprise scale engagement.

Acknowledgements

- Mummy-Pappa, without your encouragement it would not have been possible for me to be here where I am today. I would never miss a chance to say a 'Big big thank you'.

  Anurag, your presence in my life has positively shaped my life and career. Thank you for being there in my life and supporting me in everything that I want to do and encouraging me to do things which would help me to grow in every aspect of life. You understand me, help me to progress, love me like an idiot, and even take care of me like a small child. Thank you and I love you a lot.

  Also a big thanks to all my friends (Isha, Ashvanee, Siddhartha, Palash and Bhanu) for being there with me in all my ups and downs. Bhavna mam, Shakti sir, Kiran sir and Amit sir thank you for guiding me during start of my career, this learning and growing in professional way is all because of you all.

  Mitesh, my guide and mentor always, thank you for giving me the opportunity to co-author this book with you.

  Last but not least, I would like to thank the BPB Team for giving me the opportunity to write this book for them.

  — Ankita

- Ruby, all that you are, is all that I'll ever need. Thank you for being there. Thank you for inspiring me and pushing me to do the right things always and being there in difficult times. Your presence made my life easier in tough times. Every life has an amazing story. Thank you for being part of one of the BEST stories of my life. You are by far the most amazing, beautiful, loving, kind, and ANGRY woman in the world. I included that last one, so you know that I am being honest☺!

  I would like to thank Masi-Malav, my family members, Daksh-Parul Didi-Amit Jiju, Apoorva-Saurabh, Mayank Bhai and Bhabhi, Navrang, Dharmesh, Akkusss, Nalini and her Family, Anupama-Mihir and Priyanka-Hemant, Rohini, Yohan, Radhika, her parents and Mukund, Ramya-Srivats, Radhika's all cousins, Piyushi, Prajakta – Keep Singing, Priyanka S, Gauri, Mitul, Kanak, Bapu, Vimal, Ashish, Bhavna, Amit R, Vijay, Rinka, Parinda, Arpita and her family, Kim and Yaashi, Jai Jamba, Nitesh, Munal, Jyotiben, Niralee-Khushboo, Rohan C, Mayur, Chintan, Vijay, Nikul, Paresh, Raju, Yogendra, Jayesh and his family, Ramesh and his family, Munni Bhabhi and her family, Jyoti N, Bharti, Chitra Madam, Kittu and family, Aarohi, Poonam Aunty, Uncle, Laukik and Bhabhi, Oracle Team, Deepika, Aniket, Prasanna, Mahendra, Arvind, Dinesh, Viral, Chaitali, My village, school and college friends, and teachers for being there always.

Special thanks to Gowri-Arya, Sourabh Mishra, Sid, Sudeep, Rita-Yashvi, Ajay, Sneha, and Ankita, Palash for always being there.

Ankita, I have always believed that you are my little champion, and you inspire me to work hard. Miles to go!

I would like to thank BPB Team for giving me this opportunity to write this book for them.

—*Mitesh*

Preface

DevOps is a software development practice that focuses on culture change and brings quality and faster time to market in Application Lifecycle Management. DevOps practices implementation is popular in all customer discussions. At times, it is considered as a value add. The combination of people, processes, and tools brings the culture change initiative to reality.

The DevOps pipeline or CI/CD pipeline is a popular word used. What does it mean? The pipeline includes different operations in different environments. Continuous Integration (CI) and Continuous Delivery (CD) are some of the most popular DevOps practices. Continuous Integration involves development, code analysis, unit testing, code coverage calculation, and build activities which are automated using various tools. Continuous Delivery is all about deploying your package into different environments, so that end-users can access it. There are different ways to create a pipeline/orchestration that involves Continuous Integration, Continuous Delivery, Continuous Testing, Continuous Deployment, Continuous Monitoring, and other DevOps practices. Each tool provides different ways to create a pipeline.

In this book, we will discuss Jenkins. Jenkins is an open-source automation tool that offers an easy way to set up a CI/CD pipeline for almost any combination of languages, tools, and source code repositories. The Jenkins project was started in 2004 (originally Hudson). Initially, Jenkins was more popular for Continuous Integration, but after the release of Jenkins 2.0, Jenkins is utilized to automate and orchestrate the entire Application Management Lifecycle. The Jenkins community offers more than 1,500 plugins that empower Jenkins users to create orchestration by integrating almost all popular tools in different categories.

A pipeline is the most talked about concept that refers to the groups of stages or events or jobs that are connected in a specific sequence with sequential or parallel execution flow based on the use case. There are different ways to create a pipeline in Jenkins. In this book, we will create the Declarative Pipeline and also discuss the Multibranch pipeline that facilitates to create different Jenkinsfiles for different branches in the code repository. Jenkins will automatically discover branches where the Jenkinsfile is available. The Jenkinsfile contains the scripted or declarative pipeline. It is managed in Version Control, and hence, it is easy to maintain. Blue Ocean provides pipeline visualization and pipeline editor to create the Declarative pipeline quickly.

The main objective of this book is to provide an easy path for beginners who want to create the Declarative Pipeline for programming languages such as Java, Android, iOS, AngularJS, NodeJS, Flutter, Ionic Cordova, and DotNet. Each chapter based on a specific programming language focuses on a Pipeline that includes Static Code Analysis using SonarQube or Lint tools, Unit test execution, calculating code coverage, publishing unit tests and code coverage in uniform reports, verifying the quality of code coverage with Quality Gate, creating a build/package, and distributing a package to a specific environment based on the type of programming languages. You will learn the following in the 11 chapters of this book:

Chapter 1, introduces all the areas which encompass the field of DevOps practices. It discusses the definition of DevOps, DevOps history, benefits of DevOps culture, DevOps and Value Streams, DevOps Practices (objective, benefits, challenges, tools, best practices, and outcomes), Continuous Planning, Continuous Code Inspection, Continuous Integration (CI), Cloud Computing and Containers, Continuous Delivery and Continuous Deployment, Continuous Testing, Continuous Monitoring, Continuous Feedback, Continuous Improvements / Innovations, and Measurements. This chapter focuses on Cognitive biases in specific sections and how DevOps practices implementation helps to address it. It also emphasises on how the Nudge theory can help the culture transformation process.

Chapter 2, introduces you to Jenkins 2.X, history of Jenkins, pre-requisites to install Jenkins, how to run Jenkins, different Pipeline types such as Build pipeline, Scripted pipeline, Declarative pipeline, and Blue Ocean.

Chapter 3, discusses how to implement Continuous Integration and Continuous Delivery for a sample Java application. This chapter provides step-by-step instructions to import code from the repository, sonarqube integration, create Azure App Services – Platform as a Service to host Java Web Applications, Unit Tests execution and Code coverage, Static Code Analysis (SCA) using SonarQube, build a wAR or package file, upload a package file to Artifactory, download a package from Nexus and Artifactory, deploy to the Azure App Services Dev Environment, promotion (Approval) request to deploy to the QA environment, and rollback.

Chapter 4, discusses how to implement Continuous Integration and Continuous Delivery for an Android Application using Pipeline as Code in Jenkins. This chapter provides step-by-step instructions to create a multi-stage pipeline for an Android App, how to import a repository, how to perform Lint Analysis for an

Android application, execute Unit tests, calculate Code coverage, verify build quality, create an APK file, and configure Continuous Delivery by deploying the Package/APK to the App Center.

Chapter 5, discusses how to implement Continuous Integration and Continuous Delivery for an iOS Application using a declarative pipeline in Jenkins. The chapter covers step-by-step instructions to create a multi-stage pipeline for the iOS App to configure Continuous Integration, understand how to perform Lint Analysis for an iOS application, how to execute Unit tests and calculate Code coverage, verify build quality based on Unit test coverage, to create an IPA file and deploy it to the App Center.

Chapter 6, covers how to implement Continuous Integration and Continuous Delivery for an Angular Application using Pipeline as Code in Jenkins. It covers step-by-step instructions for a multi-stage pipeline that includes Junit and Cobertura configuration in karma.conf.js, Lint, Unit tests, and Code Coverage configuration in Package.json, Unit Tests and Code Coverage calculation, end-to-end test execution, and NPM Audit, verify build Quality, deploy an Angular application to a docker container, and deploy an Angular application to Azure Kubernetes Services (AKS).

Chapter 7, discusses how to implement Continuous Integration and Continuous Delivery for a Node.js Application using a Declarative pipeline in Jenkins. It also covers how to implement Continuous Integration and Continuous Delivery for the Node.js Application. It includes step-by-step instructions to create a multi-stage pipeline for the NodeJS Express App with Lint, Unit tests, and Code Coverage configuration in Package.json, how to configure Unit Tests and Code Coverage using Jest, configure build Quality plugin, archive files, and deploy Node.js Express Web App to Azure App Services. In the other section, it includes step-by-step instructions to create a multi-stage pipeline for the NodeJS Application with Lint, Unit tests, and Code Coverage configuration in Package.json, a configuration of Unit tests and Code coverage using Mocha, configuration of build Quality plugin using Pipeline as Code.

Chapter 8, discusses how to implement Continuous Integration and Continuous Delivery for Hybrid Mobile Apps developed in Ionic Cordova and Flutter using Pipeline as Code in Jenkins. It covers a multi-stage pipeline for Hybrid Mobile applications for tasks such as code analysis, Unit test execution and Code coverage, builds quality check, and distributes app package to App Center.

Chapter 9, discusses how to implement Continuous Integration and Continuous Delivery for a Python Application using Pipeline as Code in Jenkins. It covers a multi-stage pipeline for a Python application for tasks such as Static Code Analysis (SCA) using SonarQube, Unit test execution and Code coverage, and build quality check.

Chapter 10, discusses how to implement Continuous Integration and Continuous Delivery for a DotNet application using Pipeline as Code in Jenkins. It covers a multi-stage pipeline for a DotNet application for tasks such as Static Code Analysis (SCA) using SonarQube, Unit test execution and Code coverage, and build quality check.

Chapter 11, covers best practices to implement DevOps Practices using Jenkins.

Downloading the coloured images:

Please follow the link to download the
Coloured Images of the book:

https://rebrand.ly/90v3r

Errata

We take immense pride in our work at BPB Publications and follow best practices to ensure the accuracy of our content to provide with an indulging reading experience to our subscribers. Our readers are our mirrors, and we use their inputs to reflect and improve upon human errors, if any, that may have occurred during the publishing processes involved. To let us maintain the quality and help us reach out to any readers who might be having difficulties due to any unforeseen errors, please write to us at :

errata@bpbonline.com

Your support, suggestions and feedbacks are highly appreciated by the BPB Publications' Family.

Did you know that BPB offers eBook versions of every book published, with PDF and ePub files available? You can upgrade to the eBook version at www.bpbonline.com and as a print book customer, you are entitled to a discount on the eBook copy. Get in touch with us at :

business@bpbonline.com for more details.

At **www.bpbonline.com**, you can also read a collection of free technical articles, sign up for a range of free newsletters, and receive exclusive discounts and offers on BPB books and eBooks.

BPB is searching for authors like you

If you're interested in becoming an author for BPB, please visit **www.bpbonline.com** and apply today. We have worked with thousands of developers and tech professionals, just like you, to help them share their insight with the global tech community. You can make a general application, apply for a specific hot topic that we are recruiting an author for, or submit your own idea.

The code bundle for the book is also hosted on GitHub at **https://github.com/bpbpublications/Hands-on-Pipeline-as-Code-with-Jenkins**. In case there's an update to the code, it will be updated on the existing GitHub repository.

We also have other code bundles from our rich catalog of books and videos available at **https://github.com/bpbpublications**. Check them out!

PIRACY

If you come across any illegal copies of our works in any form on the internet, we would be grateful if you would provide us with the location address or website name. Please contact us at **business@bpbonline.com** with a link to the material.

If you are interested in becoming an author

If there is a topic that you have expertise in, and you are interested in either writing or contributing to a book, please visit **www.bpbonline.com**.

REVIEWS

Please leave a review. Once you have read and used this book, why not leave a review on the site that you purchased it from? Potential readers can then see and use your unbiased opinion to make purchase decisions, we at BPB can understand what you think about our products, and our authors can see your feedback on their book. Thank you!

For more information about BPB, please visit **www.bpbonline.com**.

Table of Contents

CHAPTER 1
Introducing DevOps

> **"There is always room for improvement."**
>
> *— Anonymous*

In the waterfall model, all activities in application lifecycle phases are implemented serially and only once! Why do you need an extensive documentation? Isn't it a pain? No testing/verification and validation are performed until an application is ready. Requirements change over time and because of that, all the work that is documented needs to be changed! Expectations change and hence the application changes over time based on the market, technical evolution, and other factors such as demands! Failures are detected too late and issues come at a time that is no point of return! In such a scenario, the Happy Team becomes a MYTH!

To deal with the known issues of the traditional development approach, Agile development methods came into the picture. Integrative and incremental development of features brings customer feedback into the development. Customers know what they are going to get after each iteration. It is not an approach where things are considered serially. A lot of communication and effective collaboration (arguably) takes place between stakeholders to understand the requirements or explain expectations. All stakeholders are continuously involved. To meet the speed of the incremental and iterative model, automation is necessary to speed up things concerning application lifecycle management activities. Here comes the challenge;

manual processes bring delay in such an incremental and iterative approach. With agile, all issues and inefficiencies are magnified like never before.

The question is how to automate? Can we start using some tools directly that automates application lifecycle management activities? Is there something more to automation than just tools?

The answer is Yes!

DevOps, Continuous Practices, or DevOps Practices! DevOps is a culture transformation! It helps to bring about change and adopt a change smoothly. We will understand how issues and inefficiencies are magnified and how DevOps practices implementation help in the digital transformation or cultural transformation.

Structure

In this chapter, we will discuss the following topics:

- What is DevOps?
- Benefits of DevOps
- DevOps and Value Streams
- DevOps practices implementation using tools
    - o   Continuous Code Inspection
    - o   Continuous Integration (CI)
    - o   Cloud computing and containers
    - o   Artifact management
    - o   Continuous delivery
    - o   Continuous testing
    - o   Continuous deployment
- Conclusion
- Questions and exercises

Objectives

After studying this unit, you should be able to:

- Understand the concept of DevOps
- Discuss the types of Continuous practices such as Continuous Integration and Continuous Delivery
- Understand the importance of the mindsets of people, processes, and tools
- Discuss the different DevOps practices

What is DevOps?

DevOps is a disruptive shift in how to manage the mindsets of people, way of working, and the Application Lifecycle Management Cycle. It is a process of transforming culture rather than implementing tools or a tool-specific approach. DevOps is all about culture transformation using a combination of people, processes, and tools. DevOps is known to be associated with practices such as continuous code inspections, continuous integration (CI), continuous delivery (CD), continuous testing, continuous monitoring, continuous feedback, continuous improvement, and continuous innovation. Now, DevOps practices also accommodate Infrastructure Provisioning in the cloud, Infrastructure as a Code, Configuration Management, and Pipeline as Code too. In this chapter, we will see what the DevOps culture is, how vision, people, processes, and tools help in culture transformation, and the benefits of implementation of continuous practices. Before going ahead with defining DevOps, let's have a quick look at DevOps history.

DevOps history

This flow is based on my exploration and experience. That's how I realized how we started our DevOps culture transformation:

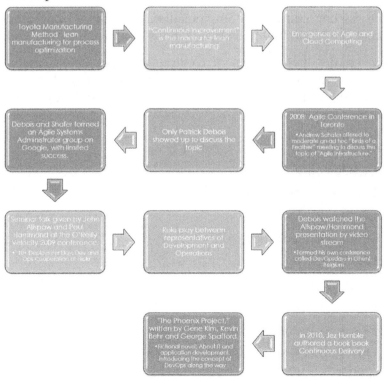

Figure 1.1: *DevOps history*

Now, let's define DevOps. It is a part of the quality-related discussion in organizations.

In simple language, DevOps is all about effective collaboration and communication between different stakeholders such as development, operations, quality, and security teams for better quality, and faster time to market. There are no set of guidelines or methodologies available for DevOps practices implementation:

Let's first understand the responsibilities of the Dev and Ops teams before defining DevOps:

Dev	Ops
• Write robust applications using design patterns and best practices	• Automated provisioning and de-provisioning of environments
• Maintain code quality and standards	• Scaling up/down, in/out
• Write practical unit tests and utilize active test-driven development	• Manage Infrastructure as a Code (**IaC**) to maintain version and visibility
• Verifying behavior of an application	• Configuration management, monitoring and measurements

Table 1.1: Dev and Ops

Based on the existing culture, the implementation roadmap may differ from one organization to another as **NO** two organizations can have the same culture.

DevOps is a culture that consists of continuous practices that help to achieve faster time to market for an application with the highest quality by Continuous Improvement and Continuous Innovation by involving people, processes, and tools.

NOTE

What is DevOps not?
- DevOps is not a methodology.
- DevOps is not a tool.
- DevOps is not a technology.
- DevOps is not a framework.
- DevOps is not a process.
- DevOps is not scripting.
- DevOps is not automation only.
- DevOps is not a set of design patterns where problems and solutions are well defined.

The organization culture can be affected by cognitive biases as it is all about changing culture, and hence, resistance is inevitable. In this chapter, we will take a look at some cognitive biases and their solutions at some intervals with no specific context.

DevOps practices implementation needs visibility. It requires a vision. It also requires transparency and acceptance of the AS-IS scenario. Hence, it is important to assess the ground situation in the organization and derive a roadmap for effective adoption of the roadmap of this cultural transformation journey.

DevOps transformation depends on the following three major aspects:

- People
- Processes
- Tools

Let's understand each aspect in more detail.

People

DevOps is all about people, processes, and tools. It is important to note that people still have a high priority. People have a different notion about what DevOps is, but some are not even aware of it. People are tightly coupled with the existing culture and hence, transformation is difficult.

Each organization has a different culture and different set of practices exists, and hence, it is challenging to change things until people change their attitude and mindset.

Here are the following sets of people:

- People who have a vision about change
- People who lead the change
- People who welcome change
- People who drive the change
- People who resist change
- People who are confused regarding the change

If people resist and if they are not ready for the change, then it is very easy to predict the failure of the culture transformation initiative as people drive the change and not tools. From management to development/scrum team's level, all stakeholders must be ready for the culture transformation initiative for better quality and speed in the lifecycle. It is important to have transparency in the transformation exercise as it helps to understand where implementation needs improvement and what we are doing right in the DevOps maturity model.

But, how to inspire change? Is there any formula that can assist in the culture transformation initiative? Yes!

The formula for change provides a space to assess the relative strengths affecting the success possibilities of change initiatives concerning the culture transformation:

$$D * V * F > R$$

The formula for change was created by *David Gleicher* and refined by *Kathie Dannemiller* later. Let's try to understand this formula in the context of DevOps:

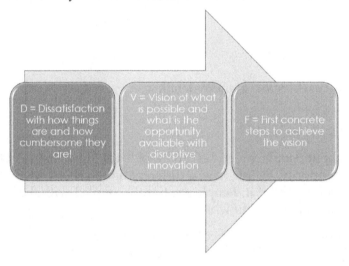

Figure 1.2: The formula for change

TIP

Declare war on existing issues.

Business is an exciting battle with limited time, considering the competitive market and evolution. Hence, it is essential to target root causes that are holding the organization back. It is important to assess existing issues first. Once the issues are identified, then proper solutions can be thought through:

- Manual processes
- Repetitive work
- Rigidness of processes
- No flexibility
- Huge capital expenditure
- No visibility

Let's look at the dissatisfaction felt by people due to the existing culture and inefficient processes. What are the existing pain points or problems faced by project teams or organizations with existing cultures? The answer is manual and inefficient processes, bureaucracy, and so on.

The second aspect is the vision. What is the vision and benefits organization/ business unit/project teams aim to achieve with the culture transformation?

Answer: Better quality of product, faster time to market, and continuous improvements, and so on.

The third aspect is the concrete steps needed to achieve the vision. How to achieve the vision? Which best practices or DevOps practices implementation will accelerate the culture transformation?

Answer: Phase-wise implementation of Continuous Practices.

If the product of these three factors ($D * V * F$) is greater than $R = Resistance$, then change is possible. If any of the factors is absent (zero) or low while D, V, and F are multiplied, then the multiplication will be zero or low, and therefore, it may not overcome the resistance.

Change is the mindset of the organization culture which is not impossible to achieve, but it is not easy to achieve as well. The reason behind these difficulties lies in the subjective realities created by people and sometimes it leads to the situations that are not considered rational. Let's see some of the cognitive biases because of which people resist change in the organization and how DevOps practices helps to fix it.

Cognitive bias	Resistance	Solution
Bandwagon effect	The tendency to do (or believe) things because many other people do (or believe) the same. Everyone is doing DevOps and that's why organizations want DevOps.	It is better to have the DevOps assessment framework and measurements in place to find out the AS-IS scenario and benefits that can be achieved using DevOps practices.
Anchoring or focalism	The tendency to rely too heavily on existing practices while making decisions, not to integrate feedback frequently, and learn from lessons to improve practices to improve the existing organizational culture.	Create a chart of things that went well and things that went wrong, introspect in a retrospective meeting and decide action items to improve, and create a plan to integrate action items in the coming sprints based on priorities.
Ostrich effect	Ignoring an evident but not so practical traditional approach and ignoring better approaches.	Use the vision and first steps of change formula to convince people and change mindsets.

Status quo bias	The tendency to like things to stay relatively the same and not to adopt new practices even though they are useful and in trends.	Adopt DevOps practices in a phase-wise manner and strive for continuous improvements.
Availability cascade (Anti-Pattern)	Repeat something long enough and it will become true.	In the case of DevOps practices implementation, this is true in the context. The more you repeat the process of automation, the more you gain confidence, and the more you realize benefits.
Default effect	Project teams complain about work overload and hence not willing to implement DevOps practices.	If DevOps practices implementation is considered as a choice between several options, the tendency to favor the default one helps in convincing the teams. It also applies to tools that are going to be utilized in automation.
Law of the instrument	An over-reliance on a familiar tool or methods of existing practices, ignoring or under-valuing alternative DevOps practices which are more useful in terms of faster time to market and quality.	It is essential to have a vision for a cultural change and go ahead with it by using an assessment framework or maturity model.
Empathy gap	In cultivating the DevOps culture, the tendency to underestimate the influence or strength of feelings, in either oneself or others, is a roadblock. Even if it is a resistance in practice implementation, that has to be taken seriously and addressed.	Patience and pilot implementation with improvement numbers helps to convince people.
Mere exposure effect	The tendency to express undue liking for traditional practices merely because of familiarity with them and ignoring the continuous practices of the DevOps culture.	It is essential to find bottlenecks and improve existing practices in the application lifecycle management. Find the areas of dissatisfaction and implement the first steps to convince people.

Exaggerated expectation	The tendency to expect or predict more extreme outcomes from automation or DevOps practices implementation than those outcomes that happen. It disappoints people and the growth stops.	It is better to keep realistic expectations, learn from failures, and improve. Hence, phase-wise implementation matters.
Functional fixedness	Existing culture in terms of processes and technology limits a person to using an object only in the way it is traditionally used.	It is essential to find bottlenecks and improve existing practices in the application lifecycle management. Find the areas of dissatisfaction and implement the first steps to convince people.
Neglect of probability	The tendency to completely disregard the probability of failures of DevOps practices implementation due to cultural differences when deciding under uncertainty.	Be realistic, measure the change, improve, and innovate continuously.
Optimism bias	The tendency to be over-optimistic, overestimating favorable, and pleasing outcomes.	Be realistic, measure the change, improve, and innovate continuously. Not all projects are fit for DevOps practices implementation.
Ambiguity effect	The tendency to avoid options regarding the automated approach and continuous practices implementation for which the probability of a favorable outcome is unknown.	Phase-wise implementation based on the maturity model, realize the benefits, and go for the next phase.
Outcome bias	The tendency to judge a decision by its eventual outcome instead of being based on the quality of the decision at the time it was made.	It is essential to implement continuous practices phase-wise, realize the benefits, and then implement another practice.
Curse of knowledge	When better-informed DevOps Evangelists find it extremely difficult to think about problems from the perspective of project teams or development teams.	The simple answer here is to communicate and collaborate.

Automation bias	The tendency to depend excessively on automated systems without verification and improvements based on learning which can lead to erroneous automated information overriding correct decisions.	Try -> Analyze -> Revise -> Try Again should be the cycle the Scrum team needs to focus on. Even with automation, it is essential to analyze or monitor the behavior of existing processes. continuous monitoring, continuous improvements, and continuous innovations helps to improve the organization culture
Declinism bias	Often the predisposition to view the past favorably and future negatively is a common practice when any culture is going to take place. It is a game of patience.	Phase-wise implementation of continuous practices brings faster outcomes and productivity gains. Hence, people realize the value of change and that triggers the mindset change!

Table 1.2: Cognitive biases

So, how to overcome resistance in phases? The following is the typical path that is taken by organizations:

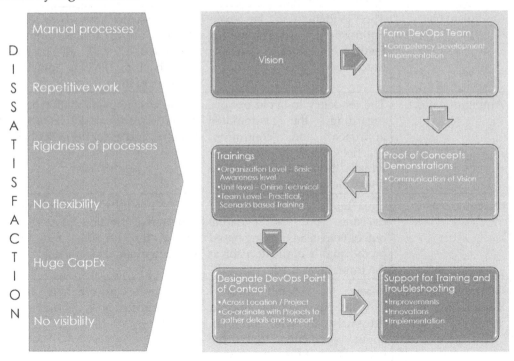

Figure 1.3: Culture Transformation - Vision

TIP

Collaboration and communication is important.

Take command and control but don't be too authoritarian and not too weak in the culture transformation process:

- Create a chain of command - Delegate responsibilities - Become a leader and not the boss.
- Identify people who are willing to change and are a source of knowledge that helps implantation of automation in the organization, rely on them but be open and firm towards the main goal.
- Divided leadership is a sure way towards failure - All stakeholders have to be on board for DevOps practices implementation.
- Ensure you get information from all the stakeholders.
- Communication and collaboration are vital to form strategy – improvement and evolvement is a key.

Organization-wide DevOps practices implementation is tricky. Big bang implementation doesn't work. It creates chaos. The best way to adopt this culture change is the phase-wise implementation of or phase-wise adoption of different practices based on the confidence and maturity of people, processes, and tools.

In the next section, we will discuss people and processes.

People and processes

Let's drill down a bit more on the mindset change and see how it can be done more effectively? The assessment framework, maturity model, frameworks, and processes help to fix resistance due to culture change. Effective processes can help to boost the culture transformation initiative to the next level. It is important to standardize processes and convince different stakeholders to strive for quality and speed.

Set processes for important quality gates before the application goes into a production environment. Make some quality gates mandatory and some in phase-wise implementation. It is important to understand the mindset of people while setting up processes. We can't expect the development to fix all the code quality-related issues in one go. The team must be given a chance to fix issues based on criticality level and increase the criteria overtime to the team that doesn't burn out. It is important to repeat any change exercise multiple times so teams become confident and realize benefits. This helps to gain confidence in new processes.

Another important aspect is to set certain practices or processes as default, and it has to be fulfilled in DevOps practices implementation to move ahead in the DevOps transformation initiative. The DevOps Maturity model helps in such a scenario. We will discuss the Maturity model later in this chapter.

Is there any proof or documented framework or theories for a mindset change?

Yes, there are many theories and concepts available that can be utilized for a mindset change in the organization. However, one of the most suitable theories is the nudge theory. The Nudge theory is all about nudging people and making changes in policies and implement things that are beneficial in the long term. Nudges are small changes in the current behavior which creates long-term beneficial effects.

NOTE

Richard Thaler was awarded the Nobel economics prize for his contributions to behavioral economics in 2017. He is known as the Father of the nudge theory. In 2008, *Richard Thaler* and *Cass Sunstein* authored the book *Nudge: Improving Decisions About Health, Wealth, and Happiness*. It brought the nudge theory to prominence. Nudges are not about mandating something.

Example: Putting an apple at eye level is considered as a nudge. Banning fast food is not considered as a nudge.

The DevOps team has to be a nudge unit to change the culture in the organization in a way that changes people's mindset and behavior in a way without forcing them any options or significantly changing their economic incentives.

TIP

Calm to transform culture – it takes time. Circumstances don't make a champion; they reveal her! Don't lose heart and balance during chaos in the beginning:

- Do not get frustrated by the rigidness of people when you try to make a change in the organization.
- Maintain calm and presence of mind, and do not let yourself be intimidated by the rigidness of people.
- Do not panic if culture transformation efforts fail; focus on what you want to achieve.
- Make decisions quickly to improve existing practices.
- Rely only on yourself, minimize reliance on others but remember collaboration and communication is key to success in the long term.

Nudges should be small changes in the overall culture that are easy and inexpensive to implement. Many types of nudges can help to cultivate the DevOps culture in an organization. Let's see how different types of nudges help in DevOps practices implementation:

Default nudge

- It is an effective way to influence behavior in the organization for DevOps practices implementation.
- Keep DevOps practices implementation as a *'default'* if it is not opted out with valid reasons.
  - o Research and experimental studies show that making an option a default increases the chance of them to be selected and performed; this is called the default effect.
- Keeping DevOps practices implementation as default is an essential example of nudges or soft paternalist policy.

The social proof nudge

- It is easy to convince customers and project teams by showcasing DevOps practices implementation by other teams and the benefits they have achieved.
  - o Everyone wants to adopt new and efficient things and by providing proof of successful execution of DevOps practices implementation, it is easy to convince different stakeholders.
- By demonstrating tools, processes, and frameworks, we can nudge others to change the mindset and go for tools as well to implement DevOps practices.

Numerical anchors nudge

- Measurement metrics with numbers can help to nudge stakeholders or teams to change the mindset.
  - o Example: Before DevOps practices implementation, deployment used to take 30 minutes while after DevOps practices implementation, it takes 5 minutes.
- The cumulative calculation becomes huge, and teams understand gain in terms of time and productivity.

Option restriction nudge

- Options restriction works better than giving them an option on use any tool you like and any DevOps practices which are feasible. It creates confusion and delays.
  - o Keep specific options in terms of DevOps practices implementation such as implement CI.
  - o Keep all critical and major bugs in the solved state before deployment.
  - o Use open-source tools for automation, use Jenkins or Azure DevOps for CI/CD automation.

Competition nudge

- One of the essential nudges in the business unit or an organization is competition nudge.

- Spread the word that specific project or unit is utilizing DevOps practices and managing productivity gains.
- It encourages other teams and units in the organization to compete and incorporate DevOps practices in their existing culture.

Table 1.3: Nudges

TIP

Create a sense of urgency. When there are only options to improve due to existing issues, fight harder for culture transformation. There is nothing to lose if things are not improving with the existing culture:

- Do not wait to be ready - Use a phase-wise implementation approach for culture transformation.
- Act as if it is the only approach that can improve existing practices.
- Stay restless and be out of your comfort zone to change the mindset of people and seek change in processes.

In the next section, we will discuss the role of tools in the culture transformation.

Tools

Let's repeat this statement 100 times: DevOps is a culture. DevOps succeeds in an environment that is Tools Agnostic. Here are some of the evaluation criteria when we want to select tools to implement DevOps practices: ease of use, learning curve, distributed architecture, extensibility using plugins, features based on technology evolution, compatibility with existing culture, and future roadmap.

All tools provide more or less similar kind of features and functionality. It is all up to the organization and existing culture of an organization to make sure how the tool fits in the requirements. Nowadays, all tools provide integration with popular tools available in the market with the use of plugins or extensions.

TIP

Pick your battles based on the existing skillset. Leverage your existing DevOps skillset and to target for improvements, use open source tools and visualize larger picture on how the strategies can be used for commercial tools:

- Do not rely on technology and tools, rely on your knowledge - DevOps is a tool agnostic approach for culture transformation.
- Take one step at a time - Agile approach in DevOps practices implementation.

- Learn to say no if demands don't fit in the current roadmap - example, usage of Containers and Kubernetes for resource management while the team is still working on Continuous Integration for all the projects available in the organization or business unit.

- Know your limits – The COE team has a limited number of people. Based on the existing skillset, we need to decide what work we can accomplish.

We have understood DevOps and its three important aspects as of now. Let's take a look at some of the benefits.

Benefits of DevOps

Let's understand business and technical benefits realized by multiple organizations after culture transformation is achieved using DevOps practices:

Business benefits	Technical benefits
• Improved communication and collaboration between teams • Happy people • Faster time to market • Quality releases • Productivity gains • Transparency in process execution • Measurement of achievements, for example, improvement in deployment time • Agile teams • Reliability and reusability	• Early detection of failures • High availability • Stable and consistent environment • Efficient utilization of resources • **Easy rollback:** Enhanced recovery time • Single-click deployment • Continuous deployment • Monitoring • Cross skilling

Table 1.4: Business and Technical Benefits

DevOps practices help to improve activities that are blocking the flow of product from development to deployment. It is important to identify bottlenecks in the entire value stream and fix them using culture transformation activities and automation. We need to identify and assess the existing situation; we need to find bottlenecks and we should try to fix them. Value Stream Mapping (VSM) comes to rescue us in such a situation.

VSM is one of the most talked about topics in DevOps practices implementation in recent days. We will discuss Value Streams and its related aspects in the next section.

DevOps and Value Streams

High quality with speed is a need of the hour. To maintain pace with the organization's culture transformation with technology evolution and market trends, Agile and DevOps are getting popular in organizations. Both help to increase communication and collaboration between stakeholders. Agile and DevOps introduces automation as well! Let's understand Value Stream and Valsu Stream Mapping.

- **Value Stream:** It describes the flow of activities carried out by the development team (in the context of DevOps) to deliver values from ideas to outcomes. It means that it is important to have complete visibility in the end-to-end activities that are involved in the application lifecycle. That is called Value Stream Mapping.

- **Value Stream Mapping:** It allows stakeholders to find AS-IS situations, analyze the AS-IS situation concerning DevOps practices implementation or automation or application lifecycle management. VSM is used to illustrate, analyze, and improve the steps involved in the delivery of an outcome to customers.

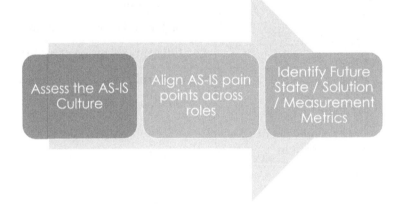

Figure 1.4: Value Stream Mapping

It also includes the following activities:

- Vision for a future state (DevOps Maturity Model can help here):
- Start with proof of concept
- Eliminate Waste – Find bottlenecks (Automated approach in the application lifecycle management using tools)
- Priorities work (phase-wise implementation of continuous practices)
- Identify boundaries and limitations
- Identify improvement items

- Insights into improvements (measurements and metrics)
- While continuous improvement is the ultimate goal, but we need to be realistic considering the use case

Value Stream Mapping can come in to a picture where repeatable steps exist with manual activities. Yes, Agile and DevOps practices contain repeatable steps or iterations, and hence, VSM becomes important in DevOps practices implementation as well as culture transformation activity.

DevOps is a culture where stakeholders are responsible for end-to-end activities involved from development to delivery. It is a continuous cross-functional approach that has its roots in Agile. VSM highlights the most important things for organizations to improve the AS-IS situation and eliminate waste. It helps to prioritize the work and at times, it indicates phases of implementation to build trust in DevOps practices. Let's understand how DevOps practices or Continuous practices help to achieve the goal - Phase-wise implementation or to eliminate waste.

The culture transformation initiative needs assessment and the DevOps maturity model to excel. Assessment is an exercise with a larger scope and meant for assessing organization-wide practices to verify readiness for culture transformation using DevOps practices implementation. We will discuss the DevOps Readiness Assessment Framework and Maturity Model in brief in the next section.

DevOps assessment and maturity model

Culture transformation requires assessment of existing culture and practices, guidelines, implementations of DevOps practices, and measurement of success.

Assessment framework

DevOps assessment helps to build a case in front of the top management for culture transformation. It is essential to consider the DevOps transformation as a journey and Continuous Process rather than a one-time effort. Hence, it is essential to assess the AS-IS scenario of an organization or business unit or a project and lead the culture transformation approach accordingly. DevOps is a holistic approach to transforming the existing culture of an organization using disruptive innovations and new practices by adopting the Automation First approach. The DevOps assessment framework will help to find issues and suggest recommendations accordingly.

Maturity model

The DevOps maturity model indicates where you are in terms of a defined maturity model at the start of the journey. The main objective of the maturity model is to understand what to achieve and what is acceptable in the DevOps transformation process. It presents an end-to-end picture of culture transformation. The maturity model indicates where an organization is in terms of the DevOps transformation, where an organization can be to improve quality and increase faster time to market, and where an organization will be when the DevOps transformation process is in the mature stage!

It is essential to decide the minimum level of maturity all projects should achieve and what can be the best-case scenario.

NOTE

Chapter 2: DevOps Assessment – Measure the 'AS-IS' Maturity in book Hands-on Azure DevOps covers detailed information on DevOps Readiness Assessment.

- Categories
- Questions and answers
- Charts
- Information gathering
- Workshop
- Assessment report
- Vision
- AS-IS scenario – significant issues
- Assessment results
- Origins of existing issues
- DevOps practices adoption recommendations
- Maturity model

DevOps practices implementation

Continuous practices play an important role in culture transformation. The following Figure indicates some if not all, Continuous Practices:

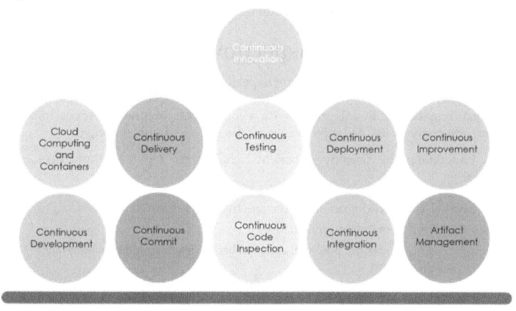

Figure 1.5: *Continuous Practices*

What are the activities and operations involved in different DevOps practices at a high level? Let's understand the preceding Continuous Practices that we are going to cover in this book using the Jenkins Pipeline.

TIP

Showcase benefits – case studies

Convince people that DevOps will help them after assessment. Make the stakeholders think that they will succeed, bluff if needed. Stakeholders will be happy if they will be convinced about the benefits:

- Convince people wisely based on past experiences and case studies and mapping them with the technology available to come to the conclusion.

- Showcase capabilities of the DevOps CoE Team by creating or demonstrating PoCs of Continuous Integration and Continuous Delivery.

- Threatening people don't work in culture transformation – collaboration and communication is important.

Continuous practices implementation is the best in a phase-wise implementation as prioritized by VSM or Assessment workshop. It helps to understand the benefits of automation and make the entire process stable based on continuous learning!

Let's start our small journey to understand continuous practices in brief. In the next section, we will discuss Continuous Code Inspection.

Continuous Code Inspection

Continuous code inspection allows you to perform static code analysis and highlight bugs, vulnerabilities, and other code issues related to standards. Quality profiles and quality gates can be integrated with a continuous integration server. In short, **static code analysis (SCA)** helps to analyze the code without running it.

Let's understand the objectives, benefits, challenges, tools, best practices, and outcomes:

Objectives	The following are the main objectives to perform static code analysis: • To maintain code quality • To identify potential code quality issues during the development phase • To cultivate the habit to write better quality of code with continuous improvement • To programming errors, finding bugs, or ensuring conformance to coding guidelines
Benefits	The following are the benefits of implementing continuous code inspection practice in the organization: • SCA Tools are open-source, affordable or available with SDKs • Automated code analysis • Repeatable • Details analysis on the AS-IS scenario of code • Customizable • No human intervention except initial configuration for code analysis • Huge rule set and efficient scanning of a large codebase

Challenges	The following are some of the challenges faced by an organization while implementing continuous code inspection. • To integrate the code using development tools to get the results as and when code is written • To cultivate the mindset to avoid the issues in the code that have already occurred in past code inspections • To develop a habit to write code that matches industry and technical standards • To fix the benchmark for code quality in different programming languages and different domains
Tools	The following is the list of tools related to continuous code inspection: • SonarQube • Android Lint • SwiftLint • Checkstyle
Best Practices	The following are some of the best practices related to continuous code inspection: • Code reviews, pair programming • Static code analysis • Create rules based on organization culture • Customize rule set based on the culture of an organization • Project-wise or programming language-wise profiles • Configure code coverage • Integrate with the CI tool • Quality gate configuration within the CI tool • Schedule SCA daily to find all issues and configure. Notifications

Outcome	The following are the outcomes or artifacts after continuous integration takes place in general:
	
	• Code analysis result
	
	  o Priority/category-based bugs – code issues, security vulnerabilities
	
	  o Maintainability related issues
	
	  o Quality gate results

Table 1.5: Continuous Code Inspection

It is important to fix code analysis issues based on category wise. All fixes at once approach may demoralize the development team.

Let's understand some of the features provided by SonarQube:

- 20+ programming languages: C#, CSS, Flex, Java, JavaScript, PHP, Python, SCSS, TypeScript, HTML, XML, and so on.
- Detects bugs, security vulnerability, and code smells (Maintainability).
- Quality gate to enforce a code quality practice.
- Built-in integrations are provided for MSBuild, Maven, Gradle, Ant, and Makefiles.
- Support for execution of analysis from all CI engines: Jenkins, VSTS, TFS, and Travis-CI.
- Webhook mechanisms to notify pass/fail notifications.
- Unified rules for the analysis of projects.

Other tools also should be verified in similar lines for the functionality and integrations. In this book, we covered code analysis using SonarQube, Lint tools, and Flutter-specific analyzer. The idea is to utilize open source tools for such code analysis and in certain cases, utilize native or specific tools that are used for specific programming languages.

Code analysis is the first step of verification. Good quality of code reduces failures at later stages. It is easier to manage and maintain code. Once code is reviewed and verified, the next logical step is to perform compilation, unit test execution, and creating a package. In the next section, we will discuss Continuous Integration.

Continuous Integration (CI)

Continuous Integration is the DevOps practice to integrate the new feature implementation or a bug fix in the existing **distributed version control systems** such as Git that triggers code quality checks, unit test execution, and build. Continuous Integration is easy to implement, and hence for DevOps starters, it works as a solid base on which the rest of DevOps practices can stand.

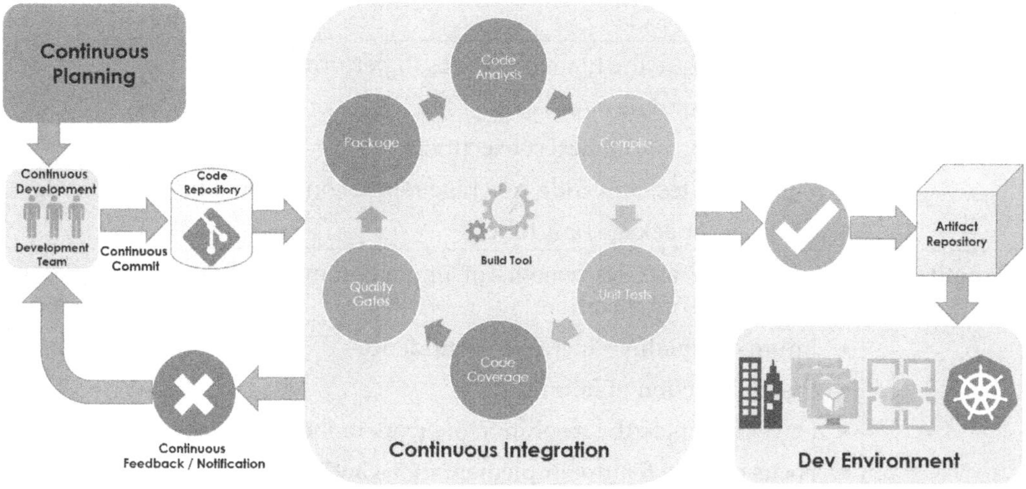

Figure 1.6: *Continuous Integration*

TIP

Counter the resistance

Being aggressive and imposing automation is not the way to go when we are going for culture transformation. Understand the resistance and showcase the root causes of issues/existing practices to the stakeholders and explain how DevOps practices implementation will help:

- Turn the stakeholder's resistance into acceptance by demonstrating the benefits of continuous practices in comparison with the existing manual activities.

- Remove your emotions - DevOps practices may not fit in all the projects. It has to be decided on a case to case basis. Examples, number of people, duration of the project, revenue of the project, environment of the project, willingness of the customer to implement automation in the existing project, and so on.

- Attempt to convince stakeholders by convincing them using case studies or PoCs.

- Keep calm.

Let's understand the objectives, benefits, challenges, tools, best practices, and outcomes:

Objectives	The following are the main objectives to perform: • To fail fast and recover fasts • Compilation and unit test execution • Publishing test and code coverage reports on the Jenkins dashboards • To create a package or artifact
Benefits	The following are the benefits of implementing continuous integration practice in the organization: • Improved quality - increased confidence • Faster detection of failures • Fewer efforts in the resolution of errors in the early stage of issues • Focus on new feature implementations and bug fixes • Transparency and visibility across stakeholders • Improved communication and collaboration • A solid base of culture transformation movement • Collective responsibility, accountability, and ownership • Reduce risks • Reduce repetitive manual processes
Challenges	The following are some of the challenges faced by an organization while implementing continuous integration: • Build automation to compile source code files, to execute unit tests, and to create a package file • Expertise in build automation tools such as Ant, Maven or Gradle is required • Unit tests implementation – to develop a mindset in the team so the team can understand the importance of test-driven development
Tools	The following is the list of tools related to Continuous Integration: • Jenkins • Microsoft Azure DevOps • Atlassian Bamboo • TeamCity

Best practices	The following are some of the best practices related to continuous integration: • Commit code frequently - feature completion/bug fix • Run builds on the system to verify • Never commit broken code • Integrate notifications on failures • Fix broken builds immediately • Write automated unit tests (Coverage %) • Easy access to packages generated after successful build and quality gates verifications • Configure notifications for failures
Outcome	The following are the outcomes or artifacts after Continuous Integration takes place in general: • Code quality reports • Code quality gate verification • Unit tests reports • Code coverage reports based on unit tests • Package creation for distribution or deployment

Table 1.6: Continuous Integration

Continuous Integration helps in communication and collaboration between different stakeholders. It helps to detect issues faster and if notifications are configured, it is helpful in better communication. Branch policies or pull requests are also one of the better ways to collaborate effectively.

The main objective of this book is to keep a uniform format of all reports such as unit test results and code coverage reports. Published results should be in the same format irrespective of programming languages. We have successfully demonstrated these capabilities using plugins available in Jenkins. The same type of reports help to analyze all different types of applications easily and hence, we focused on uniform reports irrespective of code coverage tools such as Jacoco, Cobertura, or XCCov.

Once the Continuous Integration stage is completed successfully, the next logical step is to deliver or deploy it into specific environment such as dev, test, stage or production. Environments can contain resources such as physical, virtual, cloud, containers, or hybrid based on the need. In the next section, we will cover details about cloud computing and containers.

Cloud computing and containers

Cloud computing is a disruptive innovation in recent times. As per the **National Institute of Standards and Technology (NIST)** definition, the following are the aspects of Cloud computing:

- **Cloud deployment models:** There are four cloud deployment models:
  - o **Public cloud:** We can access the public cloud services over the Internet. Anyone who has a credit card or enterprise account or free tier can access public cloud services.
  - o **Private cloud:** A private cloud is the cloud deployment model that serves the need for a single organization that builds it and owns it. A private cloud is built behind the organization firewall and the complete infrastructure is in control of an organization.
  - o **Hybrid cloud:** A hybrid cloud is a cloud deployment model that has a mixture of other cloud deployment models such as public cloud and private cloud. The main objective behind this design is to keep business-critical applications and data on-premises (behind firewall) in a more secure environment or perceived to be a more secure environment such as a private cloud and rest of the components on a public cloud.
  - o **Community cloud:** A community cloud is a deployment model where resources are shared among the organizations who share common interests or security requirements or compliance requirements or performance requirements.

- **Cloud service models:** There are three Cloud service models:

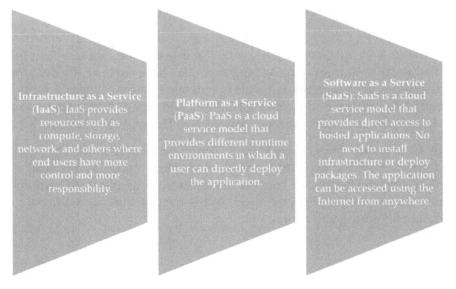

Figure 1.7: Cloud Service Models

- **Essential characteristics:** There are five essential characteristics:
    - o On demand self-service
    - o Broad network access
    - o Resource pooling
    - o Rapid elasticity
    - o Measured service

Now, let's talk about containers in brief.

A container can package application code, libraries, and configurations. The container engine is installed on the host OS. Hence, all containers share a single host, and that can be a security threat. However, all containers are run as isolated processes and managed by a container engine. Many containers can run on a single host operating system.

Docker is an open-source tool to create, deploy, and manage containers on a different host operating system using resource isolation features, such as cgroups and Linux kernels.

Docker comes in two flavors:

- Docker Community Edition
- Docker Enterprise Edition

NOTE

More details on cloud computing and containers with experiences are available in *Chapter 3: Agile, DevOps, and Cloud Computing* with Microsoft Azure of the book.

Let's understand the objectives, benefits, challenges, tools, best practices, and outcomes:

Objectives	To utilize infrastructure resources effectively with high availability and fault tolerance.
Benefits	The following are the benefits of utilizing cloud computing and containers practice in the organization: • Service models and deployment models • Agility • Scalability • Elasticity • Competitive edge • Pay as you use - cost saving • High availability • Disaster recovery

Challenges	The following are some of the challenges faced by an organization while implementing cloud computing and containers-based resource environment: • Security and privacy concerns • Best practices implementation • Governance
Tools	The following is the list of tools/service providers related to cloud computing and containers: • Amazon Web Services • Microsoft Azure • Google Cloud Platform • VMware • OpenStack • Docker • Kubernetes • EC2 Container Service • Azure Containers
Best Practices	The following are some of the best practices related to cloud computing and containers: • Cloud computing • Leverage cloud-based infrastructure for agility and cost-effectiveness • Provide role-based access to all infrastructure or platform resources • Create templates based on technology stack and requirements • Leverage PaaS for applications that require no specialized environment for quick availability of the deployment environment • Configure monitoring and alerts for important resources or environments • Use IaaS feature using APIs or CLIs made available by virtualized environments or services made available by cloud providers • Containers • A single application per container • Build the smallest image possible • Use Docker instances for CI/CD practices implementation • Don't store data in containers • Use official images
Outcome	The following are the outcomes or artifacts after cloud computing and containers take place in general: • Ready to deploy environment in the cloud or using containers • IaaC

Table 1.7: Cloud Computing and Containers

In this book, we have used different types of environment and step-by-step description is available on how to create an environment using Cloud or Container resources. We have used Platform as a Service offering from Microsoft Azure cloud for web application deployment while in some cases, we have used Docker containers and Kubernetes as well. A detailed discussion on Cloud, Containers, and Kubernetes is out of the scope of this book.

Most of the automation servers such as Jenkins or Azure DevOps provide support to integrate the Cloud environment and containers. Based on the number of environments and teams, it is difficult to track and maintain artifacts. It is also important to make security and governance a priority while managing these artifacts. The artifact repository helps to manage different versions of artifacts effectively. It also provides integration with different automation tools such as Jenkins, Atlassian Bamboo, Azure DevOps, and so on.

In the next section, we will cover details about Artifact management.

Artifact management

An artifact repository supports the artifact lifecycle and allows you to manage DevOps practices more efficiently by managing the version of different artifacts. It manages packages ready for deployment or dependencies that can be used to create packages itself:

Objectives	To manage application packages such as WAR, APK, IPA file, or dependencies such as Maven dependencies – Jar files.
Benefits	The following are the benefits of utilizing the Artifact repository in the organization: • Integration with the CI server such as Jenkins or Automation tool such as IBM Urbancode Deploy helps to maintain multiple versions of package files. • Rollback is easier while using the artifact repository as multiple versions are available. • Integration with tools available for automation such as Maven, Jenkins, npm, Docker, Java, and others. • It serves as a shared library for artifacts. • Compliance control for all dependencies used by teams in applications and complete control of in-house developed libraries within an organization.
Challenges	The following are some of the challenges faced by an organization while implementing the Artifact repository: • The learning curve is medium to difficult • Downtime management if the repository is not as a Service

Tools	Artifactory - **https://jfrog.com/open-source/**
	Nexus Repository - **https://www.sonatype.com/nexus-repository-oss**
Best Practices	The following are some of the best practices related to cloud computing and containers:
	• The naming structure should be easy to interpret
	• Configure access control – Authentication and Authorization
	• Configure retention policy
Outcome	The following are the outcomes or artifacts after continuous integration takes place in general:
	• Versioned artifacts
	• Shared dependencies

Table 1.8: Artifact Management

In this book, we have used the Jfrog Artifactory and App Center to manage versions of different artifacts for different types of programming languages based on feasibility.

Artifact repositories make it easier to deploy artifacts in different environments and also play a big role in rollback. Automated deployment and rollback are important practices in the DevOps culture. In the next section, we will cover details about Continuous Delivery.

Continuous delivery

The objective of continuous delivery and continuous deployment is to deploy an application in Dev, test, UAT, production environment in an automated manner.

It helps in incremental releases after short spans of development or sprint in agile terms. Let's understand the objectives, benefits, challenges, tools, best practices, and outcomes:

Objectives	Automated deployment to a production environment with or without some governance/approvals.
Benefits	The following are the benefits of implementing Continuous Delivery and Continuous Deployment practice in the organization:
	• Accelerate application delivery
	• Faster time to market with continuous feedback
	• Productivity gains
	• Easy rollback

Challenges	The following are some of the challenges faced by an organization while implementing continuous delivery and continuous deployment. • To write scripts or use plugins to deploy an application in the specific environment • To set an approval process for governance • Proper access to the remote systems to deploy an application
Tools	The following is the list of tools related to Continuous Delivery and Continuous Deployment: • Plugins • Shell Script • Batch script • App Center • TestFlight • Other tools
Best Practices	The following are some of the best practices related to continuous delivery and continuous deployment: • Use Release Management Techniques such as Blue-Green Deployment or Canary Release for minimum downtime and higher user satisfaction • Use Release Management tools or Plugins available in Automation tools to manage releases and rollback in different environments • Automate feasible processes to gain maximum efficiency • Configure deployment activity as a part of the pipeline using Plugins or Release Management tools
Outcome	The following are the outcomes or artifacts after continuous integration takes place in general: • Automated deployment of artifacts • Governance • Approval or review process before deployment

Table 1.9: Continuous Delivery

In this book, we have covered Continuous delivery extensively in most of the chapters. We have covered web application deployment to Azure App Services, Docker containers, Azure Kubernetes Services while in case of mobile and hybrid applications, we have distributed app packages to App center using plugins available in Jenkins or using command line tools that are supported by Cloud Service CLIs.

Once artifacts are deployed in a specific environment, the next logical step is to verify and validate for expected outcome. Testing can be performed on different environments based on the existing processes and policies of an organization. In the next section, we will cover details about continuous testing.

Continuous testing

Continuous testing helps to verify the functional aspects of an application in an automated manner and to keep application production-ready after all verifications. Let's understand the basic difference between manual and automated testing in the context of scaling testing mechanisms:

Description	Manual testing	Automated testing
The productivity of the testing team	Difficult to achieve due to repeated tasks	High as repeated tasks can be automated and saved time can be invested in other activities
Learning curve	Easy	Medium
Multiple iterations with speed	No	Yes
Supports Agile principles	No	Yes
Suitable for the DevOps culture	No	Yes
Accuracy	No	Yes
Quality	No	Yes
Reliability	Less	High
Faster delivery/faster time to market/execution time	No	Yes
Possibility of early detection of bugs	Less	High
Transparency	No	Yes
Cost-effective	No	Yes
Easy maintenance	No	Yes
Parallel execution with a distributed architecture	N/A	Yes
Scalability	No	Yes
Need for human intervention	Yes	Minimum
Suitable for short term projects and strict deadlines	Yes	No
Highly skilled and technically aware resources required?	No	Yes
Prone to human error	Yes	Only if the automation script has issues
Investment required for training, coaching, and tools?	No	Yes – Significant Time and Money investment

Table 1.10: Manual vs. automated testing

In an agile world, speed and quality matter while the need for verification and validation has exponentially increased. In this scenario, manual testing no longer satisfies those essential requirements. Continuous testing is the answer to speed and quality for testing. Manual testing is still used in some cases where automation is not feasible.

Let's understand the objectives, benefits, challenges, tools, best practices, and outcomes:

Objectives	To verify the functional and non-functional aspects of an application in an automated manner and to keep the application production-ready after all verifications.
Benefits	The following are the benefits of implementing continuous testing practice in the organization: • Brings quality and improvement as a part of a continuous process or pipeline • Helps to detect issues in early stages • Accelerate application delivery • Faster time to market with continuous feedback • Improve test coverage • Transparency
Challenges	The following are some of the challenges faced by an organization while implementing continuous testing: • Understanding requirements • Trained resources to write functional test cases • Testing framework for reusability • Software licenses • Running the same test cases multiple times • Testing for multiple platforms/device models is time-consuming • Testing application on the different models, screen sizes, screen resolutions, OS • Long testing cycles across a variety of devices lead to high costs • Apps must be tested for each new OS version – Beta as well • Creating a Stub Management System – for example, third-party API that is consumed by middleware is not available all the time for new services – In such a case, the Stub Management System can provide dummy data in the JSON format to the middleware until API is ready with live data. To be ready with such a system is a challenge.

Tools	The following is the list of tools related to continuous testing: • Selenium • Appium • Apache JMeter • OWASP ZAP • Cucumber • MobSF
Best Practices	The following are some of the best practices related to continuous testing: • Functional tests should validate use cases such as accessibility, positive scenarios, negative scenarios, localization and internationalization • Execute smoke tests that can be executed by the automation server to verify the most important functionality • Configure load testing earlier and execute continuously to receive continuous feedback with short cycles using automation and cloud computing • Integrate performance testing to verify availability, scalability, reliability, speed, responsiveness, and resource usage of your application and infrastructure
Outcome	The following are the outcomes or artifacts after continuous integration takes place in general: • Test reports • Validation and verification of the existing state of an application

Table 1.11: Continuous testing

Are there any disadvantages of automation? Automation has to be stable and verified before we blindly use it. All activities have to be monitored for improvements.

Continuous testing is the process of executing automated tests as part of the software delivery pipeline to obtain feedback on the business risks associated with a software release candidate as rapidly as possible. Here are some important types of testing that can help to accelerate time to market. If not automated, then such manual testing requires lot of human efforts and it becomes a bottleneck at times:

- **Functional testing**
    - o Functional/regression testing is a vital part of the success of the application.
    - o It ensures the correctness of features and functionality of an application in a quick time.
    - o It is important to highlight that functional tests are written from business and end user's perspective.

o Automated functional test execution helps to increase accuracy and highlight issues in a timely manner.

o In agile development, automation of functional test execution helps in faster time to market, increased reliability, productivity gains, and increased customer satisfaction.

o Ease of use, innovation, customization, flawless functionality, and personalized user experience is the need of the hour in a huge and competitive market.

o Automated functional testing removes the bottlenecks of faster release of a mobile application.

- **Performance testing**

  o Performance testing includes load testing, scalability testing, Availability testing, and so on.

  o The Apache JMeter application is an open-source product that is designed to load functional test behavior of applications and measure performance.

  o It provides the facility to distribute the load by master-slave configuration.

  o Faster time to market and availability with quality is extremely essential and DevOps practice implementation is a good fit to solve this issue for Mobile apps.

- **Security testing**

  o Digital transformation is a new normal in today's world.

  o Organizations are transforming their business using social media, mobile, cloud computing, and analytics to make their presence visible in an extremely competitive market.

  o Cloud and mobile-based applications are new normal and hence, cyber theft is a new way to gain monetary benefits.

  o Mobile apps are developed as native apps or hybrid apps.

  o Mobile security is extremely important considering the wide usage of mobiles in day-to-day usage and operations.

Shift left is one of the important terms discussed in DevOps practices related discussions. Shift left has its origins in lean wherein the focus is on to improve quality by moving testing in the early phase of the application lifecycle. It is more about having proper communication and collaboration in place since the beginning to ensure quality.

In this book, we will cover security testing for an Android application in *Chapter 4: Building CI/CD Pipeline for an Android App.* Functional, performance, and security test automation integration in a pipeline is supported using plugins or command line tools.

Automated testing helps to accelerate time to market and quality of the product. Once application is verified and validated, the final step is to deploy an application in the production environment. In the next section, we will discuss continuous deployment.

Continuous deployment

What is the difference between continuous delivery and continuous deployment? Let's understand the difference:

	Continuous delivery	Continuous deployment
Definition	Continuous delivery is about confidence and capabilities that every change is ready to be deployed to production immediately if required.	Continuous deployment is about confidence and capabilities that every change is deployed in the production environment.
Environment	Production-like environments such as Dev, Test, SIT, UAT, and so on.	Production
Feasible	Yes	Usually the number of organizations and projects don't prefer to deploy all changes directly to production environments.
Approvals	Manual/stakeholder approval is needed.	Manual/stakeholder approval is not needed.
Relation?	Continuous Delivery doesn't imply Continuous Deployment.	Continuous Deployment implies Continuous Delivery.

Continuous deployment implies continuous delivery.

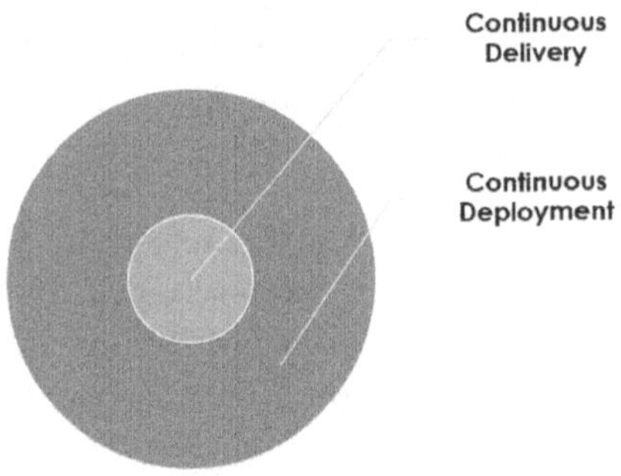

Figure 1.8: Continuous delivery and continuous deployment

Table 1.12: Continuous delivery and continuous deployment

In this book, we will cover Continuous Deployment in *Chapter 3: Building CI/CD Pipeline for Java Web Application* where we will deploy an application to Azure app services in different environments using the main production slot and other environments slots such as Dev and QA. The deployment process is usually the same in an automated fashion.

Once the application is deployed in the production environment, it is important monitor the environment as well as the application performance. Continuous feedback from the monitoring systems helps to improve the application and its runtime environment continuously. In the next section, we will discuss Continuous feedback and Continuous improvement in brief.

Continuous feedback and continuous improvement

Continuous feedback is one of the important phases in an agile development approach where learning is based on experience, feedback is based on the current market, or feedback is based on expectations are integrated into the next sprint to improve the existing practices.

Continuous improvement in the mindset and existing practices is essential to build a better organizational culture. It is the responsibility of all stakeholders, including project teams. DevOps practices implementation is a journey that should never END as progress is a continuous process. *Roy T. Bennett* has correctly said that No matter how much experience you have, there's always something new you can learn and room for improvement.

People can make the organization a better place by making daily improvements to become the best version of themselves. This is so apt for Continuous Improvement in the DevOps culture. It is the responsibility of the leadership team to provide an opportunity for teams to improve by empowering them, and the responsibility of the team is to contribute and improve with all available resources.

With all Continuous practices in place, it is easier to change the mindset of people. Hence, it helps in the culture transformation process immensely. Let's understand the culture change and its effects in brief in the last section of this chapter.

Culture change and its effects

Culture change comes with a mindset change and that only happens with incremental improvements in the behavior. The following can be some of the objectives of cultural transformation in an organization:

- Culture transformation to improve and innovate continuously..
- Culture transformation to learn from failures.

- Culture transformation to increase product quality.
- Culture transformation to improve time to market.
- Culture transformation to be relevant in the market.
- Culture transformation to enable automation in Application Lifecycle Management activities.

Cultural transformation is the application of current technologies in training products, processes, and strategies within an organization to achieve continuous improvement and innovation.

Conclusion

DevOps is a culture and it essentially supports culture transformation to increase quality and make time to market faster. DevOps practices implementation is not a short-term plan. It takes 2-5 years for culture transformation and implements DevOps practices to improve quality and to achieve faster time to market. DevOps practices implementation must be a phase-wise implementation as per the defined maturity model. It is important to perform **Proof of Concepts (PoCs)** and pilots before the full-fledged implementation of DevOps practices in projects. Transformation is not an easy exercise. It is important to assess, implement, and measure this journey for Continuous Improvement and Continuous Innovations. It requires patience and implementation based on priority decided in the workshop. DevOps is more about culture and mindset with automation, while cloud and containers are more about technology and service with automation. The agile methodology needs DevOps and cloud to get effective results. The next few chapters will focus on DevOps practices implementation using Jenkins, Microsoft Azure Cloud, and App Center.

Points to remember

- DevOps is a culture.
- Culture transformation needs a triangle of people, processes, and tools.
- Continuous Integration and Continuous Delivery are not DevOps. There are other Continuous Practices available as well.
- Culture transformation is a long-term approach – no quick fixes are available.
- DevOps is a tools agnostic approach.
- Agile and DevOps are complementary and not mutually exclusive.
- DevOps practices implementation and culture transformation are a journey and not only a single project initiative.
- Phase-wise implementation should be preferred for DevOps practices implementation.
- The maturity model should be dynamic, and it should evolve over time.

Multiple choice questions

1. **DevOps consists of:**
   a. Development
   b. Operations
   c. Operations Logic
   d. a and b

2. **DevSecOps consists of:**
   a. Development
   b. Operations
   c. Security
   d. A, b and c

3. **Agile and DevOps are not mutually exclusive.**
   a. True
   b. False

4. **Agile and DevOps don't complement each other.**
   a. True
   b. False

5. **DevOps culture consists of:**
   a. People
   b. Processes
   c. Tools
   d. All of these
   e. None of these

6. **The DevOps maturity model should evolve with time:**
   a. True
   b. False

7. **Which are the following benefits that can be achieved using DevOps practices implementation**
   a. High quality
   b. Faster time to market
   c. Productivity gains
   d. Continuous improvement

  e. Continuous innovation

  f. All of these

  g. None of these

Answer

1. d
2. d
3. a
4. b
5. d
6. a
7. f

Questions

1. What is DevOps?
2. What is Continuous Integration?
3. What is Continuous Delivery?
4. What is Continuous Deployment?
5. What is Continuous Testing?
6. What is Cloud Computing?
7. What is the role of containers?
8. How containers are better than virtual machines?
9. What is the difference between Continuous Delivery and Continuous Deployment?
10. Why Value Stream is important?
11. What are the continuous practices that help culture transformation?
12. Why DevOps practices implementation has to be phase-wise?
13. What is the importance of the maturity model?
14. How does the assessment framework help in consulting exercises?

Introducing Jenkins 2.0 and Blue Ocean

> "The improvement of understanding is for two ends: first, our increase of knowledge; secondly, to enable us to deliver that knowledge to others."
>
> — *John Locke*

Jenkins 2.0 provided new features such as Pipeline as Code—the technical aspect, a new setup experience, and other UI improvements—enhancements with the Jenkins interface. The entire user experience had a drastic change. Easy navigation to a different section in the job configuration was an eye-catching difference.

In this chapter, we will focus on the overview of Jenkins and evolution of the pipeline from Build pipeline, Scripted pipeline, Declarative pipeline, and Blue Ocean.

Structure

In this chapter we will discuss the following topics:

- Introducing Jenkins 2.X
    - o History
    - o Overview of Jenkins
    - o Prerequisites
    - o How to run Jenkins?

- Pipelines
  - o Build pipelines
  - o Scripted pipeline
  - o Declarative pipeline
  - o Blue Ocean
- Conclusion
- Questions and exercises

Objectives

After studying this unit, you should be able to:

- Understand prerequisites before installing Jenkins
- Install Jenkins
- Change Port and JENKINS_HOME
- Understand basic installation and configuration of Jenkins
- Understand best practices of the Jenkins configuration

Introducing Jenkins 2.X

Let's start by getting some information about Jenkins. The first question is what is Jenkins?

History

Let's take a quick look at the history of Jenkins and see how it has evolved over the years, including its current footprint:

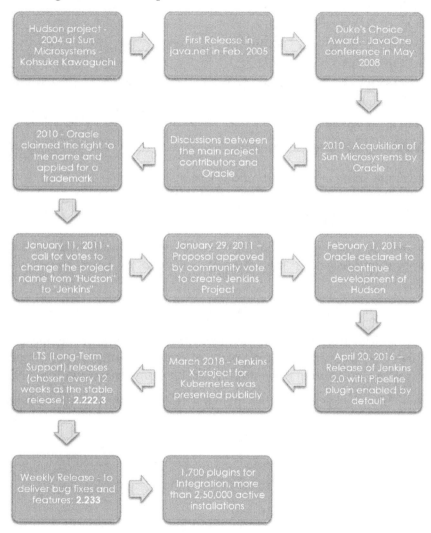

Figure 2.1: *Jenkins history*

Jenkins provides a simple way to create a pipeline that includes continuous integration and continuous delivery.

NOTE

What DevOps is not?
- DevOps is not a methodology.
- DevOps is not a process.
- DevOps is not a tool or technology.
- DevOps is not a framework.
- DevOps is not a set of design patterns where problems and solutions are well defined.
- DevOps is not scripting.
- DevOps is not automation only.

Let's understand some more details about Jenkins.

Overview of Jenkins

Jenkins is an open-source tool that provides integration with existing tools used in the application lifecycle management to automate the entire process based on feasibility.

NOTE

It is essential to decide tools for the DevOps practices implementation and agree upon its usage as a standard practice. It helps to improve and innovate with expertise in the implementation of DevOps practices using the tool.

It is essential to decide toolsets based on the existing culture of an organization and also introduce new tools based on the requirements of the evolvement of the culture and DevOps practices implementation.

Training should be given to associates by keeping the scope of the tools in culture transformation in mind.

Jenkins provides the following features:

1. Open-source tool with huge community support.

2. Easy installation - platform-agnostic (Generic Java package (.war), Docker, FreeBSD, Gentoo, Arch Linux, macOS, Red Hat/Fedora/CentOS, Ubuntu/Debian, OpenBSD, openSUSE, OpenIndiana Hipster, and Windows).

3. Easy way to configure Continuous Integration, Continuous Testing, Continuous Delivery, and Continuous Deployment.

4. It supports arguably all languages as it provides plugin-based architecture. In case plugins are not available, CLI or command execution helps to set up Continuous practices – Extensible:

- **Plugin categories:** .NET Development, Android Development, .NET Development, Agent Launchers and Controllers, Android Development, Artifact Uploaders, Authentication and User Management, Build Notifiers, Build Parameters, Build Reports, Build Tools, Build Triggers, Build Wrappers, Cloud Providers, Cluster Management and Distributed Build, Command Line Interface, Database, Deployment, DevOps, External Site/Tool Integrations, Groovy-related, iOS Development, Library plugins (for use by other plugins), List view columns, Maven, Misc (administrative-monitor), Misc (adopt-this-plugin), Misc (agent), Misc (analysis), Misc (api-plugin), Misc (aws), Misc (azure), Misc (bitbucket), Misc (bitbucket-server), Misc (ca-apm), Misc (cmp), Misc (codebuild), Misc (configuration-as-code), Misc (confluence), Misc (deprecated), Misc (docker), Misc (email), Misc (emailext), Misc (git), Misc (github), Misc (gitlab), Misc (google-cloud), Misc (jira), Misc (kubernetes), Misc (localization), Misc (logging), Misc (monitoring), Misc (notification), Misc (npm), Misc (openshift), Misc (performance), Misc (pipeline), Misc (plugin-external), Misc (plugin-misc), Misc (plugin-post-build), Misc (plugin-test), Misc (queue), Misc (rocketchatnotifier), Misc (slack), Misc (spot), Misc (spotinst), Misc (stash), Misc (webhook), Misc (website), Misc (windows), Miscellaneous, Other Post-Build Actions, Page Decorators, Python Development, Ruby Development, RunConditions for use by the Run Condition plugin, Scala Development, Security, Source Code Management, Source Code Management related, Testing, Uncategorized, User Interface, Views
- Plugins are written in Java and as Jenkins has this extensibility, it is easier to integrate new tools based on market trends
- Organization write their plugins to integrate internal tools with open source Jenkins

5. Default plugin installation at the time of the initial setup.

6. Simple and easy configuration of tools, proxy, environment variables, etc.

7. Distributed Architecture - Controller / Master Agent architecture to scale and distribute a load of processing along with ease of use, fast execution, and parallel execution.

8. A huge leap from being popular as a Continuous Integration server to become an Automation server after the release of Jenkins 2.0.

9. Rich community and support.

10. Huge knowledge base and documentation available for beginners.

Jenkins installation and configuration process is different after Jenkins 2.0 release. Now, there are suggested plugins that you can install in one go. It takes a huge burden away from the Jenkins engineer's shoulder. You don't need to remember and document which plugins are required and which dependencies are required. Another important option available is to skip this new configuration and install Jenkins in the usual manner as it was done earlier.

The major change is an introduction and big push for the Pipeline as Code rather than creating pipelines or orchestration using the traditional pipeline using plugins such as a build pipeline.

The most important thing was to focus on Pipeline as Code and commit the pipeline into a repository so that versions could be maintained as it was maintained for code. Visualization is an important part of an end-to-end automation pipeline and Jenkins 2.x focuses on this part significantly.

A multi-branch pipeline provides a way to have different pipeline scripts for different branches. Jenkins automatically detects branches with the Jenkinsfile and starts its execution. It is one of the fastest ways to recover from Jenkins failures as well. Reason? Because the pipeline is available in the repository. Jenkins will fetch branches available in the repo that has the Jenkinsfile and your pipeline will be ready immediately if the environment is available for execution.

Considering UI enhancements and pipeline-related changes, it looks like effective use of design thinking in new Jenkins 2.0. In the next section, we will discuss prerequisites to install Jenkins.

Prerequisites

The following are the prerequisites to install Jenkins on a specific system as per our experience:

- The Jenkins official documentation recommends 256 MB of RAM, although more than 512 MB is recommended. However, we suggest 4 to 8 GB RAM to manage the CI/CD pipeline across multiple projects. One of the common reasons is the way system configuration is available in the organization as well as with a personal laptop or system.

- The Jenkins official documentation recommends 10 GB of drive space; however, we suggest 50-80 GB of free space on a disk drive.

- The Jenkins official documentation recommends Java 8 or 11 (either a JRE or Java Development Kit (JDK) is fine); however, we suggest JDK installation only.

> **TIP**
>
> Always use the Controller/Master Agent Architecture. It is not wise to install tools on the Jenkins server for automation.
>
> Another important reason is that the entire environment setup has to be done but this might not work effectively if the development team is not able to give time to the setup. Hence, it is easier to use a developer's system as an agent and effectively use it in Jenkins. The entire work is delegated to an agent where the environment is already configured. This saves time of the installation and configuration of tools and helps focus on automation activities.

In the next section, we will discuss how to run Jenkins and start using it.

How to run Jenkins?

The following are the commands to run Jenkins:

> **TIP**
>
> The generic WAR file usage is the easiest way to install and configure Jenkins across operating systems. You have complete control over its operation and you are aware of the uniform approach of the Jenkins installation; hence, it is easy and fast.
>
> It is important to note that the installation of Jenkins as a service helps to manage Jenkins better in a way such that at the startup of the system, Jenkins starts automatically.

1. Start Jenkins using the command line by using the Generic Java package (.war):

   ```
   1.   java -jar jenkins.war
   ```

   Go to **http://localhost:8080.**

2. Change the port to run Jenkins with the following command:
   ```
   java -jar jenkins.war --httpPort=9999
   ```

   The following is the output of the preceding command to start Jenkins:

   ```
   1.   Picked up _JAVA_OPTIONS: -Xmx512M
   2.   Running from: F:\1.DevOps\2020\jenkins.war
   3.   webroot: EnvVars.masterEnvVars.get("JENKINS_HOME")
   4.   .
   ```

```
5.  .

6.  .

7.  .

8.

9.  2020-04-25 15:42:30.741+0000 [id=33]      INFO      jenkins.
    install.SetupWizard#init:

10.

11. *********************************************************

12. *********************************************************

13. *********************************************************

14.

15. Jenkins initial setup is required. An admin user has been
    created and a password generated.

16. Please use the following password to proceed to installation:

17.

18. a8ce35dccd3a4ec6911647816c602733

19.

20. This may also be found at: F:\1.DevOps\2020\Jenkins_Home\
    secrets\initialAdminPassword

21.

22. *********************************************************

23. *********************************************************

24. *********************************************************

25.

26. 2020-04-25    15:42:51.700+0000    [id=47]                 INFO
    h.m.DownloadService$Downloadable#load: Obtained the updated
    data file for hudson.tasks.Maven.MavenInstaller

27. 2020-04-25 15:42:51.700+0000 [id=47]      INFO    hudson.util.
    Retrier#start: Performed the action check updates server
    successfully at the attempt #1

28. 2020-04-25 15:42:51.712+0000 [id=47]      INFO       hudson.
    model.AsyncPeriodicWork#lambda$doRun$0: Finished Download
    metadata. 23,838 ms

29. 2020-04-25 15:43:13.069+0000 [id=21]      INFO       hudson.
    WebAppMain$3#run: Jenkins is fully up and running
```

3. Go to **http://localhost:9999**. It will redirect you to unlock the Jenkins page where you need to provide the administrator password available in the console or at `Jenkins_Home\secrets\initialAdminPassword`:

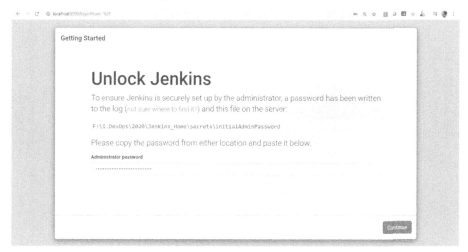

Figure 2.2: Unlock Jenkins

4. Click on **Install Suggested Plugins**.

TIP

If the Jenkins server is behind a proxy, then you need to provide proxy details and go ahead with the installation. In some cases, skip plugin installation. Go to **Manage Jenkins -> Manage Plugins -> Advanced** and configure proxy details and verify the connection and then install plugins.

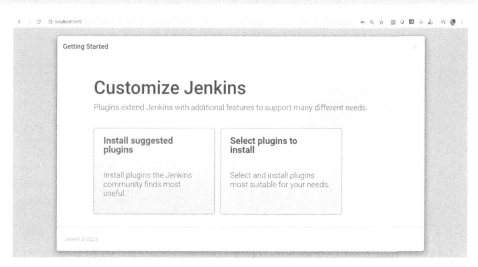

Figure 2.3: Customize Jenkins

Have patience! Wait until all plugins are installed:

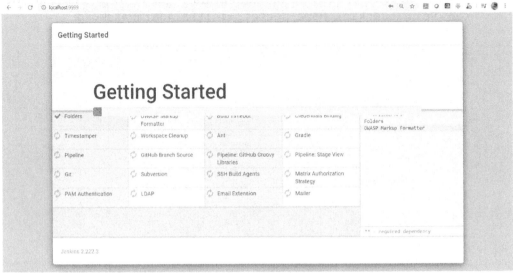

Figure 2.4: Plugins installation

5. If the plugins installation fails, then click on **retry**.

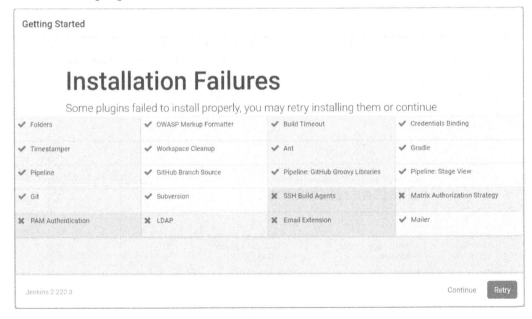

Figure 2.5: Plugins installation failures

6. Once all plugins are installed, create your first admin user and click on **Save** and **Continue**.

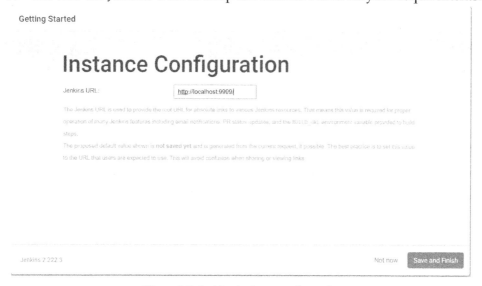

TIP
Remember your credentials!

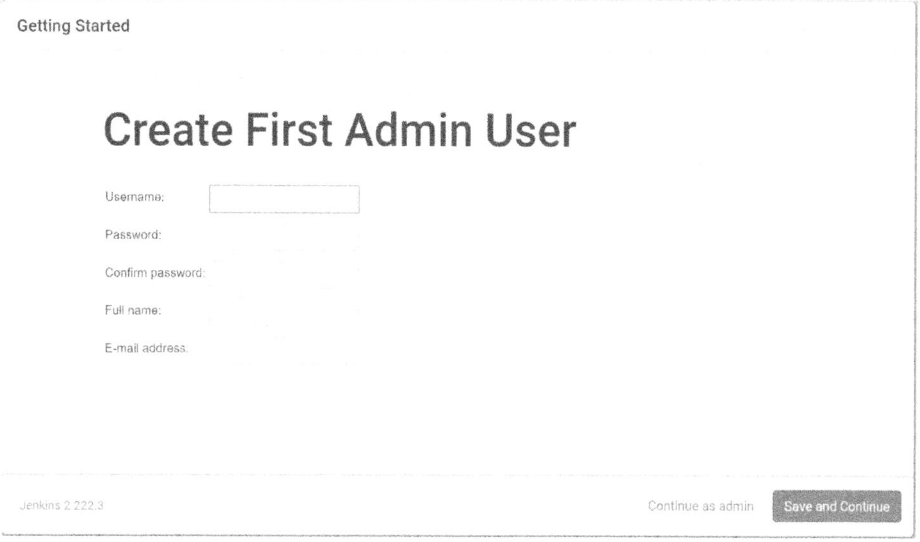

Figure 2.6: Admin user

7. Provide the Jenkins URL or keep the default based on your requirements:

Figure 2.7: Jenkins instance configuration

TIP
Use the IP address or domain name in place of the localhost if required to access Jenkins in the network. If it is not changed, then none can access it outside your system.

8. Once the Jenkins setup is complete, click on **Start** using Jenkins:

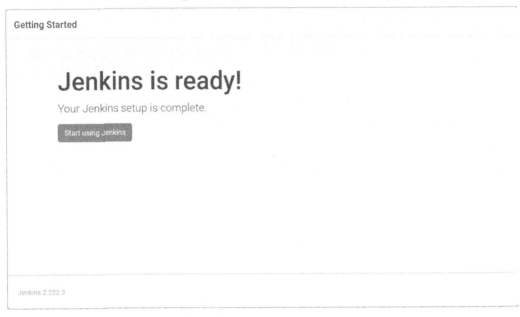

Figure 2.8: Jenkins set-up is complete

9. Verify the Jenkins Dashboard. Click on **Manage Jenkins**:

Figure 2.9: Jenkins Dashboard

10. Click on **Configure** system to monitor the Jenkins configuration.

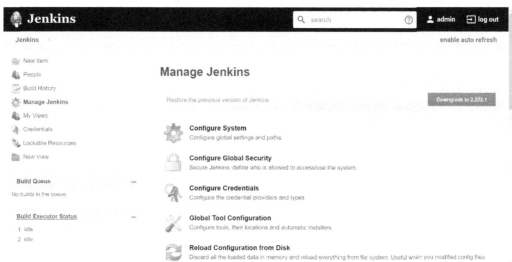

Figure 2.10: *Manage Jenkins*

11. Verify the JENKINS_HOME directory and Jenkins' URL. If you want to change the Jenkins URL, then modify it in this section.

TIP

Always configure backup and restore practices and processes for JENKINS_ HOME or keep a manual backup based on the feasibility to avoid any disaster in future.

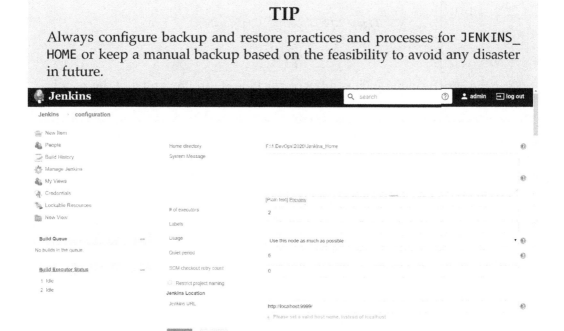

Figure 2.11: *Configure Jenkins*

12. Go to **Manage Jenkins | Global Tool Configuration**.

Here, you can configure all tools that Jenkins will use to automate application lifecycle management activities.

You can provide a path if the tools are already installed or configured, or you can install them automatically from this section only:

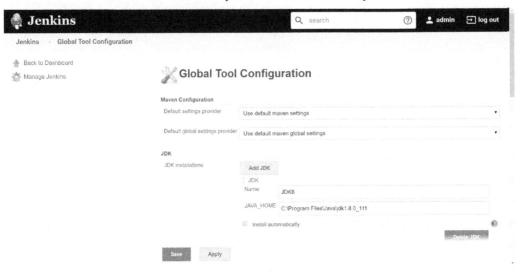

Figure 2.12: Global Tool Configuration

TIP

Keep the generic name such as **jdk8** or **jdk11** and configure all tools here with the path. It is easy to use tools in the pipeline without any issues.

13. Go to **Manage Jenkins | Nodes**. This is the section where we can manage **Controller / Master- Agent** nodes.

As of now, only the Controller/Master node is available that is the system on which Jenkins is installed.

14. Click on the **Controller / Master** node name:

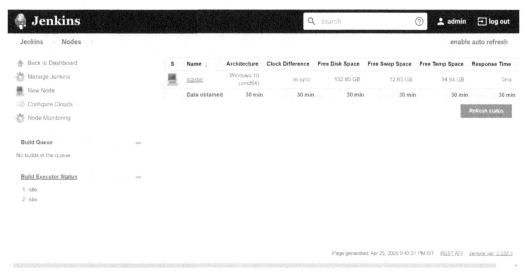

Figure 2.13: *Nodes in Jenkins*

15. Click on **Configure** and observe the usage of # of executors based on the help section:

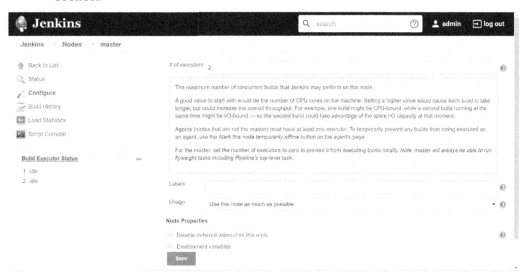

Figure 2.14: *Node Configuration*

16. What is the default JENKINS_HOME directory in Windows?

    `C:\Users\<USERNAME>\.jenkins`

17. How to change the default JENKINS_HOME directory in Windows?

18. Go to **System Properties** and click on **Advanced**:

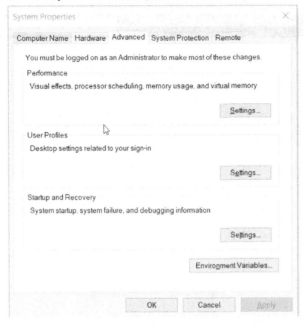

Figure 2.15: System Properties

19. Click on **Environment Variables**:

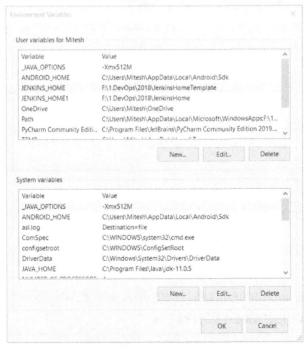

Figure 2.16: Environment Variables

20. Once you start Jenkins, you can find the `JENKINS_HOME` on the console:

```
1.   F:\1.DevOps\2020>java -jar jenkins.war
2.   Picked up _JAVA_OPTIONS: -Xmx512M
3.   Running from: F:\1.DevOps\2020\jenkins.war
4.   webroot: EnvVars.masterEnvVars.get("JENKINS_HOME")
```

Pipelines

Jenkins 2.0 and later versions have built-in support for delivery pipelines. Jenkins 2.x has improved usability and it is fully backward compatible. In today's competitive market, all organizations are competing to release better quality products and maintain a faster time to market.

Even before Jenkins 2.0, plugins helped to utilize Continuous Delivery as well but Jenkins 2.0 brings backs the focus on end-to-end automation. pipelines help to organize and manage the orchestration of the Application Lifecycle Management easily and robustly.

Pipelines use **domain-specific language (DSL)** to visualize and orchestrate the Application Life Cycle Management activities. It essentially means **Pipeline as Code (PaaC).** The highlight of this feature is that users can commit Pipeline as Code (essentially, a script) in the repository and keep many versions of it.

Sounds familiar? Yes, we all do it while managing code in Code repositories, isn't it?

NOTE

Jenkins already had build pipeline plugin for creating orchestration or pipeline based on upstream-downstream relationships of Jenkins Jobs. The scripted pipeline was also introduced and later declarative pipelines that are utilized for Pipeline as Code. Azure DevOps is using the YAML file for pipeline creation using Pipeline as Code.

Jenkins and Azure DevOps both have a feature to create a pipeline script using UI. No expertise is needed in the scripting language. Overall, understanding of tools and technology serves as a purpose to create Pipeline as Code.

In short, we can use a **domain-specific language (DSL)** to create an automation pipeline that will orchestrate the static code analysis, build, test, and deploy operations. It can also include load testing, security testing, and many other operations based on the existing culture of an organization and requirements of the project.

The reason why pipelines are getting more popular is the usage of Jenkins over the years. It is all about patterns. Usage of Jenkins and build pipeline makes users realize the complexities of Jenkins management over time. It is easier to use the Build pipeline plugin in Jenkins to create pipelines using upstream and downstream jobs. Most beginners follow this approach but over a period of time, it becomes difficult to manage.

Let's understand the traditional pipeline using the build pipeline plugin.

Build pipeline

The following are the reasons why Pipeline as Code is preferred over the traditional approach of using upstream and downstream connected jobs:

1. Each task has a corresponding unique build job or project; hence, there are too many jobs to create and manage.

2. A business unit or organization manages multiple projects.

3. The Build Pipeline configuration is in Jenkins itself, and so in case of any failure, it is a rework.

4. It is difficult to track changes in the pipeline created using Build Pipeline.

5. Go to **Manage Jenkins | Manage Plugins | Available** tab and select **Build Pipeline** plugin for installation.

Let's create the following three simple freestyle jobs:

*   SonarQubeAnalysis
*   Build
*   Deploy2Tomcat

Let's try to configure orchestration. Perform the following steps:

1. Go to SonarQubeAnalysis job in Jenkins and click on **Configure**. Go to the **Post-build Actions** section and click on the **Add post-build** action and select **Build** other projects.

    We need to execute a Build job once this job is successfully completed.

Figure 2.17: Build other projects

2. Verify the Downstream projects on the Job's dashboard:

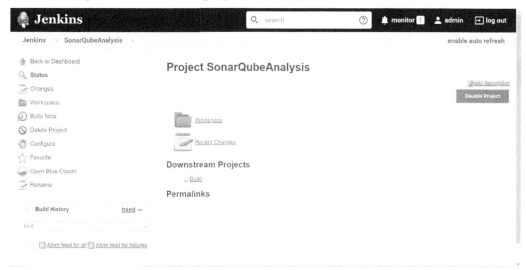

Figure 2.18: Downstream Projects

3. Verify the Upstream projects on the Job's dashboard:

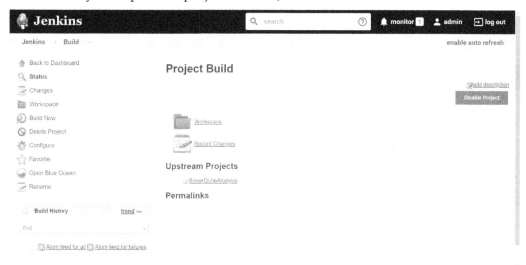

Figure 2.19: Upstream Projects

4. Go to **Build** job in Jenkins and click on **Configure** and then go to the **Post-build Actions** section. Click on the **Add post-build** action and select **Build** other projects.

We need to execute the **Deploy2Tomcat** job once the **Build** job is completed.

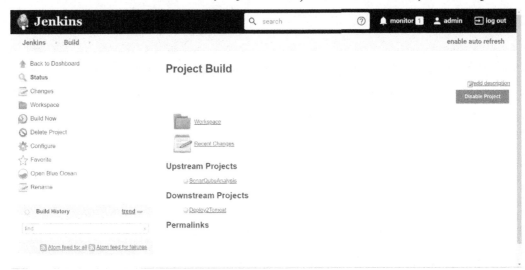

Figure 2.20: Upstream and Downstream Projects

5. Create Build Pipeline View from the Jenkins Dashboard:

Figure 2.21: Build Pipeline View

6. Select **Initial Job** as SonarQubeAnalysis as we need to start our pipeline from this job:

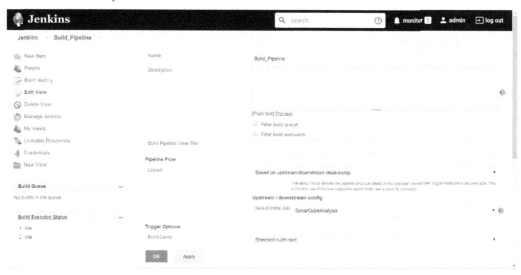

Figure 2.22: Build Pipeline Configuration

7. Execute the pipeline:

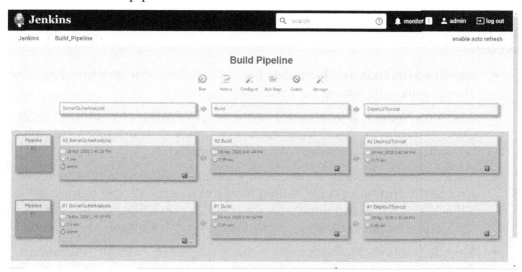

Figure 2.23: Build Pipeline View

Now, let's understand how Pipeline as code helps you to fix the manual configuration as it supports the following:

- **Domain-Specific Language (DSL)** helps to create pipelines through the DSL or Jenkinsfile.

- Pipeline as Code can utilize all programming concepts.

- Common approach and standards for all teams.

- Version control of the pipelines as it is also a script and managed in version control systems such as SVN or Git.

The pipeline helps to define and implement Continuous Integration, Continuous Testing, and Continuous Delivery pipeline using DSL in Jenkins. The Jenkinsfile contains the script to automate Continuous Integration, Continuous Testing, and Continuous Delivery or it is available in the Jenkins pipeline Job. The visible benefit of creating a Jenkinsfile in order to include Pipeline as Code is its version control in the repository. Hence, Infrastructure as a Code has a sister in the name of Pipeline as Code.

The following two ways help to create a pipeline:

- Jenkins Dashboard
- Jenkins file

It is the best practice to use the Jenkinsfile. Let's understand some basic pipeline concepts:

- **Pipeline (Declarative):** It models CI/CD pipeline or it contains stages or phases of the Application Lifecycle Management.

- **Agent or Node:** It is a system (virtual or physical) that is utilized in the Controller/Master Agent Architecture of Jenkins. The Jenkins execution takes place on the Controller/Master or Agent Node.

- **Stage:** It is a collection of tasks. For example, compilation of source files, Unit test Execution, and publishing Junit test reports. We can represent it as a Block. To understand it more easily, consider it as a Source Code Analysis or Continuous Integration or Continuous Testing or Continuous Delivery.

- **Step:** It is a task. Multiple tasks make a stage. For example, execution of the script, execution of the maven command, execution of the SonarQube analysis command, and execution of the Gradle command, and so on.

There are two types of pipelines in Jenkins as of today. It means that the Jenkinsfile can contain two different types of style/syntax and yet it can achieve the same thing. Yes, DevOps Practices implementation.

Scripted pipeline

Scripted pipelines follow the Imperative programming model. Scripted pipelines are written in the Groovy script in Jenkins. All Groovy blocks/constructs help to manage the flow as well as error reporting. A scripted pipeline doesn't have a Restart Stage feature, post-build actions, error checking and reporting (`try-catch-finally` blocks), and notifications constructs. It requires Groovy programming skills; hence, it has a steep learning curve. It is not easy to understand, manage, and maintain.

Let's see some important points about scripted pipeline:

- Available since long with Jenkins.

- *How to do* approach to create pipelines.

- Complex in comparison to a Declarative pipeline.

- The groovy syntax is the last limitation; hence, complex but we can easily utilize it in complex pipeline structures.

- The Imperative programming paradigm of computer programming in which the program or script has a collection of steps or tasks that defines how this script should achieve the outcome.

- A node block is a root of the Scripted pipeline syntax.

The following code is the structure of the scripted pipeline:

```
1.  node {
2.      /* Stages and Steps */
3.  }
4.
5.  node {
6.      stage('SCA') {
7.          // steps
8.      }
9.      stage('CI') {
10.         // steps
11.     }
12.     stage('CD') {
13.         // steps
14.     }
15. }
```

Let's see the Scripted pipeline template available in the pipeline:

1. Create a Pipeline job in Jenkins:

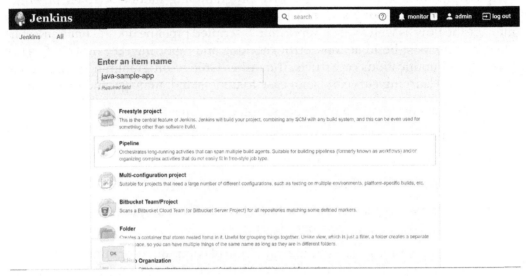

Figure 2.24: Pipeline Job

2. Go to the **Pipeline** section in the Job.
3. Select the **Scripted Pipeline** template.
4. Click on **Save**:

Figure 2.25: Scripted Pipeline

5. Click on the **Pipeline Syntax**.

6. Use **Snippet Generator** to create script commands to use in the pipeline:

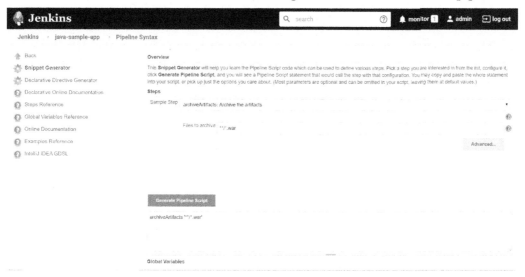

Figure 2.26: *Pipeline Syntax - Snippet Generator*

7. Similarly, the Declarative Directive Generator section is used to create a script in the declarative syntax:

Figure 2.27: *Declarative Directive Generator*

Let's understand the Declarative pipeline.

Declarative pipeline

The Declarative pipeline follows a declarative programming model. Declarative pipelines are written in the DSL in Jenkins that is easy to understand and clear. It doesn't have a Restart Stage feature, Post-build actions, error checking and reporting (try-catch-finally blocks), and notifications constructs. The Declarative pipeline has a script {} block to execute the Scripted pipeline inside a Declarative pipeline:

```
1.   pipeline {
2.       agent any
3.       stages {
4.
5.           stage('Rollback') {
6.             steps {
7.               bat 'echo "RollBack..."'
8.               script {
9.                       Successful_Build = readFile 'C:\\Users\\
     Mitesh\\2019\\JENKINS_HOME\\workspace\\Rollback.txt'
10.               echo Successful_Build
11.
12.               rtDownload (
13.                 serverId: "artifactory",
14.                 spec:
15.                 """{
16.                   "files": [
17.                     {
18.                              "pattern": "example-repo-local/
     example/${Successful_Build}/example.4.2.5-SNAPSHOT.war",
19.                       "target": "Rollback/"
20.                     }
21.                   ]
22.                 }"""
23.               )
24.             }
25.
26.           }
```

```
27.             }
28.
29.         post {
30.             success {
31.                 script {
32.                     Successful_Build = "${BUILD_TAG}" // this is
    Groovy
33.                     echo Successful_Build // printing via Groovy
    works
34.                     writeFile(file: ''C:\\Users\\Mitesh\\2019\\JENKINS_
    HOME\\workspace\\Rollback.txt', text: "${Successful_Build}" )
35.                 }
36.             }
37.         }
38.     }
39. }
```

Let's see some important points about a declarative pipeline:

- Recent feature introduced in Jenkins.

- *What to do* approach to create a pipeline.

- Easy to understand and developed for being user friendly.

- Fixed structure of pipeline; hence; Simple and good for beginners.

- The Declarative programming paradigm of computer programming in which the program or script has a collection of steps or tasks that defines what this script should achieve as an outcome.

- A pipeline block is a root of the Declarative pipeline syntax.

- Once the pipeline templates are ready for a specific type of project and specific to the programming language, it is easy to replicate the pipelines and work directly with scripts.

The following code is a sample Declarative pipeline:

```
1. pipeline {
2.     /* Stages and Steps */
3. }
4. pipeline {
5.     agent any
6.     stages {
7.         stage('SCA') {
```

```
 8.              steps {
 9.                  //
10.              }
11.          }
12.          stage('CI') {
13.              steps {
14.                  //
15.              }
16.          }
17.          stage('CD') {
18.              steps {
19.                  //
20.              }
21.          }
22.      }
23.  }
```

Let's see the declarative syntax template:

1. In the pipeline job that we created earlier, select **Hello World Template.**

2. Click on **Save**:

Figure 2.28: Sample Declarative pipeline

3. Click on **Build** now and verify the stage view.

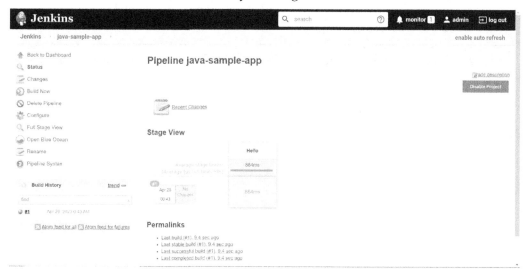

Figure 2.29: *Stage View*

In the next section, we will discuss Blue Ocean.

Blue Ocean

Blue Ocean provides an easy way to create a Declarative pipeline using a new user experience available on the Blue Ocean dashboard. It is like creating a script based on selecting components or steps or tasks. Most of the automation tools and services provide similar functionalities to attract beginners to adapt to the new Jenkins. It is a mature and transparent representation of an end-to-end automation pipeline. We can access the log stage-wise and access the script directly from the Jenkins Dashboard. It provides a view that includes multiple branches if the branches have the Jenkinsfile. We can create the Jenkinsfile using Blue Ocean if it is not available, and if the Jenkinsfile is already available with a valid syntax, then Jenkins detects the Jenkinsfile and starts the execution if a valid runtime environment is available. Blue Ocean provides a pipeline editor where we can directly enter the script or add stages and steps using UI elements. Stages are represented properly, including parallel stages execution or the stage is skipped during the execution based on conditions. Stage-wise logs are available to provide quick insights in case of failures and you don't need to scan the entire log to find an issue.

Let's understand how to start the Blue Ocean pipeline configuration:

1. Go to **Manage Jenkins | Manage Plugins | Available** and select **Blue Ocean** and **Install** without restart.

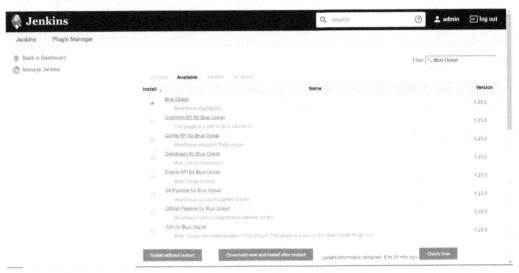

Figure 2.30: Available Plugins

2. Verify the successful installation of the Blue Ocean plugin and its dependencies:

Figure 2.31: Jenkins Update Center

3. After the Blue Ocean plugin is installed, it verifies the left-hand side sidebar where the new option has emerged.

4. Click on **Open** Blue Ocean.

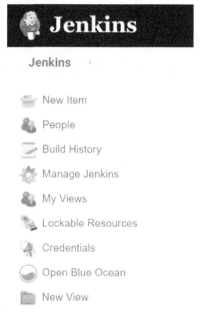

Figure 2.32: Blue Ocean in Jenkins Dashboard

5. Verify the Blue Ocean Dashboard. It provides a new user interface.

6. Click on `Create New Pipeline`:

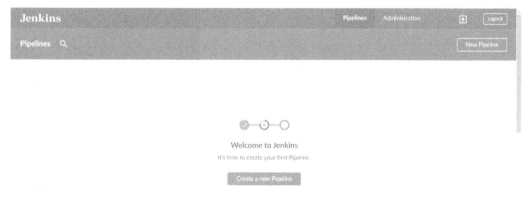

Figure 2.33: Blue Ocean Dashboard

7. Click on **GitHub** as our code is available in GitHub.

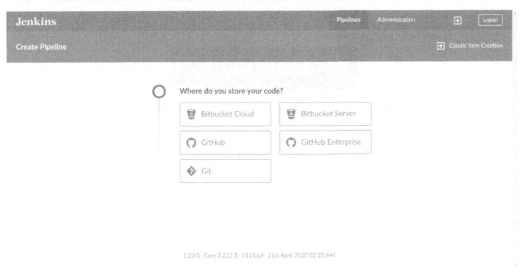

Figure 2.34: Source Code

8. Create an Access Token.

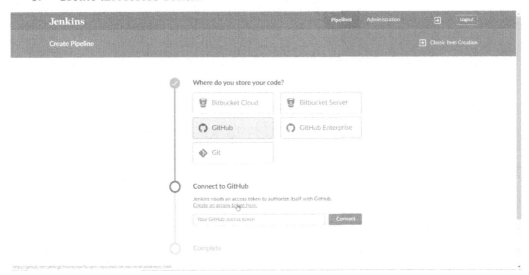

Figure 2.35: Connect to GitHub

9. Provide a name for an access token and click on **Create**.

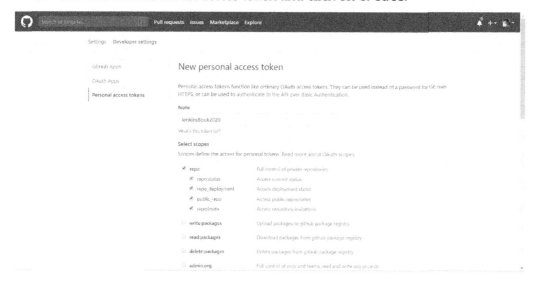

Figure 2.36: *Personal Access Token - GitHub*

10. Copy Personal Access Tokens from GitHub.

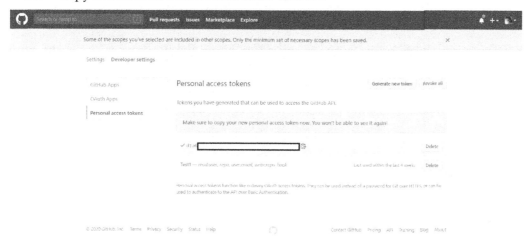

Figure 2.37: *PAT in GitHub*

11. Select the **Organization** where all the code is available. Select **Repository**:

Figure 2.38: GitHub Organization in Blue Ocean

12. If all goes well, verify the branch available on the Blue Ocean Dashboard:

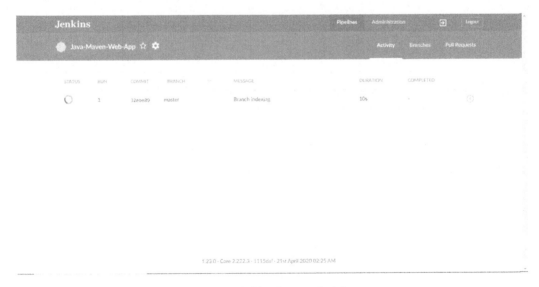

Figure 2.39: Blue Ocean - Activity

13. Go to the Classic Jenkins Dashboard. Click on the **Pipeline**:

Figure 2.40: Jenkins Dashboard for pipeline

14. Verify the Branch:

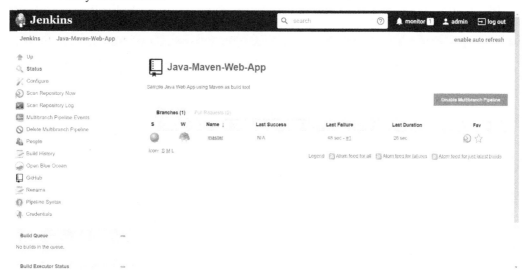

Figure 2.41: Branches

15. Click on **Scan Repository Log**. Here, verify in which branch the Jenkinsfile is used:

Figure 2.42: Scan Repository Log

16. If you want to keep only specific branches, then use Filter by name (with Wildcards):

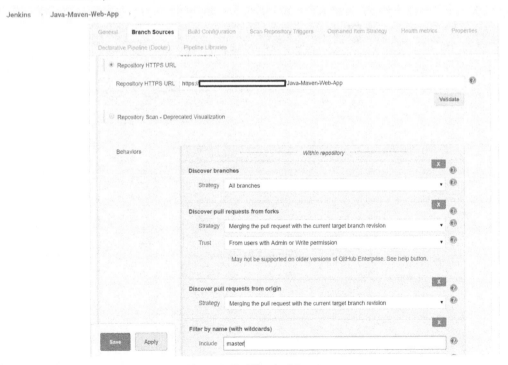

Figure 2.43: Filter by Name

17. If the Jenkinsfile is not in the root directory, then provide the path so that the pipeline can be executed:

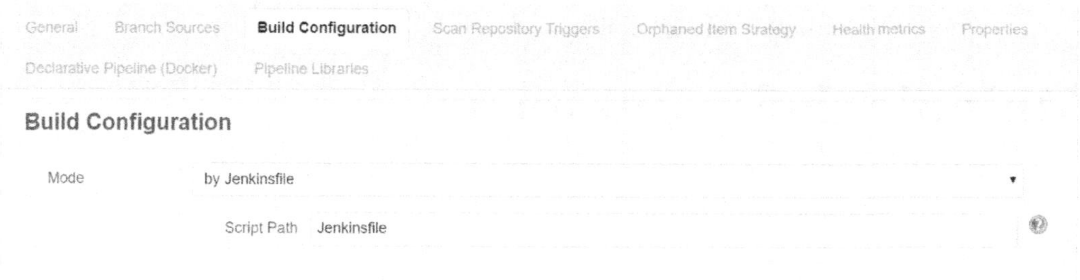

General   Branch Sources   **Build Configuration**   Scan Repository Triggers   Orphaned Item Strategy   Health metrics   Properties

Declarative Pipeline (Docker)   Pipeline Libraries

Build Configuration

Mode   by Jenkinsfile   ▼

            Script Path   Jenkinsfile

Figure 2.44: Jenkinsfile location

A Jenkinsfile contains the pipeline code in the scripted pipeline or declarative pipeline. By default, the pipeline created using Blue Ocean is stored in the Jenkinsfile. If the Jenkinsfile is already available in the repository, then Blue Ocean detects it and starts executing the pipeline while creating the pipeline on the Blue Ocean dashboard.

Conclusion

DevOps is critical to an organization's desire to become Agile. It requires better communication and collaboration between the Development and Operations teams. It also creates a scenario where associates are cross skilled across different technologies for better alignment and implementation. DevOps practices implementation helps an organization to achieve the goals of digital transformation.

In this chapter, we covered introduction to Jenkins, the history of Jenkins and how it evolved over the years, features of Jenkins, prerequisites to install Jenkins, how to run and configure Jenkins, Pipelines, Build pipeline, Scripted pipeline, Declarative pipeline, and Blue Ocean.

In the next chapter, we will cover how to create a pipeline using Blue Ocean for a Java web application.

Points to remember

- **Build pipeline:** Traditional way to create a pipeline using upstream and downstream jobs.

- **Scripted pipeline:** Boon for developers to create dynamic pipelines using programming constructs.

- **Declarative pipeline:** Boon for beginners to write a pipeline script using a Domain-Specific Language.

- **Blue Ocean:** Easy way to create a declarative pipeline using a completely new user experience in Jenkins.

- **Jenkinsfile:** File that contains Scripted or Declarative pipeline by default.
- **Multi-branch pipeline:** Pipeline that executes the script for all branches where the Jenkinsfile is available and valid.

Multiple choice questions

1. **Which of the following ways can be used to create a pipeline?**

    a. Build pipeline Plugin

    b. Scripted pipeline

    c. Declarative pipeline

    d. Blue Ocean

    e. All of the above

2. **The following code is correct in the scripted pipeline (True or False):**

```
pipeline {
    /* Stages and Steps */
}
```

    a. False

    b. True

3. **The following code is correct in the declarative pipeline (True or False):**

```
node {
    /* Stages and Steps */
}
```

    a. False

    b. True

Answer

1. e
2. a
3. a

Questions

1. What is Jenkins?
2. Explain the different ways to create a pipeline.
3. Explain the difference between the scripted and declarative pipeline.
4. Explain the significance of Blue Ocean.

CHAPTER 3

Building CI/CD Pipeline for a Java Web Application

"Change is your friend, not your foe; change is a brilliant opportunity to grow."

— *Simon T. Bailey*

Blue Ocean provides a simple way to create a pipeline using a simple user interface as well as a code editor to configure the **Continuous Integration (CI)** and **Continuous Delivery (CD)** pipeline for Java-based web applications. Blue Ocean is a topping on the Declarative pipeline that is Pipeline as Code feature from Jenkins. We can deploy an application to Platform as a Service offering such as Azure App Services or Amazon Elastic Beanstalk. In this book, we will cover the CI/CD implementation of a Java-based web application with Jenkins. We will also provide some valuable Notes related to DevOps and its culture, challenges, market trends, and so on for a better understanding.

Structure

In this chapter, we will discuss the following topics:

- Introduction
- Blue Ocean Multi-Stage pipeline for Java App
    - o Continuous Integration

- Create a Project in the Blue Ocean pipeline
- Import Repository from GitHub
- SonarQube connection in Jenkins
- Create Azure App Services – Platform as a Service to host a Java Web Application
- Unit Tests and Code Coverage
- Static Code Analysis Using SonarQube
- Create a WAR or Package file
- Upload a Package file to Nexus and Artifactory

o Continuous Delivery
- Download a package from Nexus and Artifactory
- Deploy to the Azure App Services Dev Environment
- Promotion (Approval) Request to Deploy to the QA Environment

o Rollback

- Conclusion
- Questions and exercises

Objectives

After studying this unit, you should be able to:

- Understand how to perform Static Code Analysis for a Java/Spring application
- Execute Unit Tests
- Calculate Code Coverage
- Verify Build Quality
- Create a WAR file/Package using Maven goals
- Deploy a WAR file to Azure App Services

Introduction

One of the leading organizations in the insurance sector needs to accelerate application delivery with high quality. The leadership of an organization is very clear on the implementation approach. They want the phase-wise implementation of DevOps practices. They want to automate manual processes for code analysis, unit testing, build, functional testing, and deployment. The need of the hour is to implement Continuous Integration and Continuous Delivery. This is an application selected as a pilot while there are other 10 early adopters Java-based web applications that are waiting in the queue.

The following is the list of tools and deliverables that will be integrated into the pipeline:

Tools	
Version Control	GitHub
Code Analysis	SonarQube, SonarQube Scanner
Unit Tests	Junit
Code Coverage	Jacoco
Build	Maven
Artifact Repository	Artifactory
Deployment Environment	Microsoft Azure – Azure App Services
Continuous Integration	Jenkins
Continuous Delivery	Jenkins
Pipeline	Pipeline as Code, Jenkinsfile, Blue Ocean
Expected deliverables or features in an automated pipeline	

- Installation and Configuration of Jenkins
- Distributed Architecture / Master Agent Architecture
- Role-based access
- Configuration of a CI/CD pipeline using Pipeline as Code
- Configuration of a CI/CD pipeline that deploys the WAR file to Azure App Services
- Documentation
  - o Documentation of defined processes and implementations
  - o Technical documentation – How to guides
- Best practices documentation for the usage of Jenkins / Blue Ocean

Table 3.1: *Tools and deliverables*

In the next section, we will create a pipeline for a Java application using the Blue Ocean interface in a step-by-step manner.

Blue Ocean multi-stage pipeline for a Java app

In this chapter, we will try to cover CI/CD for a sample Java application. Below is a big picture of CI/CD pipeline implementation in this chapter.

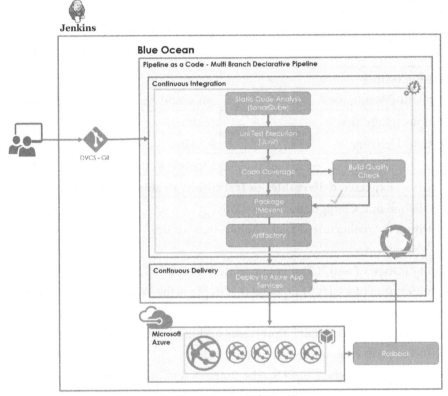

Figure 3.1: Big picture for CI/CD of Java app

In this chapter, we can use any Maven-based web application to implement Continuous Integration and Continuous Delivery.

In Jenkins, for the execution of the Maven CI pipeline, we need the following plugins to be installed:

- Maven integration plugin
- Pipeline Maven integration plugin
- Cobertura plugin
- SonarQube Scanner for Jenkins
- Azure app service plugin
- Script security

To install the preceding plugins, go to **Manage Jenkins | Manage Plugins | Available | Search** plugin and click on install without the restart button.

Continuous Integration – Java application

In this section, we will configure Continuous Code Inspection (Static Code Analysis) and Continuous Integration using Jenkins – the Declarative pipeline (Blue Ocean – Pipeline as Code - Jenkinsfile).

Continuous code inspection allows you to perform static code analysis and highlight bugs, vulnerabilities, and other code issues related to standards. **Continuous Integration** is the DevOps practice to integrate new feature implementation or a bug fix in the existing **distributed version control systems** such as Git that triggers code quality checks, unit test execution, and build.

> **NOTE**
>
> Continuous Integration is one of the most popular DevOps practices due to its easy implementation and benefits. However, there is no written rule to start with it. There are several projects where the Ops team initiates and performs release automation using tools or scripts.

Let's create a project in Blue Ocean to start with.

Create a project in the Blue Ocean pipeline

We are assuming here that the Jenkins setup is completed and the Blue Ocean plugin is installed successfully and it is available for use. Let's create a new pipeline:

1. Go to the Jenkins dashboard and click on **Open Blue Ocean**.

Figure 3.2: Jenkins Dashboard

2. Click on **Create a new Pipeline**:

Figure 3.3: Blue Ocean Dashboard

3. Select **GitHub** from the available repository option on the Blue Ocean dashboard:

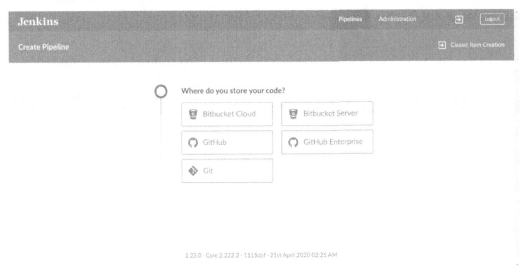

Figure 3.4: Create Project

4. Let's configure GitHub in a step-by-step manner in the next section.

Import repository from GitHub

To connect with the GitHub repository, Jenkins needs an access token so it can authorize itself with GitHub:

1. Click on the **Create an access token** link available on the Blue Ocean dashboard:

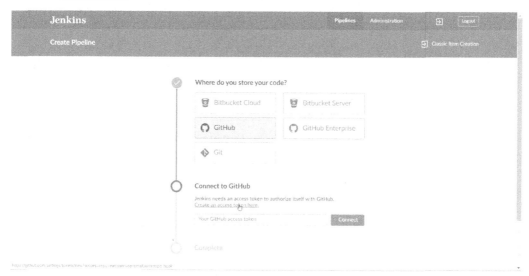

Figure 3.5: Connect to GitHub

2. Provide a name to an access token:

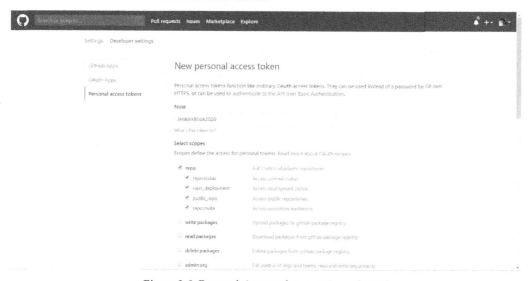

Figure 3.6: Personal Access token creation – GitHub

3. Copy the new access token and save it in a safe place in case you want to refer to it later:

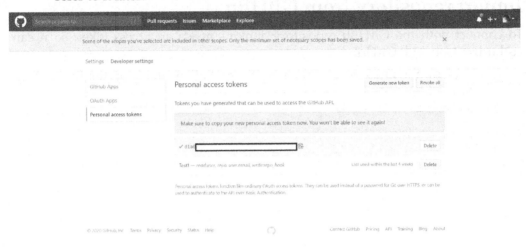

Figure 3.7: PAT in GitHub

4. Paste the access token copied from **GitHub** on the Blue Ocean dashboard where we are trying to create a pipeline.

5. Click on **Connect**:

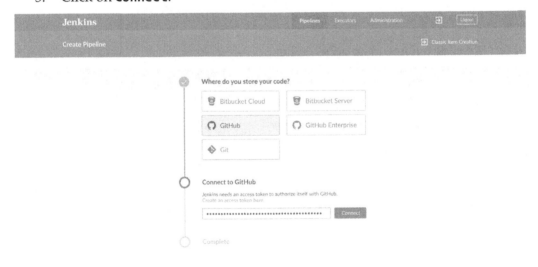

Figure 3.8: Connect to GitHub using PAT

6.   Select the **Organization** from GitHub that contains specific repositories that you want to use in the Blue Ocean pipeline:

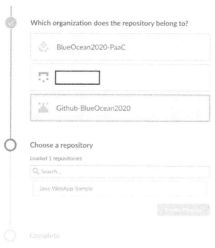

Figure 3.9: GitHub Organisation in BlueOcean

7.   Select a repository and click on **Create Pipeline**:

Figure 3.10: GitHub Repository in BlueOcean

8. Pipeline creation is work in progress as per the dashboard:

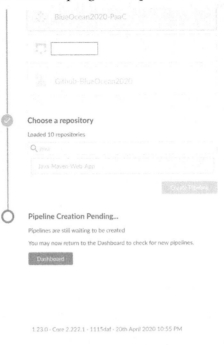

Figure 3.11: Pipeline Creation

9. Search for the pipeline on the Blue Ocean dashboard and click on it:

Figure 3.12: Search pipeline on BlueOcean Dashboard

As there is not a single branch in the chosen repository that has the Jenkinsfile, it will show the message that you don't have any branches that contain the Jenkinsfile. If there is a Jenkinsfile available in any branch, then that branch name will appear in Blue Ocean and the execution will start based on the availability of the agent mentioned in the Jenkinsfile. The Jenkinsfile contains a declarative pipeline script for the end-to-end automation.

Figure 3.13: Create pipeline for Java Maven Web App

It is used for both scripted and declarative pipeline. Blue Ocean allows you to configure steps on the Blue Ocean dashboard and it automatically creates the Jenkinsfile for you:

1. Provide agent details. We can delegate execution to the master or slave agent or virtual machines from cloud providers such as Azure and AWS or Docker containers:

Figure 3.14: Configure pipeline

2. First, we will configure **static code analysis (SCA)** using SonarQube in the Blue Ocean pipeline:

SonarQube connection in Jenkins

Perform the following steps:

1. Go to the **Manage Jenkins | Manage Plugins | Available | Search** SonarQube Scanner plugin and click on install without the **Restart** button:

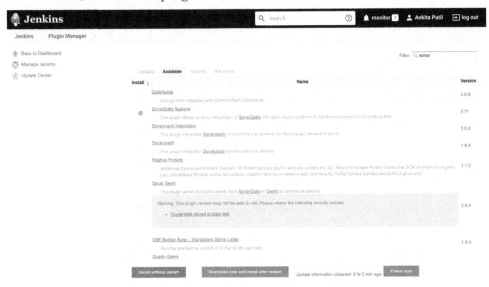

Figure 3.15: SonarQube Scanner Plugin installation

2. Verify the plugin installation in the Update Center:

Figure 3.16: Plugin install without restart

3. Go to **Manage Jenkins | Configure System | SonarQube** servers and click on **Add SonarQube**:

Figure 3.17: *SonarQube configuration in Jenkins*

4. Give the **Name** and **Server URL** of SonarQube:

Figure 3.18: *SonarQube server details in Jenkins*

5. Create a SonarQube authentication token. Go to the SonarQube dashboard |
   My Account:

Figure 3.19: *SonarQube Dashboard*

6. Then, go to the **Security** tab. You will find the **Token** section there in the
   Generate Tokens section. Give an appropriate name to the token and click
   on the **Generate** button to its right:

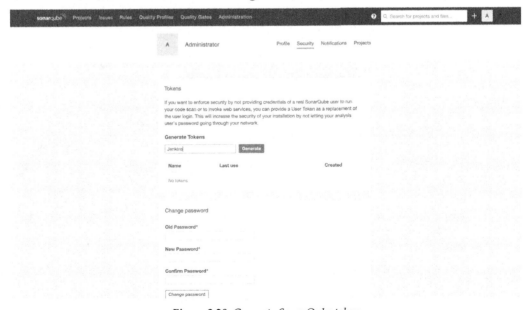

Figure 3.20: *Generate SonarQube token*

7.   Copy the generated token to use it in Jenkins:

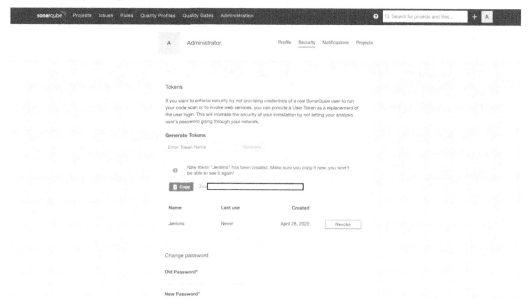

Figure 3.21: *SonarQube token*

8.   Go back to the Jenkins SonarQube configuration page and add the created token in Jenkins:

Figure 3.22: *Add SonarQube token to Jenkins*

NOTE

Measurement is easy in existing applications as we already know the AS IS scenario concerning lead time and other factors due to manual activities. Benefits measurement in the new application is difficult as DevOps practices implementation starts with the initial stage of the projects; hence, it is challenging to calculate the overall effort as well to find data with which new data should be compared with.

9. Select **Secret text** from the drop-down menu of **Kind**:

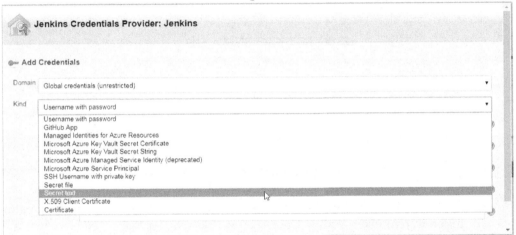

Figure 3.23: Jenkins Credentials for SonarQube token

10. Paste the copied token in the **Secret** column and provide an ID to a token for reference identification of the token configuration for SonarQube. Click on the **Add** button to save the token in Jenkins.

Figure 3.24: Secret and ID for SonarQube token in Jenkins Credentials

11. Select the created secret from the drop-down menu of the SonarQube authentication token by the ID we provide in Jenkins credentials:

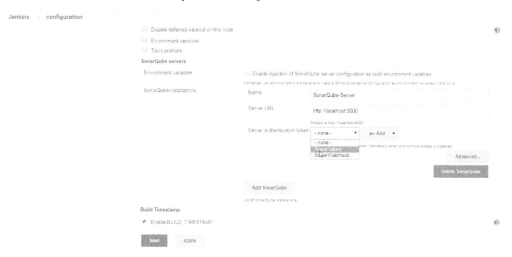

Figure 3.25: SonarQube authentication token in Jenkins

12. Now, click on the **Advanced** button to provide advanced settings. Configure the Webhook token in SonarQube. To create a webhook, go to **SonarQube | Administration | Configuration | Webhooks**, and click on the **Create** button on the right-hand side to create a webhook. Provide name, URL as **http://localhost:8080/sonarqube-webhook/**, and a secret for connection with Jenkins. Click on the **Create** button to save:

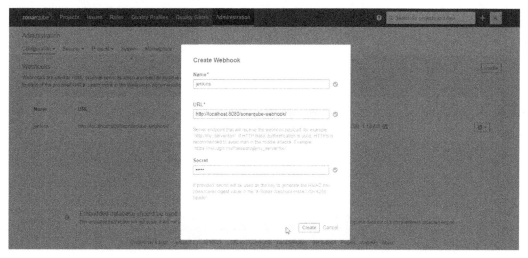

Figure 3.26: SonarQube webhook

13. Add the SonarQube Webhook token to Jenkins just like we added the SonarQube authentication token as the secret text:

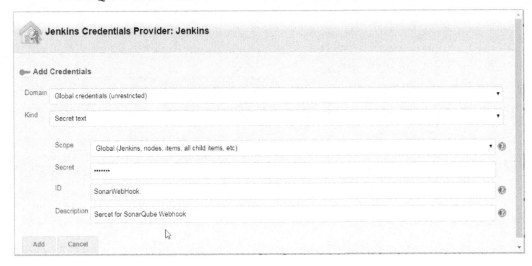

Figure 3.27: Jenkins credentials for SonarQube Webhook

14. Select the added webhook secret from the drop-down menu of Sonar Webhook of the Jenkins configuration of SonarQube:

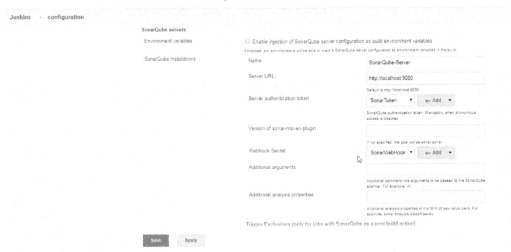

Figure 3.28: SonarQube Webhook

15. Now, save the configuration. You have configured the SonarQube connection with Jenkins. Before going further with the Jenkins pipeline, we will create a deployment environment in Cloud.

Create Azure app services – Platform as a service to host

Azure App Services help to host web applications or APIs or backends in a multi-tenant hosting environment. It supports several built-in images, and if the runtime environment is not available, then built-in Docker images can be created for Linux platforms. It has support for Java, Node.js, PHP, Python, .NET Core, and Ruby. For Java, supported versions are Tomcat 8.5, 9.0, Java SE, and WildFly 14 (all running on JRE 8). The following are the categories of pricing for virtual machines:

- Free and Shared tiers: Worker processes on shared VMs
- Standard and Premium tiers: Dedicated VMs

Let us try to create the Azure App Service in a resource group.

NOTE

Operations teams or Continuous Delivery utilizes cloud computing nowadays, and that opens a gate for automation. Various configuration management tools, as well as cloud-native templates and services, are available to automate resource provisioning.

Azure App Services to host Java web application

Let us understand this from the following steps:

1. Log into Azure with a valid subscription. Go to the home page and search for the Azure service named App Services:

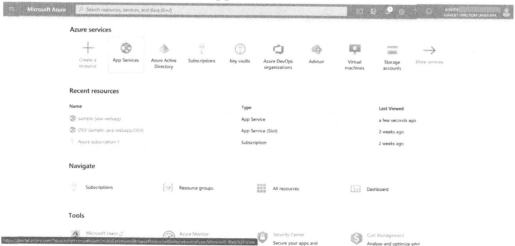

Figure 3.29: *Azure App Services*

2. You will be navigated to the App Service dashboard once you select the service. To create an App Service, click on the **Add** button on the left-hand side of the **App Services** page as shown in the following screenshot:

Figure 3.30: Create Azure App Service

3. Enter all the required details. Select the valid subscription using which you want to create the app service. Create or select a resource group in which you want to create the app service:

Figure 3.31: Create Azure App Service

4. Provide a valid name in the **Name** column and **Publish**. Select **Java 8 – Tomcat 9** from the drop-down list:

Figure 3.32: *Create Azure App Service*

5. Now, provide the **Service Plan** details. Create and select a service plan for your application:

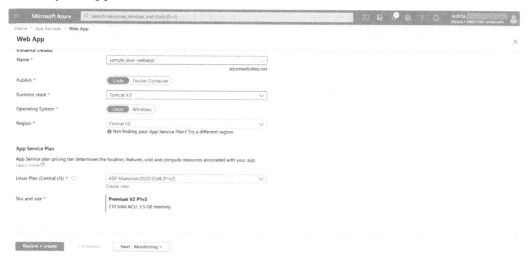

Figure 3.33: *Create Azure App Service*

6. Click on **Next**. Add monitoring if you want to get application insights. Here, we are not selecting monitoring:

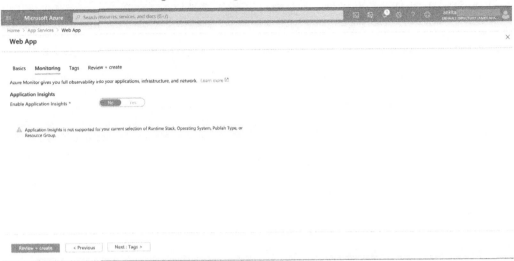

Figure 3.34: Create Azure App Service

7. Go ahead and click on the **Next** button. Provide the appropriate **Tag** if required. Or else leave it blank and click on **Next: Review + Create**:

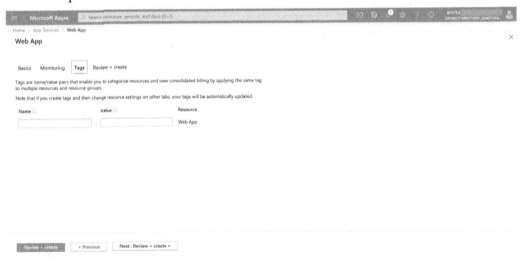

Figure 3.35: Create Azure App Service

8. Review all the details you added, and if everything seems fine, then click on the **Create** button:

Figure 3.36: *Create Azure App Service*

9. Once you click on the **Create** button, you will be redirected to the deployment page as shown in the following screenshot:

Figure 3.37: *Deployment of Created Azure App Service*

10. Once the deployment is complete, you can find your App Service running and ready to use for your Web app deployment. Refer to the details of the newly created Azure App Service as shown in the following screenshot:

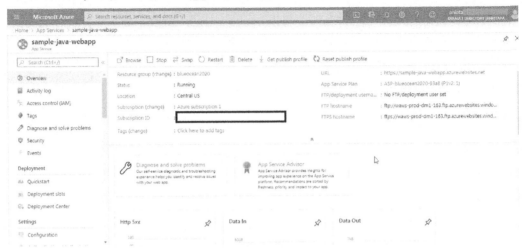

Figure 3.38: Azure App Service for Java Web App

11. Now, let us create different **Deployment** slots for creating different environments with the same App Service. For this, click on the **Deployment Slots** from the menu list in the left-hand side panel of the App Service sample-java-webapp that we just created:

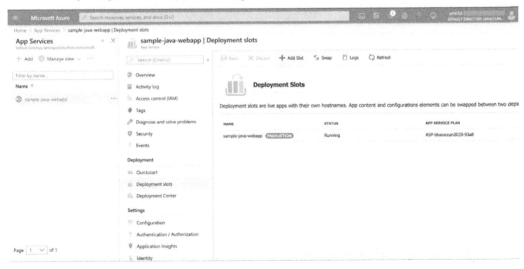

Figure 3.39: Deployment Slots

12. Click on **Add Slot** at the top of the **Deployment** slots. Provide the **Slot Name** and **Slot** from which you want to clone the setting/configuration:

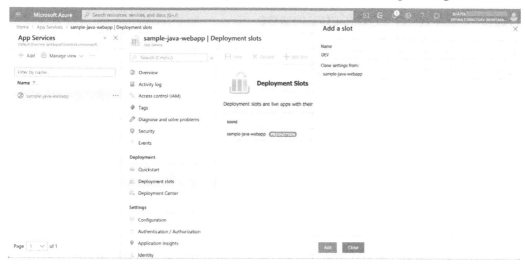

Figure 3.40: *Create Deployment Slot*

13. Click on the **Add** button to save and create the slot. Create slots for all environments you require. We have created the **DEV**, **QA**, and **STAGE** slots as shown in *Figure 3.37* (Production is the default pre-created slot when we create the Azure App Service):

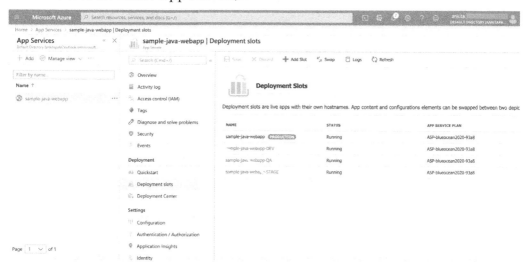

Figure 3.41: *Deployment Slots*

In the next section, we will complete the prerequisites for unit tests and code coverage.

Unit tests and code coverage

Before we start with the pipeline, let us configure the maven installation and JDK installation in the Global tool configuration:

1. Go to **Manage Jenkins | Global tool configuration | Maven**. Add the path to the maven installation on a machine:

Figure 3.42: *Maven home configuration*

2. Similarly, for configuration of the JDK installation go to **Manage Jenkins | Global tool configuration | JDK**. Add the path to the JDK installation on a machine:

Figure 3.43: *JAVA Home configuration*

NOTE

It is challenging to inject DevOps practices implementation in the existing and stable process as there is a possibility of resistance from a team that is already following processes, and the team may find it difficult transforming themselves to something new.

3. For code coverage, we use Cobertura and Jacoco. So, please add the following plugins to `pom.xml`:

```
1.    <build>
2.      <plugins>
3.        <plugin>
4.          <groupId>org.jacoco</groupId>
5.          <artifactId>jacoco-maven-plugin</artifactId>
6.          <version>0.7.5.201505241946</version>
7.          <executions>
8.            <execution>
9.              <goals>
10.                <goal>prepare-agent</goal>
11.              </goals>
12.            </execution>
13.            <execution>
14.              <id>report</id>
15.              <phase>prepare-package</phase>
16.              <goals>
17.                <goal>report</goal>
18.              </goals>
19.            </execution>
20.            <execution>
21.              <id>jacoco-check</id>
22.              <goals>
23.                <goal>check</goal>
24.              </goals>
25.              <configuration>
26.                <rules>
27.                  <rule>
28.                    <limits>
```

```
29.                    <limit>
30.                        <minimum>0.75</minimum>
31.                    </limit>
32.                  </limits>
33.                </rule>
34.              </rules>
35.            </configuration>
36.          </execution>
37.        </executions>
38.      </plugin>
39.      <plugin>
40.        <groupId>org.codehaus.mojo</groupId>
41.        <artifactId>cobertura-maven-plugin</artifactId>
42.        <version>${cobertura.version}</version>
43.        <configuration>
44.          <formats>
45.            <format>xml</format>
46.          </formats>
47.        </configuration>
48.        <executions>
49.          <execution>
50.            <phase>package</phase>
51.            <goals>
52.              <goal>cobertura</goal>
53.            </goals>
54.          </execution>
55.        </executions>
56.      </plugin>
57.      <plugin>
58.        <groupId>org.sonarsource.scanner.maven</groupId>
59.        <artifactId>sonar-maven-plugin</artifactId>
60.        <version>3.6.0.1398</version>
61.      </plugin>
62.    </plugins>
63.  </build>
64.  <reporting>
```

```
65.    <plugins>
66.     <!--  integrate maven-cobertura-plugin to project site  -->
67.      <plugin>
68.        <groupId>org.codehaus.mojo</groupId>
69.        <artifactId>cobertura-maven-plugin</artifactId>
70.        <version>${cobertura.version}</version>
71.        <configuration>
72.          <formats>
73.            <format>html</format>
74.            <format>xml</format>
75.          </formats>
76.        </configuration>
77.      </plugin>
78.    </plugins>
79.  </reporting>
```

Now, let us configure the Continuous Integration execution in the pipeline, and follow the given steps.

4. Go to the Blue Ocean pipeline we created. If you want to run the pipeline on a specific node, please select the node option in Agent setting and provide the node label, for example, `Master`:

Figure 3.44: Agent setting

5. Add a stage to the pipeline called `Continuous Integration`:

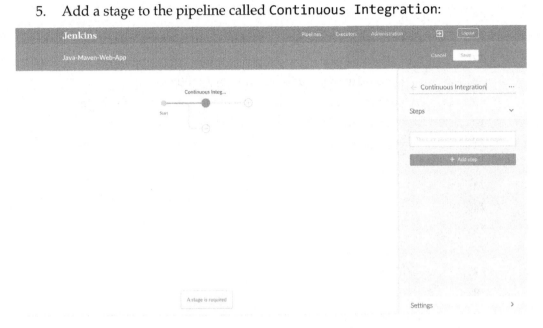

Figure 3.45: *Continuous Integration Stage*

6. Then, add a step to the same stage. Choose **Provide Maven environment** by searching in the step type:

Figure 3.46: *Provide a Maven environment*

7. Provide the required details such as JDK (`JAVA_HOME`) and maven (`MAVEN_HOME`) which we configured at the start of this topic in the global tool configuration of Jenkins. Please refer to the following screenshot to configure the Maven environment:

Figure 3.47: Provide a Maven environment

8. Scroll down for more options in the step:

Figure 3.48: Provide a Maven environment

9. Add the step to clean the project. This can be done by using the following command in a batch script:

`mvn clean`

10. So, add a new step in the **Provide Maven environment** step. Choose **Windows Batch Script** from the list of step types as shown in the following screenshot:

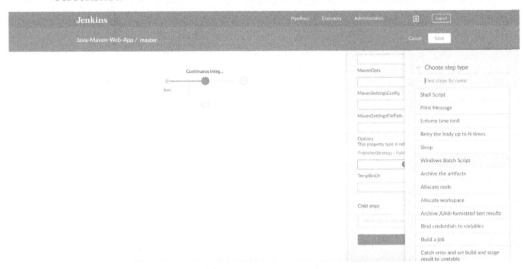

Figure 3.49: Windows batch command step

11. Add the `clean` command as mentioned earlier:

Figure 3.50: Maven clean

12. Similarly, add a new step **Windows Batch Script** after the clean step and add the unit test and code coverage report generation. Add the following command to a batch script:

```
mvn test cobertura:cobertura install
```

13. Refer to the following screenshot of the Jenkins pipeline:

Figure 3.51: *Unit Test and Code Coverage Step*

14. Now, the next step is to archive the Cobertura code coverage report. Add another step in **Prepare Maven environment** as the step type **Publish Cobertura Coverage Report** as shown in the following screenshot:

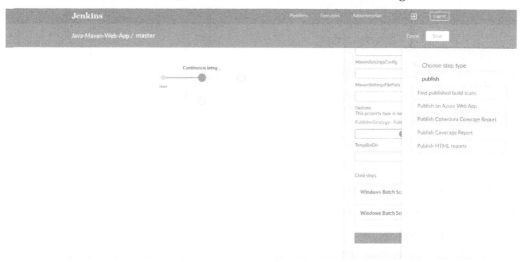

Figure 3.52: *Publish Cobertura Coverage Report step*

15. Provide the path to the report file. The default path is `target/site/cobertura/*.xml` and select the required configuration:

Figure 3.53: Cobertura report configuration

16. Once you have configured this, to check whether we have configured everything right, please save the pipeline. Once you click on the **Save** button, you will get the pop-up asking for the commit message and commit branch name:

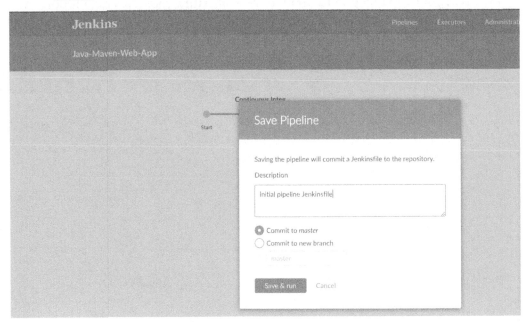

Figure 3.54: Save Configuration

17. Once you click on **Save & run** the pipeline, all the new configurations are committed in the Jenkinsfile in the GitHub repository. And then, a built is triggered on the same branch (here, we have a master branch).

   You can view the **Output/Console** logs on the build which got triggered as shown in the following screenshot:

Figure 3.55: BlueOcean console for Unit test and Code Coverage

18. So, your build is successful and we have integrated maven clean, unit test, and Code coverage to the CI pipeline. Please find the **Unit Test Result in Test** tab of the same page:

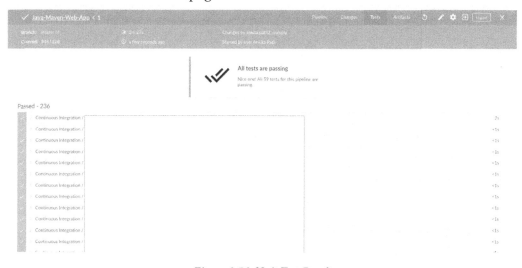

Figure 3.56: Unit Test Result

19. The Code Coverage report is published on the Jenkins main project dashboard. You can go to the main dashboard by clicking on the button on the top of the above image. You will be then redirected to the Jenkins main dashboard as shown in the following screenshot:

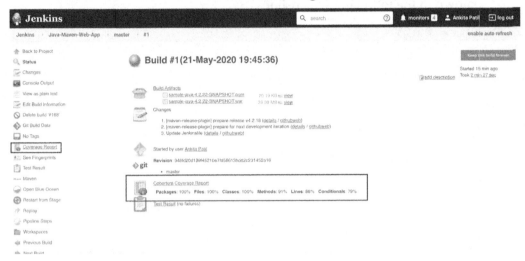

Figure 3.57: Jenkins build details

20. You can directly find the **Cobertura Coverage Report** and for a detailed report of **Code Coverage**, click on the **Coverage Report** option on the left-hand side of the panel. The detailed report of Cobertura code coverage is shown in the following screenshot:

Figure 3.58: Cobertura Coverage Report

Static code analysis using SonarQube

To do this, follow the given steps:

1. Add a new step to the Continuous Integration stage below **Provide Maven environment**:

Figure 3.59: Add step

NOTE

DevOps Readiness Assessment helps to understand the AS-IS situation and then accordingly, you need to create a roadmap for culture transformation. DevOps practices should be implemented as PoC, and then a pilot has to be done to realize the benefits. After pilot execution, a phase-wise implementation should be carried out for DevOps practices implementation.

2. Choose step type as prepare SonarQube Scanner environment:

Figure 3.60: Prepare SonarQube Scanner environment

3. Provide the required details like **InstallationName** (SonarQube Server Name which we provided in the Jenkins configuration of the SonarQube server) and the **CredentialsId** we created in Jenkins credentials for SonarQube credentials:

Figure 3.61: *Prepare SonarQube Scanner environment*

4. Now, for SonarQube Analysis, download SonarQube Scanner on the Jenkins master machine. Extract the ZIP folder and use the following command in the Windows Batch script step:

```
1.  <SonarQube  Scanner  folder  path>//bin//sonar-scanner
    -Dproject.settings=sonar-project.properties
```

5. Please create a file named `sonar-project.properties` for the provided project properties for SonarQube analysis. Refer to the following `sonar-project.properties` file which is used for this Maven sample application:

```
1.  # Required metadata
2.  sonar.projectKey=java-sonar-runner-simple
3.  sonar.projectName=Simple Java project analyzed with the
    SonarQube Runner
4.  sonar.projectVersion=1.0
5.
6.  # Comma-separated paths to directories with sources
    (required)
7.  sonar.sources=src/main
8.  sonar.tests=src/test
9.  sonar.java.binaries=target/classes
```

```
10.  sonar.java.test.binaries=target/test-classes
11.
12.  #Unit Test And Code Coverage
13.  sonar.junit.reportPaths=target/surefire-reports
14.  sonar.java.cobertura.reportPath=target/site/cobertura/
     coverage.xml
15.  sonar.coverage.jacoco.xmlReportPaths=target/site/jacoco/
     jacoco.xml
16.
17.  # Language
18.  sonar.language=java
19.
20.  # Encoding of the source files
21.  sonar.sourceEncoding=UTF-8
```

6. Add a step in the **Prepare SonarQube Scanner** environment called **Windows Batch Script** to execute the SonarQube analysis on the Maven project using the `sonar-project.properties` file:

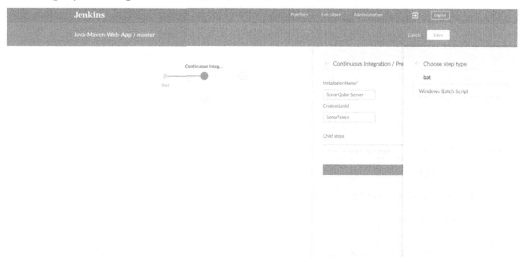

Figure 3.62: Windows batch script for SonarQube Analysis

7. Add the SonarQube Scanner script in the batch script step we just added:

Figure 3.63: SonarQube Analysis

8. Once the analysis command is configured, let us configure the next step to get the Quality Gate status after the code analysis. So, now add another step called Wait for Sonar analysis to complete and return the quality gate status as shown in the following screenshot:

Figure 3.64: Quality Gate Status step

9. Provide the required details to get the Quality Gate status from the SonarQube server like the **CredentialId** and **WebhookSecretId** we added earlier in Jenkins credentials while setting up the SonarQube server in the Jenkins configuration. Check the **AbortPipeline** checkbox to fail the pipeline if the Quality Gate fails:

Figure 3.65: Quality Gate Status step configuration

10. **Save & run** the pipeline. The output of the SonarQube analysis and Quality Gate status should be a success as shown in the following screenshot:

Figure 3.66: Quality Gate Status - Build Console log

11. The SonarQube analysis report is also published on the SonarQube server on its respective project dashboard, as shown in the following screenshot:

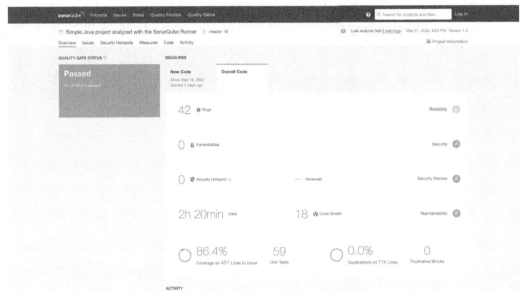

Figure 3.67: SonarQube Project Dashboard

Create WAR or package file

CI is basically for the development environment. So, the WAR which we will create is going to be **SNAPSHOT** WAR:

1. To create the WAR file, we again need to add a step **Prepare Maven environment** as discussed earlier:

Figure 3.68: Prepare a Maven environment

2. To build a WAR file, we use the following command in a Batch script so we need to add the step windows batch script:

```
1.   mvn package -Dmaven.clean.skip=true -Dmaven.test.skip=true
```

3. Add this script to the windows batch script as shown in the following screenshot:

Figure 3.69: *Maven Package batch script*

4. We now have to archive this artifact to the current build. Add a step **Archive the artifacts** as the type shown in the following screenshot:

Figure 3.70: *Archive the artifacts steps*

5. Provide the paths of files to be archived; here, we want to archive WAR files. Refer to the following screenshot for setting up the Archive:

Figure 3.71: Archive the artifacts path

6. **Save & run** the pipeline. After a successful generation of the war package, the war files are archived. One can find the archived artifacts in the top right **Artifacts** tab as shown in the following screenshot:

Figure 3.72: Archived Artifacts

In the next section, we will cover how to upload a package file to the Artifact repository.

Upload a package file to Artifactory

Before we upload the file to Artifactory, we need to get the application version from pom.xml into a build environment variable SVERSION (i.e. Snapshot Version). This step is done basically to get the latest version dynamically from pom.xml after the build is generated so that we can upload this build to Artifactory in the folder of that specific version.

The following is the arbitrary groovy script to be used for getting the version and storing it to the SVERSION and RVERSION (add in the QA stage) variables:

```
1.  def pom = readMavenPom file: 'pom.xml'
2.  VERSION = pom.version
3.  env.SVERSION = VERSION //Stable version value from pom
4.  echo env.SVERSION
5.
6.  def pom = readMavenPom file: 'pom.xml'
7.  VERSION = pom.version.replaceAll('-SNAPSHOT','')
8.  env.RVERSION = VERSION
9.  println env.RVERSION
```

Let's add steps to pipeline stage to integrate Artifactory.

1. To use this script in the pipeline, we need to add a step called the **Run** arbitrary pipeline script, as shown in the following screenshot:

Figure 3.73: Arbitrary pipeline script

2. Add the script in the text box available in the arbitrary script step:

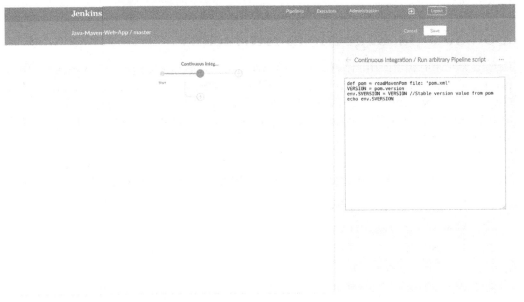

Figure 3.74 *Snapshot version script*

3. Now, focus on uploading the WAR file to the Artifactory. This can be done using a batch command which uses the Jfrog CLI tool which is to be installed on the Jenkins machine or on the agent on which the build is going to be executed. Find the Jfrog CLI command to upload an artifact to the artifactory repository below:

```
1. jfrog    rt    u    "**/sample-java.war"    Sample-Java-Web-App/org/
   springframework/samples/sample-java/%SVERSION%/ --user=%username%
   --password=%password% --url=http://localhost:8081/artifactory
```

4. The username and password are taken from the Jenkins credentials. To use these credentials, we need to use the groovy function withCredentials(). So, the entire arbitrary pipeline script is as follows:

```
1.            script {
2.              withCredentials([
3.                usernamePassword(credentialsId: 'artifactory',
4.                usernameVariable: 'username',
5.                passwordVariable: 'password')
6.              ]) {
7.                //Artifactory Credentials
8.                env.username = username
```

```
9.              env.password = password
10.
11.              //Batch command to Upload artifactory using
      above credentials
12.              bat(script: 'jfrog rt u "**/sample-java.war"
      Sample-Java-Web-App/org/springframework/samples/sample-
      java/%SVERSION%/  --user=%username%  --password=%password%
      --url=http://localhost:8081/artifactory',            label:
      'Artifactory Upload')
13.              }
14.          }
```

5. Add the preceding script in the new step **Run Arbitrary** pipeline script as shown in the following screenshot:

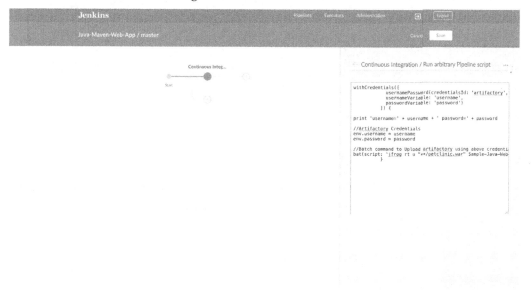

Figure 3.75: Jfrog Upload - Arbitrary pipeline script

6. Save and run the pipeline. Successful logs are shown in the following screenshot.

Figure 3.76: Jfrog upload pipeline logs

7. You can find the uploaded document in the **Repository** in the location as given in the Jfrog command `Sample-Java-Web-App/org/springframework/ samples/sample-java/%SVERSION%/` as shown in the following screenshot:

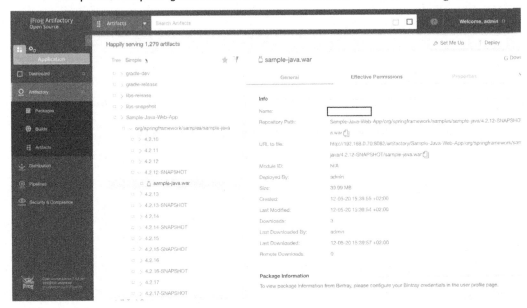

Figure 3.77: Jfrog Artifactory - a newly uploaded artifact

Continuous Delivery – Java application

Continuous Delivery (CD) is an extension or continuation of CI. CD deals with deploying packages into different environments. Multiple environments can be created for different types of testing with the invention of cloud computing. All the environments can be the same, created, and destroyed within a few minutes. The objective of CD is to make the product increment ready to deploy into production with a faster time to market and high quality. Besides, it brings the culture of discipline and standardization in the deployment process.

In the next section, we will deploy a package into the dev environment.

Download a package from Artifactory

To download the package, perform the following steps:

1. For Continuous delivery, add a new stage DEV. To download the artifact, the script used is similar to upload an artifact to the Jfrog artifactory. Find the downloaded Jfrog CLI command below:

```
1.  'jfrog rt dl Sample-Java-Web-App/org/springframework/samples/
    sample-java/%SVERSION%/sample-java.war --user=%username%
    --password=%password% --url=http://localhost:8081/artifactory
```

2. Find the entire script below which uses the `withCredentials()` function:

```
1.  withCredentials([
2.          usernamePassword(credentialsId: 'artifactory',
3.          usernameVariable: 'username',
4.          passwordVariable: 'password')
5.      ]) {
6.
7.          //Download Snapshot Artifact from Artifactiory
    using above credentials
8.              bat(script: 'jfrog rt dl Sample-Java-Web-
    App/org/springframework/samples/ sample -java/%SVERSION%/
    sample-java.war   --user=%username%   --password=%password%
    --url=http://localhost:8081/artifactory',        label:
    'Artifactory Download')
9.          }
```

3. Add the step **Run arbitrary pipeline** script to the newly added DEV stage as shown in the following screenshot:

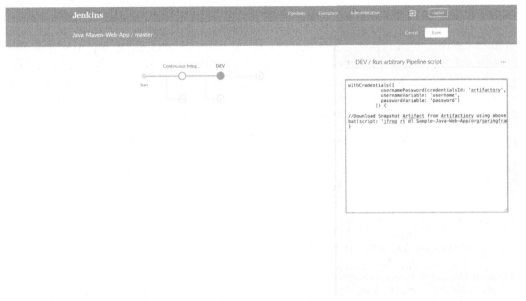

Figure 3.78: Jfrog Download Arbitrary pipeline step

4. If you click on **Save & run**, the log should look like the following screenshot:

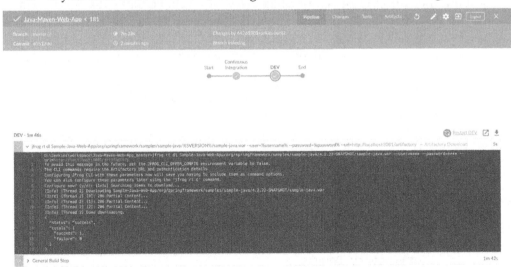

Figure 3.79: Jfrog download pipeline log

Once an artifact is downloaded from the Artifact repository, we will deploy the artifact/package/WAR file in Azure App Services that is a Platform as a Service offering from Microsoft Azure.

Deploy to the Azure app services dev environment

To deploy the war file to Azure App Services, perform the following steps:

1. Add a new step in the **DEV** stage. Choose the step type as **Publish artifact to Azure Web App** as shown in the following screenshot:

Figure 3.80: Publish to Azure Web App

2. For the connection with the Azure App service, you need to configure Azure credentials in Jenkins credentials. For this, go to the Jenkins main dashboard, you will find the **Credentials** option in the left panel. Click on it. Then, add credentials in the global credentials as shown in the following screenshot. Select the Microsoft Azure Service Principal option in kind of credential and the provide the Subscription ID, Client ID, Client Secret and Tenant IT which you can find in Azure App Service and Azure User Profile.

You can validate the connection by a click of the **verify service connection** button. It should say **Successfully verified** as shown in the following screenshot:

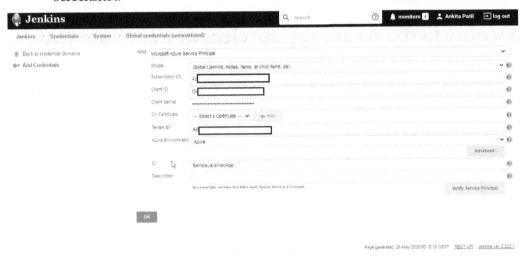

Figure 3.81: Azure Service Principal Credential - Jenkins credentials

We use this credentials ID in the step **Publish artifact to Azure Web App.**

3. Go back to the pipeline step **Publish artifact to Azure Web App** and provide the details required to deploy the WAR to Azure App Service like **AzureCredentialsID, AppName, ResourceGroup, FilePath, SlotName**, and **SourceDir** (refer to the following screenshot).

The slot name here we use is DEV as it is for a development environment.

Now, we have downloaded the artifact from the artifactory. So, we will use the same path of the war file to deploy the latest war to the Azure App Service as shown in the following screenshot (i.e. `org/springframework/samples/sample-java/'+env.SVERSION+'/sample-java.war`):

Figure 3.82: Publish to Azure Web App – AppName

4. Select **DeployOnlyifSuccessful**:

Figure 3.83: Publish to Azure Web App – DEV slot

5. **Save & run** the pipeline. The console log for the Azure App successful deployment should like the following screenshot:

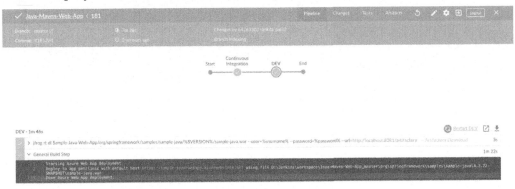

Figure 3.84: Azure Deployment - pipeline Console log

This configuration remains the same for the same Azure App service. We just need to change the **FilePath** and **SlotName** according to the environment. Verify the deployment by going to Maven application in Azure App Service or by accessing the Web application in the DEV environment.

In the next section, we will configure the approval before deploying to the QA environment.

Promotion (approval) request to deploy to the QA environment

Let's configure a step to configure approval before deployment into a specific environment.

1. To add an approval to the pipeline, first, add a stage for the approval like **Deploy to QA?** and then, add a step called **Wait for interactive input** as shown in the following screenshot :

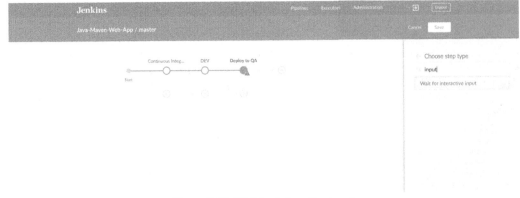

Figure 3.85: Wait for interactive input

2. Configure the values and provide the **Message, Id, Ok** (change the **Proceed** button name), **Submitter**, and **SubmitterParameter** as shown in the following screenshot:

Figure 3.86: Wait for interactive input step

3. Save and run and the step should wait until you click on one of the buttons **QA Deploy** or **Abort**. The **QA Deploy** will be selected only if you have logged-in as User which you have mentioned in the **Submitter** column of the interactive input step. Here, I have used the **admin** user and logged in as an admin user:

Figure 3.87: Console for User Input

4. Once you click on the **QA Deploy** button, the step should proceed further else abort the pipeline on the selection of the **Abort** button. Find the console log for the **QA Deploy** input selection as shown in the following screenshot:

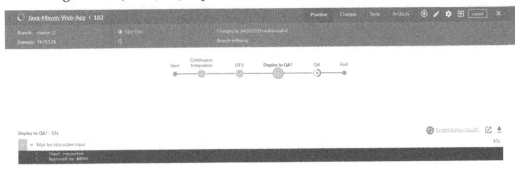

Figure 3.88: Console log QA Deploy promotion

In the next section, we will cover release management for the maven application.

Release management for the Maven application

Let's configure release plugin in pom.xml.

1. Release management in maven is done with help of the maven release plugin. Please add the following sample code to your `pom.xml`:

```
1.  <plugin>
2.    <groupId>org.apache.maven.plugins</groupId>
3.    <artifactId>maven-release-plugin</artifactId>
4.    <version>3.0.0-M1</version>
5.    <configuration>
6.      <tagNameFormat>v@{project.version}</tagNameFormat>
7.      <preparationGoals>clean verify</preparationGoals>
8.      <releaseProfiles>release</releaseProfiles>
9.    </configuration>
10. </plugin>
```

This plugin helps to accomplish the following goals:

- `release:` clean cleans the application.
- `release:prepare` prepares for a release in SCM. Tag the SCM branch with the release version and the commit new snapshot version to the `pom.xml` file in SCM.
- `release:prepare-with-pom` prepares for a release in SCM, and generate release POMs that record the fully resolved projects used.

- `release:rollback` rollbacks a previous release. This command just rollbacks the pom.xml file in local if mvn clean is not executed and SCM tagging is removed for the previous release which was executed.
- `release:perform` performs a release from SCM. Checkout the latest code from SCM and run the Maven pre-defined goals.
- `release:stage` performs a release from SCM into a staging folder/repository.
- `release:branch` creates a branch of the current project with all versions updated.
- `release:update-versions` updates the versions in the POM(s).

Here in this implementation, we are just going to use two goals `release:prepare` and `release:perform`. Once the code is successfully tested on the development environment, we release the code to other environments like QA and then Stage, and then at the end PROD.

To proceed with QA, once the **Development** team approves the code to release to QA, we prepare for release and perform the release on the code and then finally deploy the released code to the QA environment and others, if successfully tested.

2. So, now after promotion to QA, we add as a stage called QA where we add the `Prepare Maven environment` stage:

Figure 3.89: Prepare the maven environment step

3. Provide the required maven configuration as shown in the following screenshot:

Figure 3.90: Maven environment configuration

4. Now, add the following command to the windows batch script:

```
1.  mvn release:prepare release:perform -Dmaven.clean.skip=true
    -Dmaven.test.skip=true -Dmaven.deploy.skip=true
```

5. Add the step Windows Batch script:

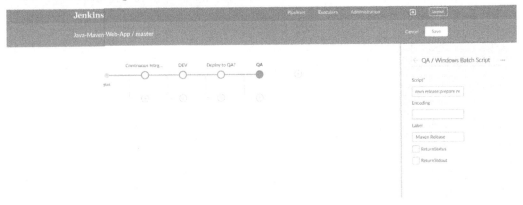

Figure 3.91: Mvn Release - Windows Batch Script

6. **Save & run** the pipeline and find the release console log once the pipeline is successfully executed:

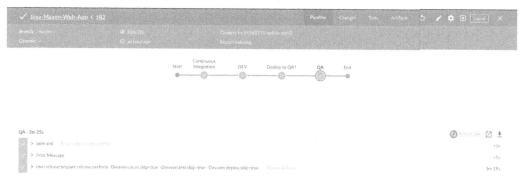

Figure 3.92: *Console for maven release execution*

7. Now, go to the **Artifacts** tab and find a new war without **SNAPSHOT** in the version of the file name:

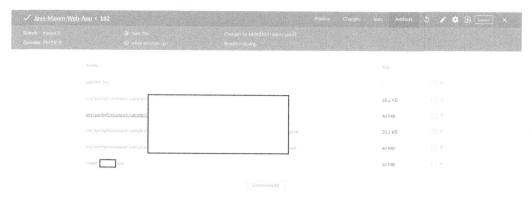

Figure 3.93: *Maven Release Artifact*

8. On successful execution of the release command, please go to your repository and see the latest commit. You should find the commits with a new `release` tag and also a new version update in the `pom.xml` file. Refer to the following screenshot:

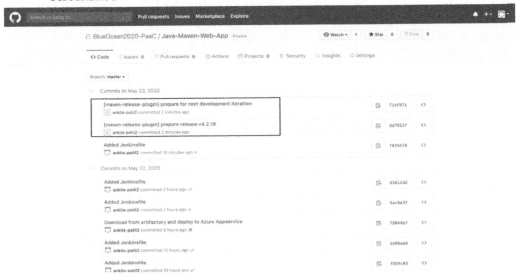

Figure 3.94: *Maven release version tagging in SCM (GitHub)*

In the next section, we will create a stage for a rollback.

Rollback

We perform a rollback in case if deployment of an application is not working as expected. Here, we have considered the scenario after deployment issues where we want to rollback:

1. First, we will use the promotion/approval interactive input step. But this time, we will ask you to input the **yes** or **no** parameter as we don't want to abort the entire pipeline.

2. This interactive input step has to be added and we need to store this parameter value in a variable. So, we will use the entire Wait for the interactive input function in the arbitrary script.

3. Please find the first part (i.e. Wait for interactive input) of the script in the following code snippet:

```
1.  def userInput = input(id: 'userInput', message: 'Do you
    want to Rollback?', submitter: 'admin', parameters:
    [choice(choices: ['Yes', 'No'], description: 'Please select
    a option below.\n Note: On Abort pipeline will be Aborted
    and Prod Stable Version will not be updated', name: 'env')])

2.  echo ("You Entered '"+userInput+ "' to Rollback")
```

4. Now, the second part is to put the condition that if the user enters yes, then she/he wants to rollback. So, in this condition, we will download the last stable build from the artifactory. To get the stable version, we have a file that stores the **Stable** version, which we read and then get the version to be downloaded. Then, deploy it to the Production environment again.

This rollback does not rollback your code in SCM that needs to be manually rollbacked to a previous stable state.

Find the if condition in the following Code:

```
1.    //script to rollback on 'Yes'
2.    if(userInput=='Yes'){
3.               echo ("Rollback in process")
4.               //get stable version value
5.               env.stableVersion = readFile 'D:\\Jenkins\\imp-
      docs\\stable-version.txt'
6.               //download stable version from Artifactory
7.             bat(script: 'jfrog rt dl Sample-Java-Web-App/org/
      springframework/samples/sample-java/%stableVersion%/*.
      war    --user=admin    --password=admin123    --url=http://
      localhost:8081/artifactory',    label:    'Release    Package
      Download from Artifactory')
8.
9.               //bat(script: 'MOVE org\\springframework\\
      samples\\    sample-java\\%stableVersion%\\*-sample-*.war
      org\\springframework\\samples\\sample-java\\4.2.11\\
      sample-java.war')
10.              //Deploy stable version back to PRODUCTION
      environment
11.               azureWebAppPublish(azureCredentialsId:
      'SampleJavaWebApp',        appName:        'sample-java-webapp',
      resourceGroup:    'blueocean2020',    deployOnlyIfSuccessful:
      true,        filePath:            'org/springframework/samples/
      sample-java/'+env.stableVersion+'/sample-java.war',
      sourceDirectory: '.')
12.               }
```

Now, if the user enters **No**, then the rollback should not happen and it should update the new release version as the stable version to the stable-version. txt file. For this, first create a file stable-version.txt at the location and then provide the path to the following script. Find the following code snippet for the script on the user input as **No**:

```
1.   //script to rollback on 'No'
2.   else if(userInput=='No'){
3.     echo ("Rollback aborted.\n Deployment Successful.\
       nUpdating Stable Version")
4.     //write stable version to file
5.     writeFile(file: 'D:\\Jenkins\\imp-docs\\stable-version.
       txt', text: env.RVERSION)
6.     echo env.RVERSION
7.   }
```

Your entire rollback script should look like the following script:

```
1.   //User input to get yes or no input for rollback
2.   def userInput = input(id: 'userInput', message: 'Do you
     want to Rollback?', submitter: 'admin', parameters:
     [choice(choices: ['Yes', 'No'], description: 'Please select
     a option below.\n Note: On Abort pipeline will be Aborted
     and Prod Stable Version will not be updated', name: 'env')])
3.     echo ("You Entered '"+userInput+ "' to Rollback")
4.
5.     //script to rollback on 'Yes'
6.     if(userInput=='Yes'){
7.       echo ("Rollback in process")
8.       //get stable version value
9.         env.stableVersion = readFile 'D:\\Jenkins\\imp-
       docs\\stable-version.txt'
10.      //download stable version from Artifactory
11.        bat(script: 'jfrog rt dl Sample-Java-Web-App/org/
       springframework/samples/sample-java/%stableVersion%/*.
       war --user=admin --password=admin123 --url=http://
       localhost:8081/artifactory', label: 'Release Package
       Download from Artifactory')
12.
13.        //bat(script: 'MOVE org\\springframework\\samples\\
       spring-sample\\%stableVersion%\\sample-java-*.war    org\\
       springframework\\samples\\sample-java\\4.2.11\\sample-
       java.war')
```

```
14.        //Deploy stable version back to PRODUCTION environment
15.                    azureWebAppPublish(azureCredentialsId:
    'SampleJavaWebApp',      appName:      'sample-java-webapp',
    resourceGroup:   'blueocean2020',   deployOnlyIfSuccessful:
    true,       filePath:       'org/springframework/samples/
    sample-java/'+env.stableVersion+'/sample-java.war',
    sourceDirectory: '.')
16.     }
17.
18.     //script to rollback on 'No'
19.     else if(userInput=='No'){
20.        echo ("Rollback aborted.\n Deployment Successful.\
    nUpdating Stable Version")
21.        //write stable version to file
22.           writeFile(file: 'D:\\Jenkins\\imp-docs\\stable-
    version.txt', text: env.RVERSION)
23.        echo env.RVERSION
24.     }
```

5. Now, let us continue with the pipeline configuration. Add the promotion and deployment steps for STAGE and PROD (You can find these steps in the entire Jenkins file at the end of this chapter.) and then add a stage for **Rollback**:

Figure 3.95: Rollback Stage

6. Now, add a step **Run arbitrary pipeline** script as shown in the following screenshot and add the preceding rollback script that we created to the text box of the step:

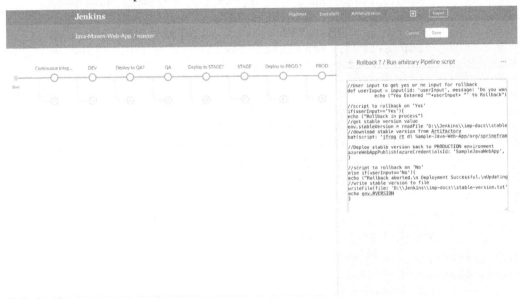

Figure 3.96: Rollback Script in Arbitrary pipeline Script

7. **Save & run** the pipeline. When the pipeline runs, you'll have to choose an option to rollback or not as shown in the following screenshot:

Figure 3.97: Console for Rollback Promotion Choice Input

8. If you select **Yes**, you will find the console with the Rollback deployment logs:

Figure 3.98: Rollback deployment logs

Else if you select **No**, the `stable-version.txt` file is edited with the new release version as shown in the console log and text file in the following screenshot:

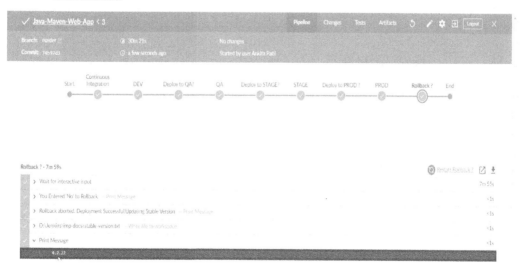

Figure 3.99: No Rollback logs

9. After the rollback stage is successful when **No** is given as input, find the text file edited with the new stable version as shown in the following screenshot:

Figure 3.100: stable-version.txt after the successful deployment

The following is the final version of the declarative pipeline:

```
1.  pipeline {
2.     agent {
3.        node {
4.           label 'master'
5.        }
6.
7.     }
8.     stages {
9.        stage('Continuous Integration') {
10.          agent {
11.             node {
12.                label 'master'
13.             }
14.
15.          }
16.
17. // Unit test execution and code coverage calculation
```

```
18.      steps {
19.        withMaven(jdk: 'JAVA_HOME', maven: 'MAVEN_HOME') {
20.          bat 'mvn clean'
21.            bat(script: 'mvn test cobertura:cobertura install',
   label: 'Unit Testing and Code Coverage')
22.            cobertura(autoUpdateHealth: true, autoUpdateStability:
   true,       classCoverageTargets:        'target/site/cobertura/',
   coberturaReportFile:                'target/site/cobertura/*.xml',
   failUnstable: true, zoomCoverageChart: true)
23.        }
24.
25. // Static code analysis using sonarqube
26.          withSonarQubeEnv(installationName: 'SonarQube-Server',
   credentialsId: 'SonarToken') {
27.              bat(script: 'D://Softwares//sonar-scanner-cli//
   sonar-scanner-4.3.0.2102-windows//bin//sonar-scanner -Dproject.
   settings=sonar-project.properties', label: 'SonarQube Analysis')
28.        }
29.
30. //Wait for the Quality Gate results from SonarQube to Jenkins
31.          waitForQualityGate(abortPipeline: true, credentialsId:
   'SonarToken', webhookSecretId: 'SonarWebHook')
32.            withMaven(jdk: 'JAVA_HOME', maven: 'MAVEN_HOME',
   publisherStrategy: 'IMPLICIT') {
33.              bat(script: 'mvn package -Dmaven.clean.skip=true
   -Dmaven.test.skip=true', label: 'Snapshot War Packaging')
34.        }
35.
36.              archiveArtifacts(artifacts: 'target/**/*.war',
   onlyIfSuccessful: true, fingerprint: true)
37.        script {
38.          def pom = readMavenPom file: 'pom.xml'
39.          VERSION = pom.version
40.          env.SVERSION = VERSION //Stable version value from pom
41.          echo env.SVERSION
42.        }
43.
44.        script {
```

```
45.         withCredentials([
46.            usernamePassword(credentialsId: 'artifactory',
47.            usernameVariable: 'username',
48.            passwordVariable: 'password')
49.         ]) {
50.
51.         print 'username=' + username + ' password=' + password
52.
53.            //Artifactory Credentials
54.            env.username = username
55.            env.password = password
56.
57.              //Batch command to Upload artifactory using above
    credentials
58.                bat(script: 'jfrog rt u "**/sample-java.war"
    Sample-Java-Web-App/org/springframework/samples/sample-
    java/%SVERSION%/    --user=%username%    --password=%password%
    --url=http://localhost:8081/artifactory', label: 'Artifactory
    Upload')
59.            }
60.         }
61.
62.      }
63.   }
64.
65. // Deploy to Azure App Services - Dev slot
66.    stage('DEV') {
67.      steps {
68.        script {
69.          withCredentials([
70.            usernamePassword(credentialsId: 'artifactory',
71.            usernameVariable: 'username',
72.            passwordVariable: 'password')
73.          ]) {
74.
75.            //Download Snapshot Artifact from Artifactiory using
    above credentials
```

```
76.                      bat(script: 'jfrog rt dl Sample-Java-Web-App/
     org/springframework/samples/sample-java/%SVERSION%/sample-
     java.war --user=%username% --password=%password% --url=http://
     localhost:8081/artifactory', label: 'Artifactory Download')
77.              }
78.           }
79.
80.      azureWebAppPublish(azureCredentialsId: 'SampleJavaWebApp',
     appName: 'sample-java-webapp', resourceGroup: 'blueocean2020',
     deployOnlyIfSuccessful: true, filePath: 'org/springframework/
     samples/          sample-java/'+env.SVERSION+'/sample-java.war',
     slotName: 'DEV', sourceDirectory: '.')
81.           }
82.        }
83.
84. // Deployment to QA Environment with Approvals
85.      stage('Deploy to QA?') {
86.         steps {
87.            input(message: 'Are you sure you want to deploy to QA
     Environment', id: 'QA', ok: 'QA Deploy', submitter: 'admin',
     submitterParameter: 'admin')
88.         }
89.      }
90.
91.      stage('QA') {
92.         steps {
93.           script {
94.             def pom = readMavenPom file: 'pom.xml'
95.             VERSION = pom.version.replaceAll('-SNAPSHOT','')
96.             env.RVERSION = VERSION
97.             println env.RVERSION
98.           }
99.
100.         withMaven(jdk: 'JAVA_HOME', maven: 'MAVEN_HOME') {
101.            bat(script: 'mvn release:prepare release:perform
     -Dmaven.clean.skip=true -Dmaven.test.skip=true -Dmaven.deploy.
     skip=true ', label: 'Maven Release')
102.         }
```

```
103.
104.        bat(script: 'jfrog rt u "**/sample-java.war" Sample-Java-
      Web-App/org/springframework/samples/sample-java/%RVERSION%/
      --user=admin  --password=admin123  --url=http://localhost:8081/
      artifactory', label: 'Release Upload Artifactory')
105.          bat(script: 'jfrog rt dl Sample-Java-Web-App/org/
      springframework/samples/sample-java/%RVERSION%/*.war
      --user=admin  --password=admin123  --url=http://localhost:8081/
      artifactory', label: 'Release Package Download from Artifactory')
106.        azureWebAppPublish(azureCredentialsId: 'SampleJavaWebApp',
      appName: 'sample-java-webapp', resourceGroup: 'blueocean2020',
      deployOnlyIfSuccessful: true, slotName: 'QA', filePath: 'org/
      springframework/samples/sample-java/'+env.RVERSION+'/sample-
      java.war', sourceDirectory: '.')
107.      }
108.    }
109.
110.    stage('Deploy to STAGE?') {
111.      steps {
112.          input(message: 'Are you sure you want to deploy to
      STAGE Environment', id: 'STAGE', ok: 'STAGE Deploy', submitter:
      'admin', submitterParameter: 'admin')
113.      }
114.    }
115.
116.    stage('STAGE') {
117.      steps {
118.        bat(script: 'echo Revision version is %RVERSION%', label:
      'New Revision Version')
119.        azureWebAppPublish(azureCredentialsId: 'SampleJavaWebApp',
      appName: 'sample-java-webapp', resourceGroup: 'blueocean2020',
      filePath:          'org/springframework/samples/sample-java/'+env.
      RVERSION+'/sample-java.war', slotName: 'STAGE', sourceDirectory:
      '.', deployOnlyIfSuccessful: true)
120.      }
121.    }
122.
123.    stage('Deploy to PROD ?') {
124.      steps {
125.        input(message: 'Do you want deploy to prod? ', id: 'PROD',
```

```
         ok: 'PROD', submitter: 'admin', submitterParameter: 'admin')
126.         }
127.      }
128.
129.     stage('PROD') {
130.        steps {
131.        azureWebAppPublish(azureCredentialsId: 'SampleJavaWebApp',
          appName: 'sample-java-webapp', resourceGroup: 'blueocean2020',
          deployOnlyIfSuccessful: true, filePath: 'org/springframework/
          samples/sample-java/'+env.RVERSION+'/sample-java.war',
          sourceDirectory: '.')
132.        }
133.     }
134.
135. // Rollback
136.
137.     stage('Rollback ?') {
138.        steps {
139.          script {
140.            //User input to get yes or no input for rollback
141.            def userInput = input(id: 'userInput', message:
          'Do you want to Rollback?', submitter: 'admin', parameters:
          [choice(choices: ['Yes', 'No'], description: 'Please select a
          option below.\n Note: On Abort pipeline will be Aborted and Prod
          Stable Version will not be updated', name: 'env')])
142.            echo ("You Entered '"+userInput+ "' to Rollback")
143.
144.            //script to rollback on 'Yes'
145.            if(userInput=='Yes'){
146.              echo ("Rollback in process")
147.              //get stable version value
148.              env.stableVersion = readFile 'D:\\Jenkins\\imp-docs\\
          stable-version.txt'
149.              //download stable version from Artifactory
150.                bat(script: 'jfrog rt dl Sample-Java-Web-App/
          org/springframework/samples/sample-java/%stableVersion%/*.war
          --user=admin  --password=admin123  --url=http://localhost:8081/
          artifactory', label: 'Release Package Download from Artifactory')
```

```
151.
152.        //bat(script: 'MOVE org\\springframework\\samples\\spring-
      sample\\%stableVersion%\\*-sample-*.war  org\\springframework\\
      samples\\sample-java\\4.2.11\\sample-java.war')
153.            //Deploy stable version back to PRODUCTION environment
154.        azureWebAppPublish(azureCredentialsId: 'SampleJavaWebApp',
      appName: 'sample-java-webapp', resourceGroup: 'blueocean2020',
      deployOnlyIfSuccessful: true, filePath: 'org/springframework/
      samples/sample-java/'+env.stableVersion+'/sample-java.war',
      sourceDirectory: '.')
155.            }
156.
157.        //script to rollback on 'No'
158.        else if(userInput=='No'){
159.            echo ("Rollback aborted.\n Deployment Successful.\
      nUpdating Stable Version")
160.            //write stable version to file
161.                writeFile(file: 'D:\\Jenkins\\imp-docs\\stable-
      version.txt', text: env.RVERSION)
162.            echo env.RVERSION
163.            }
164.        }
165.
166.        }
167.        }
168.
169.    }
170. }
```

Done!

Conclusion

We covered continuous integration and continuous delivery for the Maven-based Java application. We deployed the sample web application in Azure App Services. We configured tasks for Unit test execution, Code coverage calculation, Build quality check, and deploying the WAR file to Azure App Services that is Platform as a Service from Microsoft Azure.

In the next chapter, we will configure the CI/CD pipeline for a sample Android application.

Multiple-choice questions

1. **SonarQube provides details such as:**

   a. Bugs

   b. Vulnerabilities

   c. Code smells

   d. All of these

2. **The command mvn test can be used for unit test execution (True or False):**

   a. False

   b. True

Answer

1. **d**

2. **a**

Questions

1. What are Azure App Services?

2. Explain the usage of deployment slots.

3. What is the use of Artifactory?

CHAPTER 4

Building CI/CD Pipeline for an Android App

> "Growth is actually contagious, so if you want to reach your goals, you've got to get around people who are going in the same direction you want to be going, and you will catch the success."
>
> — *Dr. Henry Cloud*

Evolution and innovation are part of modern life and everyone wants and needs automation with speed, quality, and safety. Automobile and car manufacturers are also running in the same race. For automobile and car manufacturers, it is important to gain traction of potential customers and build a reputation. Digital approaches along with cloud infrastructure make vehicles a great user experience with safety. This entire exercise requires software to drive the evolution and innovation in this space. In short, technology resides in the car. Leading automobile and car manufacturers are trying to revamp their entire interaction with end-users. They are creating mobile apps for managing various functions of cars related to entertainment, information, navigation, safety, and other operations. The delivery manager wants to accelerate application delivery with high quality. The leadership of an organization is very clear on the implementation approach. They want the phase-wise implementation of DevOps practices. They want to automate manual processes for code analysis, unit testing, build, functional testing, and deployment. The need of the hour is to implement Continuous Integration and Continuous Delivery. In this chapter, we will cover the CI/CD implementation of an Android application with Jenkins. We will use the Pipeline as Code to create the CI/CD pipeline. Blue Ocean provides a simple way to create a pipeline using a simple user interface as well as a code editor to configure **Continuous Integration (CI)** and **Continuous Delivery (CD)** pipeline for Android applications. We will distribute an application to a specific group in the App Center. We will also provide some valuable Notes related to DevOps, culture, challenges, market trends, and so on for a better understanding.

Structure

In this chapter we will discuss the following topics:

- Introduction
- Blue Ocean multi-stage pipeline for an Android App
  - o Continuous Integration
    - Add a pipeline to the Code Repository in GitHub
    - Understand how to perform Lint Analysis for an Android application
    - Execute Unit tests
    - Calculate Code coverage
    - Verify Build Quality
    - Create an APK file
  - o Continuous Delivery
    - Deploy a Package/APK to the App Center

Objectives

After studying this unit, you should be able to:

- Understand how to perform Lint Analysis for an Android application
- Execute unit tests
- Calculate code coverage
- Verify Build Quality
- Create an APK file
- Deploy APK to the App Center

In this chapter, we will try to cover CI/CD for sample Android applications.

Introduction

The organization has selected one application as a pilot while there are other five early adopter Android applications waiting in the queue. We have the responsibility to create a CI/CD pipeline using Pipeline as Code in Jenkins in the Declarative syntax.

The following is the list of tools and deliverables that will be integrated into the pipeline:

Tools	
Version Control	GitHub
Code Analysis	Android Lint
Unit Tests	Junit
Code Coverage	Jacoco
Build	Gradle
Secret File (s)	Keystore
Distribution	App Center
Security Testing	QARK
Continuous Integration	Jenkins
Continuous Delivery	Jenkins
Pipeline	Pipeline as Code, Jenkinsfile, Blue Ocean
Expected Deliverables or Features in Automated pipeline	

- Installation and Configuration of Jenkins
- Distributed Architecture/Master Agent Architecture
- Role-based access
- Configuration of a CI/CD pipeline using Pipeline as Code
- Configuration of a CI/CD pipeline that distributes the Android package to App Center
- Documentation
    - o   Documentation of defined processes and implementations
    - o   Technical documentation – How to guides
- Best practices documentation for the usage of Jenkins/Blue Ocean

Table 4.1: Tools and deliverables

In the next section, we will create a pipeline for the Android application using the Blue Ocean interface in a step-by-step manner.

Multi-stage pipeline for an Android app using Blue Ocean

In this chapter, we will try to cover CI/CD for a sample Android application. Following is the big picture of what we will implement in this chapter:

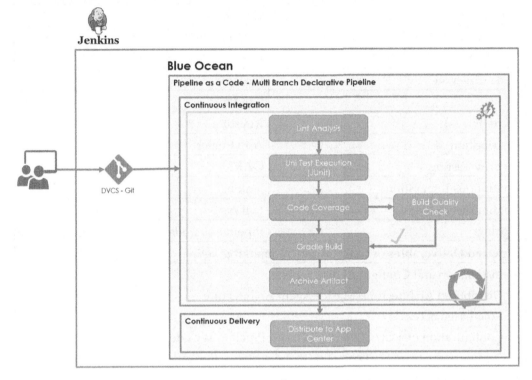

Figure 4.1: Big picture for CI/CD of an Android App

Let's configure repository for pipeline job.

1. Let's verify the existing pipeline for a sample Android application and then we will try to create it from scratch using Blue Ocean:

Figure 4.2: *Sample application with pipeline*

2. Verify the multi-branch pipeline log. There are two branches wherein one branch has the Jenkinsfile and the other doesn't have one:

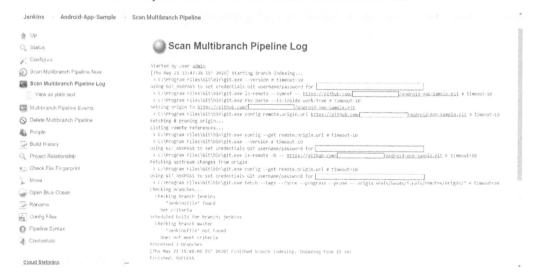

Figure 4.3: *Multi-branch pipeline log*

3. Click on the status link to get a list of branches available where the Jenkinsfile is available or branches which are filtered based on wildcards:

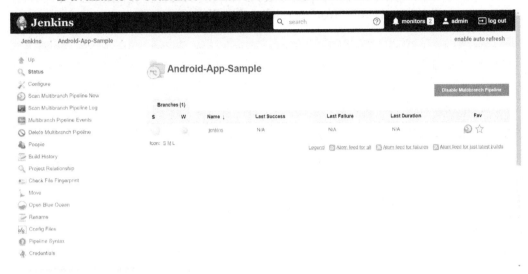

Figure 4.4: Multi-branch pipeline

4. Click on the Open Blue Ocean link on the **Project** dashboard and execute the pipeline:

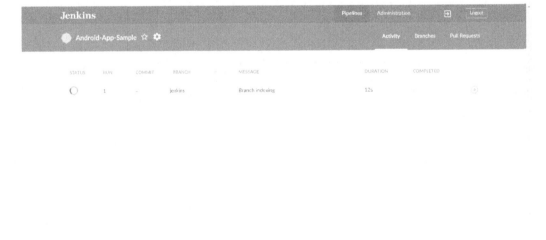

Figure 4.5: Blue Ocean interface

5. Verify the logs that are stage-wise and steps added in each stage. It is easier to navigate through the logs in Blue Ocean rather than using the traditional Jenkins console:

Figure 4.6: *Stage execution in Blue Ocean*

6. We can also verify the same console on the Jenkins console. While the pipeline is running, go to the traditional Jenkins dashboard and then go to logs:

Figure 4.7: *Stage view in traditional Jenkins Dashboard*

7. We can see that some of the **Stages** are skipped in the pipeline execution on the Blue Ocean dashboard.

    Reason?

    It is a parameterized pipeline and because it was executed for the first time immediately after we configured it in Jenkins, it started with the default parameters:

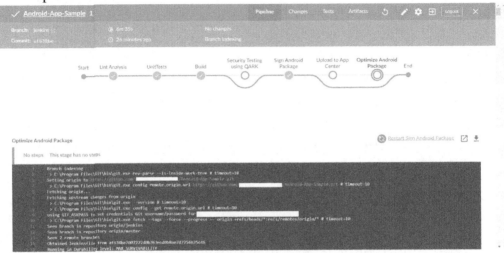

Figure 4.8: Pipeline view in Blue Ocean

8. Verify the **Restart <<StageName>>** link available on the dashboard. If you want to troubleshoot any stage execution, then you can skip stages before that stage and start the execution from a specific stage to save time and find problems in the pipeline.

9. Let's execute the pipeline again and provide parameters:

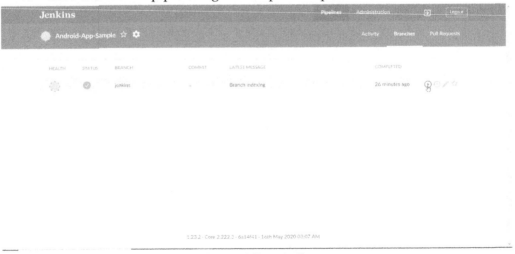

Figure 4.9: Run pipeline

10. Let's provide inputs where we don't want to execute Security Testing for a sample execution.

11. Click on **Run**:

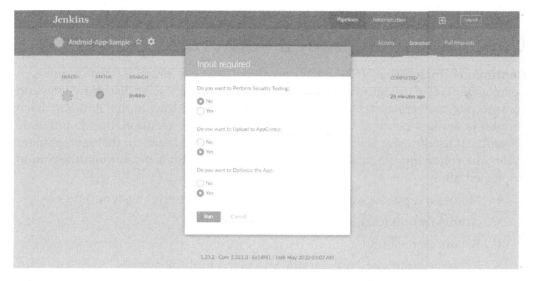

Figure 4.10: Pipeline Inputs

12. Wait until the pipeline is executed successfully:

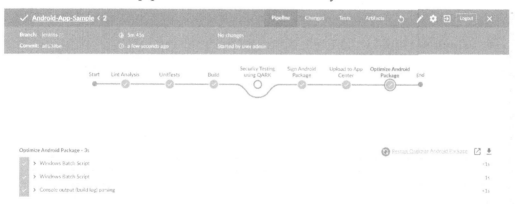

Figure 4.11: Pipeline view in Blue Ocean

Now, that we know what we want to achieve, let's try to create a pipeline for a sample code.

Let's start with Continuous Integration.

Continuous Integration – Android app

Continuous Integration (CI) is a prevalent DevOps practice that requires a development team to commit the Android app code into a shared distributed version control system several times a day based on a bug fix or feature implementation. Each commit is verified by an automated code analysis, test execution, build, and code coverage, thus allowing teams to detect and locate issues early in the development cycle. The following are tasks that can be executed in the Continuous Integration implementation:

- Maintain repository in the Distributed Version Control System (DVCS)
- Automate unit tests
- Automate the build
- Keep the build fast - use parallel jobs using multiple agents
- Calculate code coverage
- Maintain standard reporting for unit tests and code coverage
- Publish artifacts such as Lint Analysis, Unit Test results, APK file(s), Code Coverage results
- Configure Build Quality checks for an Android app

Let's consider that we have a sample Android application available in the Git repository:

Figure 4.12: Select the Repository provider

Connect to a Git repository using the credentials or SSH key configuration:

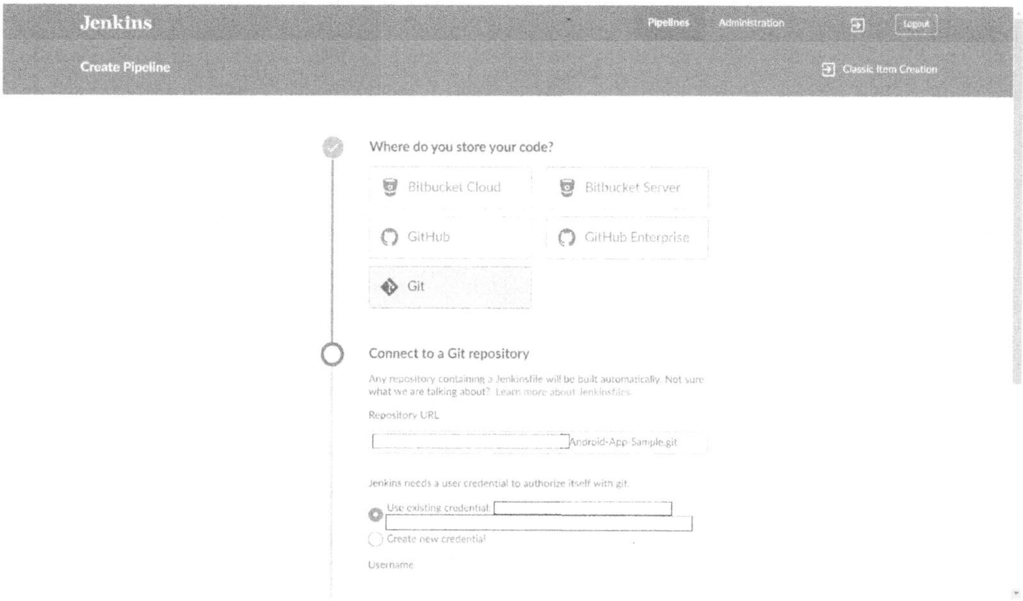

Figure 4.13: *Create pipeline in Blue Ocean*

Click on **Create Pipeline**. If the repository has branches with the Jenkinsfile, then it will start the execution once the pipeline is created successfully. If a repository does not have any branch with the Jenkinsfile, then it will ask you to create a pipeline.

In the next section, we will configure steps to execute Lint analysis.

Understand how to perform Lint Analysis for an Android application

In the Continuous Integration phase, we will start with the Lint Analysis. Lint analysis highlights structural problems in the code. It helps to increase the quality, reliability, maintainability, and efficiency of the code.

NOTE

Use `lint.xml` to verify source files with specific lint rules. Keep this file in the root folder of the Project. More details are available at **https://developer. android.com/studio/write/lint#gradle**.

The Android Lint tool is a static code analysis tool that verifies source files for potential issues such as bugs or vulnerabilities for the following attributes available in the diagram:

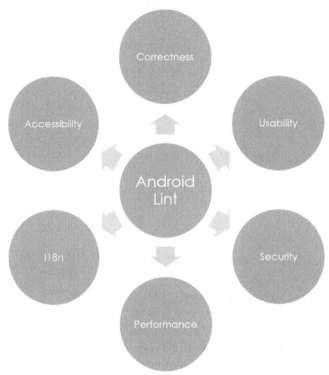

Figure 4.14: Lint Output Category

Lint tools can be utilized by the command line or in Android Studio. We will use the command line option in the Jenkins pipeline for Lint analysis.

> **NOTE**
>
> Use Continuous Integration for Android applications when the team comprises more than two developers to build, execute unit test cases, perform lint analysis (Refer *Getting the Most Out of Android Lint* - **https://www.youtube.com/watch?v=ffH-LD5uP4s** for more details), and to calculate code coverage for better quality.

If our Android project includes multiple build variants, then we can execute the lint task for a specific build variant. To find out the tasks available for the execution based on variants, we need to execute Gradle tasks or `gradlew` tasks based on the operating systems:

```
1.   > Task :tasks
2.
3.   -----------------------------------------------------------------
4.   Tasks runnable from root project
5.   -----------------------------------------------------------------
6.
7.   Android tasks
8.   -------------
9.   androidDependencies - Displays the Android dependencies of the
     project.
10.  signingReport - Displays the signing info for the base and test
     modules
11.  sourceSets - Prints out all the source sets defined in this
     project.
12.
13.  Build tasks
14.  -----------
15.  assemble - Assembles the outputs of this project.
16.  assembleAndroidTest - Assembles all the Test applications.
17.  build - Assembles and tests this project.
18.  buildDependents - Assembles and tests this project and all
     projects that depend on it.
19.  buildNeeded - Assembles and tests this project and all projects
     it depends on.
20.  bundle - Assemble bundles for all the variants.
21.  clean - Deletes the build directory.
22.  cleanBuildCache - Deletes the build cache directory.
23.  compileDebugAndroidTestSources
24.  compileDebugSources
25.  compileDebugUnitTestSources
26.  compileReleaseSources
27.  compileReleaseUnitTestSources
28.
```

```
29.  Build Setup tasks
30.  -----------------
31.  init - Initializes a new Gradle build.
32.  wrapper - Generates Gradle wrapper files.
33.
34.  Cleanup tasks
35.  -------------
36.  lintFix - Runs lint on all variants and applies any safe
     suggestions to the source code.
37.
38.  Help tasks
39.  ----------
40.  buildEnvironment - Displays all buildscript dependencies declared
     in root project 'Android-App-Sample_jenkins'.
41.  components - Displays the components produced by root project
     'Android-App-Sample_jenkins'. [incubating]
42.  dependencies - Displays all dependencies declared in root project
     'Android-App-Sample_jenkins'.
43.  dependencyInsight - Displays the insight into a specific dependency
     in root project 'Android-App-Sample_jenkins'.
44.  dependentComponents - Displays the dependent components of
     components in root project 'Android-App-Sample_jenkins'.
     [incubating]
45.  help - Displays a help message.
46.  model - Displays the configuration model of root project 'Android-
     App-Sample_jenkins'. [incubating]
47.  projects - Displays the sub-projects of root project 'Android-
     App-Sample_jenkins'.
48.  properties - Displays the properties of root project 'Android-
     App-Sample_jenkins'.
49.  tasks - Displays the tasks runnable from root project 'Android-
     App-Sample_jenkins' (some of the displayed tasks may belong to
     subprojects).
50.
51.  Install tasks
52.  -------------
53.  installDebug - Installs the Debug build.
```

```
54.  installDebugAndroidTest - Installs the android (on device) tests
     for the Debug build.
55.  uninstallAll - Uninstall all applications.
56.  uninstallDebug - Uninstalls the Debug build.
57.  uninstallDebugAndroidTest - Uninstalls the android (on device)
     tests for the Debug build.
58.  uninstallRelease - Uninstalls the Release build.
59.
60.  Reporting tasks
61.  ---------------
62.  combinedTestReportDebug - Generate Jacoco coverage reports after
     running debug tests.
63.  jacocoTestReportDebug - Generate Jacoco coverage reports after
     running debug tests.
64.  jacocoTestReportRelease - Generate Jacoco coverage reports after
     running release tests.
65.
66.  Verification tasks
67.  ------------------
68.  check - Runs all checks.
69.  connectedAndroidTest - Installs and runs instrumentation tests
     for all flavors on connected devices.
70.  connectedCheck - Runs all device checks on currently connected
     devices.
71.  connectedDebugAndroidTest - Installs and runs the tests for
     debug on connected devices.
72.  createDebugCoverageReport - Creates test coverage reports for
     the debug variant.
73.  deviceAndroidTest - Installs and runs instrumentation tests
     using all Device Providers.
74.  deviceCheck - Runs all device checks using Device Providers and
     Test Servers.
75.  lint - Runs lint on all variants.
76.  lintDebug - Runs lint on the Debug build.
77.  lintRelease - Runs lint on the Release build.
78.  lintVitalRelease - Runs lint on just the fatal issues in the
     release build.
79.  .
```

80. .

81. test - Run unit tests for all variants.

82. testDebugUnitTest - Run unit tests for the debug build.

83. testReleaseUnitTest - Run unit tests for the release build.

84.

85. Rules

86. -----

87. Pattern: clean<TaskName>: Cleans the output files of a task.

88. Pattern: build<ConfigurationName>: Assembles the artifacts of a configuration.

89. Pattern: upload<ConfigurationName>: Assembles and uploads the artifacts belonging to a configuration.

One stage is a must in the pipeline. Before creating the stage, let's configure ANDROID_ HOME and JAVA_HOME in the environment settings. Android SDK is required to build the Android app:

1. Configure Gradle in **Manage Jenkins | Global Tools** configuration:

Figure 4.15: Environment Setting in pipeline

2. On the Blue Ocean dashboard, click on the newly created pipeline and then click on the + sign to create a new stage.

3. Provide a stage name.

4. At least one step is required in the stage. Click on **Add** step:

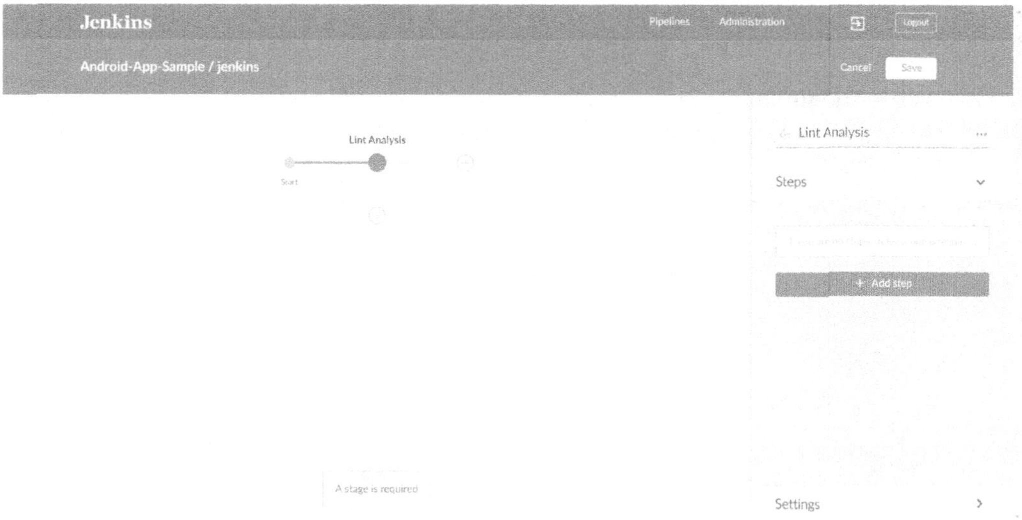

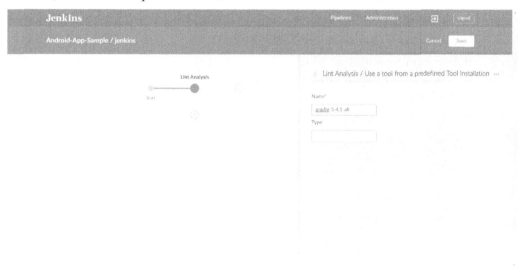

Figure 4.16: *Stage in Blue Ocean pipeline*

5. Select the step Use a tool from predefined tool installation. To use Gradle, Java is also required; hence, we will use both the tools here:

Figure 4.17: *Use a tool*

6. We will use the `gradlew` command to execute Android/Gradle tasks in the pipeline. Add the step Windows Batch Script because we are using windows to execute script for this pipeline setup.

7. Write the `gradlew.bat` lint command in the script box:

Figure 4.18: Lint task configuration

8. Once the Android lint task is executed, the next task is to configure the task to publish lint results on the dashboard.

9. If this option is not available in Blue Ocean, then we need to install the Android Lint plugin. Plugin details are available at **https://plugins.jenkins. io/android-lint/**.

10. We need to configure options based on the requirements:

Figure 4.19: Android Lint task

11. All required tasks are configured for Lint analysis in the declarative pipeline. Press *Ctrl + S* to see the script generated automatically. Click on **Save**.

It will ask in which branch you want to save:

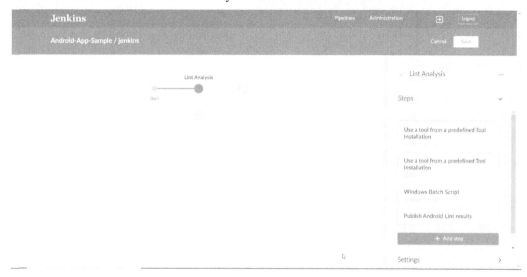

Figure 4.20: *Steps for Lint Analysis*

12. The pipeline will start the execution immediately when it gets saved in the repository. Once the pipeline is executed successfully, we can see logs as per the steps configured in the pipeline in a specific section, and hence, navigating through logs is easy compared to the traditional way of execution:

Figure 4.21: *Successful execution of Lint Analysis*

13.   Go to the traditional Jenkins dashboard and verify the Lint trend chart available after the pipeline execution:

Figure 4.22: *Lint Trends*

14.   Click on the **Lint Issues** link available in the left sidebar to get details on the issues with priority:

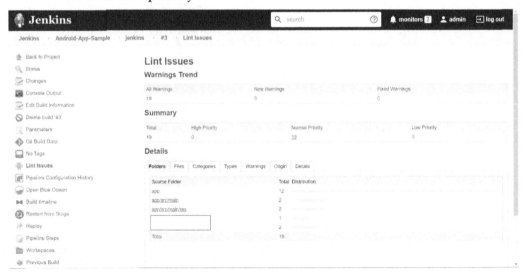

Figure 4.23: *Lint Issues*

The following is the pipeline that is automatically generated and saved in the Jenkinsfile in our code repository based on the branch:

```
1.   pipeline {
2.     agent any
3.     stages {
4.       stage('Lint Analysis') {
5.         steps {
6.           tool 'gradle-5.4.1-all'
7.           tool 'JDK8'
8.           bat 'gradlew.bat lint'
9.           androidLint()
10.         }
11.       }
12.
13.     }
14.     environment {
15.       ANDROID_HOME = 'C:\\Program Files (x86)\\Android\\android-sdk'
16.       JAVA_HOME = 'C:\\Program Files\\Java\\jdk1.8.0_111'
17.     }
18.   }
```

NOTE

We can configure lint options in the `build.gradle` file as well. Let's consider a scenario where we want to abort the execution process if there are any lint errors that exist.

```
android {
  ...
  lintOptions {
    abortOnError false
    // if true, only report errors.
    ignoreWarnings true
  }
}
```

In the next section, we will configure the Unit test execution and calculate Code coverage.

Execute Unit tests and Calculate Code coverage

We will use the Gradle plugin that generates JaCoCo reports from an Android Gradle Project: **https://github.com/vanniktech/gradle-android-junit-jacoco-plugin**:

1. Make the following changes in the root `build.gradle`:

```
1.   buildscript {
2.       // Define versions in a single place
3.       ext {
4.                       .
5.                       .
6.                       .
7.           jacoco_version = '0.8.2'
8.       }
9.       repositories {
10.          google()
11.          jcenter()
12.      }
13.
14.      dependencies {
15.                      .
16.                      .
17.                      .
18.          classpath "com.vanniktech:gradle-android-junit-jacoco-plugin:0.14.0"
19.      }
20.  }
```

2. Add the following section in app/`build.gradle`:

```
1.   apply plugin: "com.vanniktech.android.junit.jacoco"
2.
3.   junitJacoco {
4.       jacocoVersion = "$jacoco_version" // type String
5.       ignoreProjects = ["markdown"] // type String array
6.       excludes = [
```

```
7.                    '**/*Test*.*',
8.                    '**/*Activity.*',
9.                    '**/*Fragment.*',
10.                    '**/AutoValue_*.*',
11.                    '**/*JavascriptBridge.class',
12.                    '**/R.class',
13.                    '**/R$*.class',
14.                    '**/Manifest*.*',
15.                    'android/**/*.*',
16.                    '**/BuildConfig.*',
17.                    '**/*$ViewBinder*.*',
18.                    '**/*$ViewInjector*.*'
19.        ]
20.
21.     includeNoLocationClasses = true // type boolean
22.     includeInstrumentationCoverageInMergedReport = false //
    type boolean
23. }
24.
25.
26. android {
27. buildTypes {
28.            debug {
29.                testCoverageEnabled true
30.            }
31.
32. }
33.
34. }
```

3. Create a new stage for Unit tests and configure steps for Gradle and JDK along with the batch script to run the gradle task that we configured in the previous section.

4. Execute the Gradle task `jacocoTestReportDebug`. Execute the Gradle tasks command and find the available tasks for Jacoco and Code coverage.

5. Once code coverage is executed along with unit tests, archive test reports using the step **Archive Junit-formatted test results**:

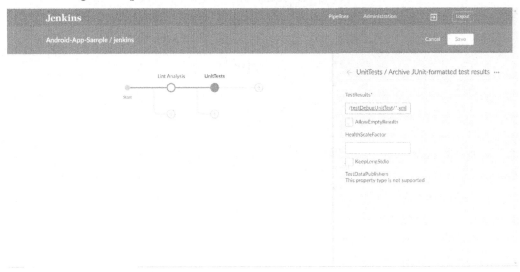

Figure 4.24: Archive Junit-formatted test results

6. Verify all the steps configured for Unit tests and code coverage:

Figure 4.25: All steps for Unit test and Code Coverage

7. Press *Ctrl + S* to get the pipeline editor and it will look as shown in the following screenshot:

```
1.    pipeline {
2.      agent any
3.      stages {
4.        stage('Lint Analysis') {
5.          steps {
6.            tool 'gradle-5.4.1-all'
7.            tool 'JDK8'
8.            bat 'gradlew.bat lint'
9.            androidLint()
10.         }
11.       }
12.
13.       stage('UnitTests') {
14.         steps {
15.           tool 'gradle-5.4.1-all'
16.           tool 'JDK8'
17.           bat 'gradlew.bat jacocoTestReportDebug'
18.           junit '**/testDebugUnitTest/*.xml'
19.         publishCoverage(adapters: [jacocoAdapter('app\\build\\
      reports\\jacoco\\debug\\jacoco.xml')], sourceFileResolver:
      sourceFiles('NEVER_STORE'))
20.         }
21.       }
22.
23.     }
24.     environment {
25.         ANDROID_HOME = 'C:\\Program Files (x86)\\Android\\
      android-sdk'
26.         JAVA_HOME = 'C:\\Program Files\\Java\\jdk1.8.0_111'
27.     }
28.   }
```

8. Execute the pipeline:

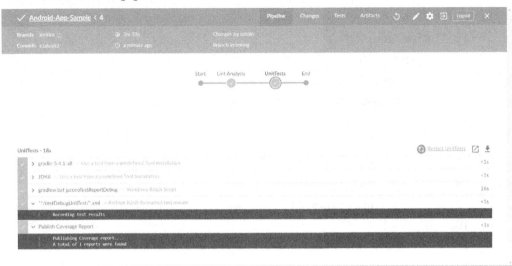

Figure 4.26: Uni Test Execution

9. Once the pipeline is executed successfully, we can see logs as per the steps configured in the pipeline in a specific section. Hence, navigating through logs is easy compared to the traditional way of execution:

Figure 4.27: Tests section in Blue Ocean

NOTE

DevOps practices implementation helps organizations to accelerate time to market with quality. It empowers teams to automate application lifecycle activities.

10. Verify the **Test Result Trend** on the Jenkins Dashboard:

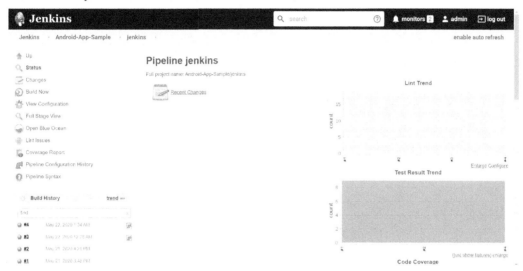

Figure 4.28: Test Results Trend

11. Verify the Code coverage chart on the Jenkins dashboard:

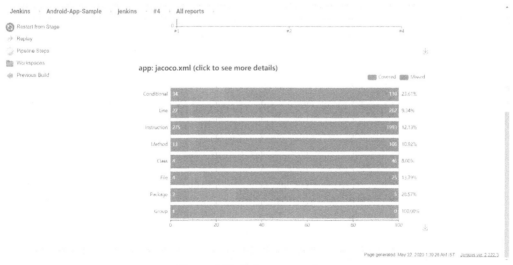

Figure 4.29: Code coverage chart

In the next section, we will verify the build quality based on the coverage report.

Verify Build Quality

To verify the build quality, perform the following steps:

1. Click on the pipeline Syntax link available in the pipeline and configure thresholds for the coverage:

Figure 4.30: Threshold configuration for Coverage

NOTE

Integrate Quality Gates in the pipelines/orchestration and the pipeline should be promoted to a specific environment based on the Quality Gate clearance only. For example, code should be promoted to QA only if the static code analysis Quality Gate is cleared or Code coverage is above the threshold. It is recommended to have quality gates in the end-to-end process.

Quality has to be part of culture and routine for Continuous Improvement and Continuous Innovation.

Thought-provoking exercise: How do you differentiate between Quality Gate and Quality Assurance as both are in place to improve quality?

2. The following is the script generated using the pipeline Syntax:

```
1.  publishCoverage   adapters:   [jacocoAdapter(path:   'app\\
    build\\reports\\jacoco\\debug\\jacoco.xml',   thresholds:
    [[failUnhealthy:   true,   thresholdTarget:   'Line',
    unhealthyThreshold:   10.0,   unstableThreshold:   20.0]])],
    failUnhealthy: true, failUnstable: true, globalThresholds:
    [[thresholdTarget:   'Method',   unhealthyThreshold:
    10.0,   unstableThreshold:   20.0]],   sourceFileResolver:
    sourceFiles('NEVER_STORE')
```

3. Go to the last successful pipeline execution and click on **Replay**. Remove the **Build and Distribution** stage to verify the Threshold configuration. Execute the pipeline from **Replay** by clicking on **Run**:

Figure 4.31: Replay the pipeline

4. The pipeline will fail after the unit test execution:

Figure 4.32: Pipeline failures due to coverage threshold

5. Verify the messages of build failure: 1) Code coverage enforcement failed: Line coverage in Report level `app: jacoco.xml` is lower than `20.00` stable threshold 2) Code coverage enforcement failed: Method coverage in **Report** level `app: jacoco.xml` is lower than `20.00` stable threshold:

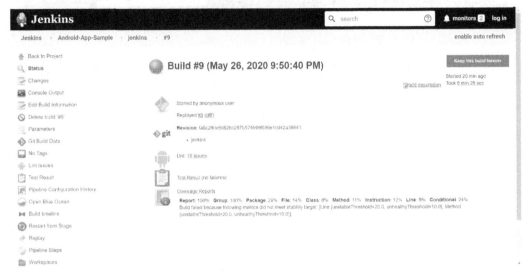

Figure 4.33: Build status

6. Click on the **Pipeline Configuration History** on the Jenkins dashboard to verify the changes in the declarative pipeline script:

Figure 4.34: Pipeline Configuration History

NOTE

DevOps practices implementation tends to be more successful when it is implemented in a phase-wise manner and not with a big bang approach. The organization evaluates benefits for pilot projects and then considers it for critical applications based on the level of confidence.

In the next section, we will configure the pipeline to create an APK file.

Create an APK file

There are multiple Gradle tasks available to build the project:

```
1.   Build tasks
2.   -----------
3.   assemble - Assembles the outputs of this project.
4.   assembleAndroidTest - Assembles all the Test applications.
5.   build - Assembles and tests this project.
6.   buildDependents - Assembles and tests this project and all
     projects that depend on it.
7.   buildNeeded - Assembles and tests this project and all projects
     it depends on.
8.   bundle - Assemble bundles for all the variants.
9.   clean - Deletes the build directory.
10.  cleanBuildCache - Deletes the build cache directory.
11.  compileDebugAndroidTestSources
12.  compileDebugSources
13.  compileDebugUnitTestSources
14.  compileReleaseSources
15.  compileReleaseUnitTestSources
```

We have already executed Lint analysis and test execution. Hence, we will run the assemble task:

1. If we want to exclude any Gradle task execution, then we can use the -x command-line argument which excludes any task. For example:

   ```
   gradle build -x test
   ```

2. Create a new stage for **Build** and configure steps for Gradle and JDK along with the batch script to run the Gradle task that we configured in the previous section:

Figure 4.35: Build steps

NOTE

Happy teams are productive teams. DevOps practices implementation increases the productivity of project teams by trying to automate manual activities and providing visibility and transparency.

3. Press *Ctrl + S* to open a pipeline editor and verify the declarative pipeline script:

```
1.  pipeline {
2.     agent any
3.     stages {
4.       stage('Lint Analysis') {
5.         steps {
6.           tool 'gradle-5.4.1-all'
7.           tool 'JDK8'
8.           bat 'gradlew.bat lint'
9.           androidLint()
10.        }
11.      }
12.
```

```
13.        stage('UnitTests') {
14.          steps {
15.            tool 'gradle-5.4.1-all'
16.            tool 'JDK8'
17.            bat 'gradlew.bat jacocoTestReportDebug'
18.            junit '**/testDebugUnitTest/*.xml'
19.          publishCoverage(adapters: [jacocoAdapter('app\\build\\
     reports\\jacoco\\debug\\jacoco.xml')], sourceFileResolver:
     sourceFiles('NEVER_STORE'))
20.            }
21.        }
22.
23.        stage('Build') {
24.          steps {
25.            tool 'gradle-5.4.1-all'
26.            tool 'JDK8'
27.            bat 'gradlew.bat assemble'
28.            archiveArtifacts '**/*.apk'
29.            }
30.        }
31.
32.    }
33.    environment {
34.        ANDROID_HOME = 'C:\\Program Files (x86)\\Android\\
     android-sdk'
35.      JAVA_HOME = 'C:\\Program Files\\Java\\jdk1.8.0_111'
36.    }
37. }
```

4. Execute the pipeline. Verify the build stage logs:

Figure 4.36: Build the app

5. Click on the **Artifact** section to verify the artifacts available to download:

Figure 4.37: Artifacts in Blue Ocean pipeline

Now, we can see that Android Packages (`.apk` files) are available. The `app-debug.apk` file can be used to test and debug APK files quickly. Build a release APK after signing the unsigned app with a private key.

We can verify the APK file using the QARK tool available at **https://github.com/linkedin/qark** to find security-related Android application vulnerabilities.

6. Install the QARK tool in CentOS and execute qark --apk path/to/app-debug.apk to verify the APK.

   If we want to keep it in the pipeline, then we may need to execute at certain times only.

7. Add parameters to ask whether Security testing needs to be performed or not in the pipeline execution:

```
1.  parameters {
2.    choice(name: 'SecurityTesting', choices: ['No', 'Yes'],
        description: 'Do you want to Perform Security Testing:')
3.  }
```

8. Use the when directive in the stage to determine whether the step needs to be executed or skipped based on the parameter value:

```
1.      stage('Security Testing using QARK') {
2.        when {
3.          expression {
4.            params.SecurityTesting == 'Yes'
5.          }
6.
7.        }
8.        steps {
9.          bat 'qark "app\\build\\outputs\\apk\\release\\app-
      debug.apk"'
10.        }
11.      }
```

For more details on the when directive, go to **https://www.jenkins.io/doc/book/pipeline/syntax/#when**.

In the next section, we will create a script to distribute the signed app using the App center.

Continuous Delivery – Android app

Perform the following steps:

1. Create a keystore with the Java Keytool utility that is available with JDK distribution.

   Keytool prompts to provide passwords for the keystore and other details. It generates the keystore as a file called jenkinsbook.keystore in the current directory. The keystore and key are protected by passwords. The keystore contains a single key, which is valid for **10000** days. The alias is a name to refer to this `jenkinsbook.keystore` when signing the application:

```
1.   C:\Program Files (x86)\Java\jdk1.8.0_192\jre\bin>keytool
     -genkey -v -keystore jenkinsbook.keystore -alias jenkinsbook
     -keyalg RSA -keysize 2048 -validity 10000

2.   Picked up _JAVA_OPTIONS: -Xmx512M

3.   Enter keystore password:

4.   Re-enter new password:

5.   What is your first and last name?

6.     [Unknown]:  Mitesh

7.   What is the name of your organizational unit?

8.     [Unknown]:  RainyClouds

9.   What is the name of your organization?

10.    [Unknown]:  Clouds

11.  What is the name of your City or Locality?

12.    [Unknown]:  Kochi

13.  What is the name of your State or Province?

14.    [Unknown]:  Kerala

15.  What is the two-letter country code for this unit?

16.    [Unknown]:  IN

17.  Is CN=Mitesh, OU=RainyClouds, O=Clouds, L=Kochi, ST=Kerala,
     C=IN correct?

18.    [no]:  yes

19.

20.  Generating 2,048 bit RSA key pair and self-signed certificate
     (SHA256withRSA) with a validity of 10,000 days

21.        for: CN=Mitesh, OU=RainyClouds, O=Clouds, L=Kochi,
     ST=Kerala, C=IN

22.  Enter key password for <jenkinsbook>

23.        (RETURN if same as keystore password):

24.  [Storing jenkinsbook.keystore]

25.  keytool error: java.io.FileNotFoundException: jenkinsbook.
     keystore (Access is denied)

26.  java.io.FileNotFoundException:         jenkinsbook.keystore
     (Access is denied)

27.        at java.io.FileOutputStream.open0(Native Method)
```

```
28.          at java.io.FileOutputStream.open(FileOutputStream.
    java:270)

29.         at java.io.FileOutputStream.<init>(FileOutputStream.
    java:213)

30.         at java.io.FileOutputStream.<init>(FileOutputStream.
    java:101)

31.          at sun.security.tools.keytool.Main.doCommands(Main.
    java:1194)

32.        at sun.security.tools.keytool.Main.run(Main.java:366)

33.      at sun.security.tools.keytool.Main.main(Main.java:359)
```

2. Keystore creation fails with access issues. Go to a directory where the access is available and use the absolute or relative path to use keytool:

```
1.  C:\Users\Mitesh\Desktop\BPBOnline\3.Hands-on    Jenkins
    Pipeline  as  Code  using  Blue  Ocean\FirstDraft\Chapter
    #4>"C:\Program   Files   (x86)\Java\jdk1.8.0_192\jre\bin\
    keytool" -genkey -v -keystore jenkinsbook.keystore -alias
    jenkinsbook -keyalg RSA -keysize 2048 -validity 10000

2.  Picked up _JAVA_OPTIONS: -Xmx512M

3.  Enter keystore password:

4.  Re-enter new password:

5.  What is your first and last name?

6.    [Unknown]:  Mitesh Soni

7.  What is the name of your organizational unit?

8.    [Unknown]:  RainyClouds

9.  What is the name of your organization?

10.   [Unknown]:  Clouds

11. What is the name of your City or Locality?

12.   [Unknown]:  Kochi

13. What is the name of your State or Province?

14.   [Unknown]:  Kerala

15. What is the two-letter country code for this unit?

16.   [Unknown]:  IN

17. Is  CN=Mitesh  Soni,  OU=RainyClouds,  O=Clouds,  L=Kochi,
    ST=Kerala, C=IN correct?

18.   [no]: yes

19.
```

```
20.   Generating 2,048 bit RSA key pair and self-signed certificate
      (SHA256withRSA) with a validity of 10,000 days
21.           for: CN=Mitesh Soni, OU=RainyClouds, O=Clouds,
      L=Kochi, ST=Kerala, C=IN
22.   Enter key password for <jenkinsbook>
23.           (RETURN if same as keystore password):
24.   [Storing jenkinsbook.keystore]
25.
26.   Warning:
27.   The JKS keystore uses a proprietary format. It is recommended
      to migrate to PKCS12 which is an industry standard format using
      "keytool  -importkeystore  -srckeystore  jenkinsbook.keystore
      -destkeystore jenkinsbook.keystore -deststoretype pkcs12".
```

3. Sign the Android package using the `jarsigner` tool available in JDK.

4. Use the following command structure to create the signed JAR file:

```
1.   <JDK path>\bin\jarsigner -verbose -keystore <Directory path>/
     jenkinsbook.keystore   -storepass   jenkinsbook   -signedjar
     <path  for  signed  apk>\app-release-signed.apk  <path  for
     unsigned apk>\app-release-unsigned.apk jenkinsbook
```

5. Verify the signed JAR file using the `-verify` attribute:

```
1.   <JDK  path>\bin\jarsigner  -verify  app\\build\\outputs\\
     apk\\release\\app-release-signed.apk
```

For example,

```
1.       stage('Sign Android Package') {
2.         steps {
3.           bat '"C:\\Program Files (x86)\\Java\\jdk1.8.0_192\\
     bin\\jarsigner.exe" -verbose -keystore "C:\\Users\\Mitesh\\
     Desktop\\BPBOnline\\3.Hands-on Jenkins Pipeline as Code
     using  Blue  Ocean\\FirstDraft\\Chapter  #4\\jenkinsbook.
     keystore" -storepass jenkinsbook -signedjar "app\\build\\
     outputs\\apk\\release\\app-release-signed.apk"       "app\\
     build\\outputs\\apk\\release\\app-release-unsigned.apk"
     jenkinsbook'
4.           bat '"C:\\Program Files (x86)\\Java\\jdk1.8.0_192\\
     bin\\jarsigner.exe"  -verify  "app\\build\\outputs\\apk\\
     release\\app-release-signed.apk"'
5.         }
6.       }
```

In the next section, we will distribute the file to the App center and optimize the package.

Deploy Package/APK to App Center

The App Center is used to distribute mobile applications to the QA team. It is also used to build, test, and distribute Android, iOS, and Windows applications. Let's configure steps to integrate Jenkins and App Center:

1. Go to **https://appcenter.ms/**.

2. Log in with the appropriate method. Provide the Username for login purpose.

NOTE

Productivity gains results in time to innovate or improve existing practices. Recognizing individuals who are change agents help them to fulfill their career aspirations.

3. Let's add a new App in the App Center by clicking on **Add new**.

4. Select **App Type, OS**, and **Platform**.

5. Click on **Add new app**:

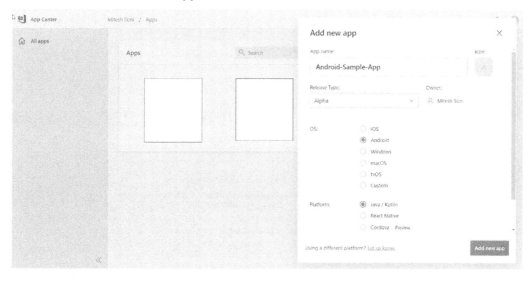

Figure 4.38: App center-Add new app

6. Here, the **App** is created:

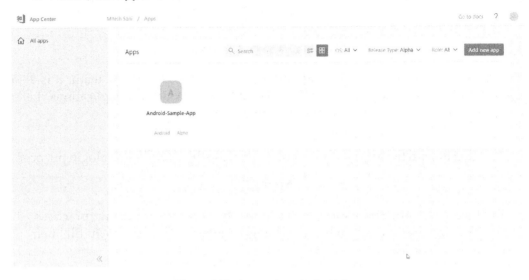

Figure 4.39: *App center - Android App*

7. Here is the **App Overview**:

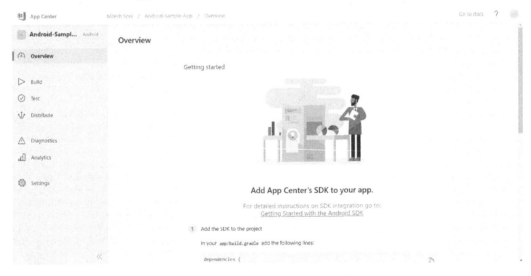

Figure 4.40: *App center - App Overview*

NOTE

The DevOps protagonists or DevOps evangelists help with the successful rollout of DevOps strategies, DevOps practices implementation, and better performance with quality.

8. As of now, there is no distribution group that is available in the Android app we created.

   Distribution groups help to organize testers and manage users who can have access to the application.

9. Click on **Add Group**:

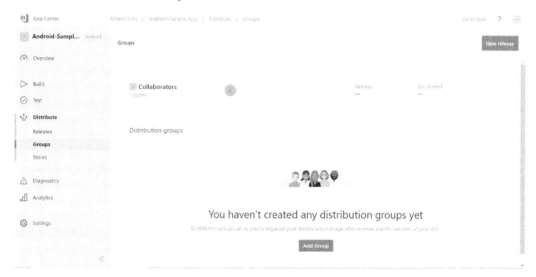

Figure 4.41: App center distribution group

10. Provide **Group name** and click on **Create Group**:

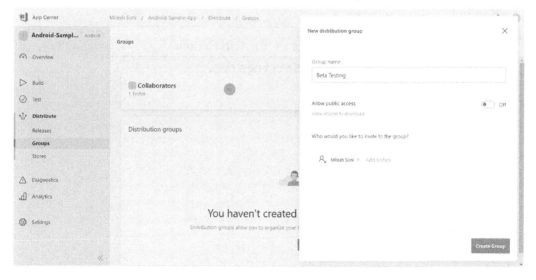

Figure 4.42: App Center - Creation of Group

11. A **New Group** is available. We will configure this group when we try to upload the Android Package from Jenkins:

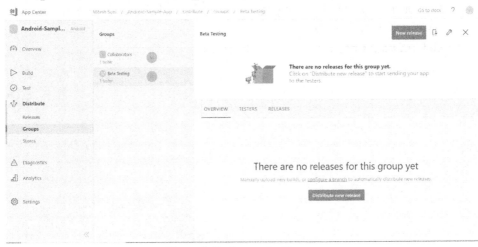

Figure 4.43: App center Groups

12. To integrate the App center in Jenkins, we will need an API token. Let's create it first.

> ### NOTE
> Mindset and culture change are the most important factors in organizations than tools and technology. Highly collaborative teams with effective communication help to change the culture and implement DevOps practices effectively.

13. Let's go to **Account Settings** of the App Center.

14. Scroll down on the **Account Settings** page:

Figure 4.44: Account Settings

15. Click on **New API token**:

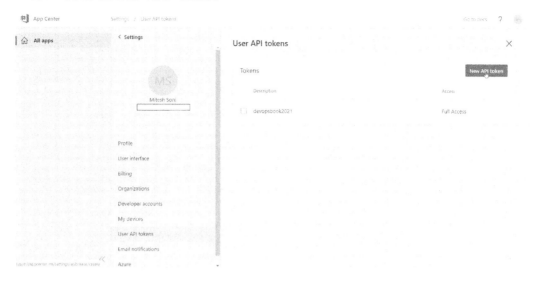

Figure 4.45: *API tokens*

16. Provide **Description** and **Access**.

17. Click on **Add new API token**:

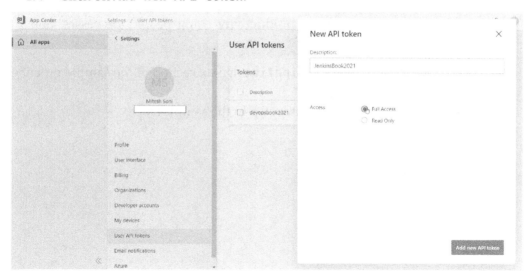

Figure 4.46: *New API Token*

18.   Copy the API token:

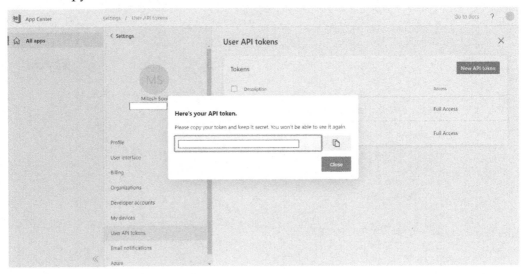

Figure 4.47: Copy the Token

NOTE
DevOps practices implementation helps to continuously focus on how to increase organizational/resource productivity using people, processes, and tools.

19.   Go to Jenkins and open the **Pipeline** syntax section of the sample pipeline project.

20.   Select **Upload** to the App Center step in the sample step.

21. Provide the values such as API Token that we created earlier, Owner name from the App center, App Name, Path to the APK file, and Distribution group that we created. Check for connectivity between Jenkins and the App Center, if we are working behind any corporate proxy:

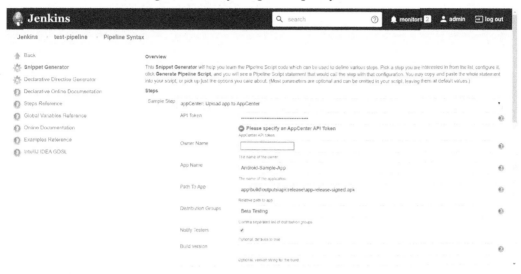

Figure 4.48: App center pipeline Syntax

22. Click on **Generate Pipeline Script:**

Figure 4.49: App Center pipeline Syntax for App Center

23. We can directly copy this script to the pipeline Editor or we can add the Blue Ocean step and provide data here as well:

Figure 4.50: Upload to app center step in Blue Ocean

24. `zipalign` performs optimization to Android application (APK) files. To know more details, go to **https://developer.android.com/studio/command-line/zipalign**.

    Use the following command structure in the Windows Batch script step in Blue Ocean:

    ```
    <ANDROID_HOME>\build-tools\28.0.3\zipalign.exe -v 4 <path to the
    signed apk>/app-release-signed.apk <path to store optimized apk>\
    app-release-optimized.apk
    ```

25. Verify the optimized APK using the following command structure:

    ```
    1.  <ANDROID_HOME>\build-tools\\28.0.3\\zipalign.exe  -c  -v  4
        <path to store optimized apk>\app-release-optimized.apk
    ```

    For example,

    ```
    1.      stage('Optimize Android Package') {
    2.        when {
    3.          expression {
    4.            params.Optimize == 'Yes'
    5.          }
    6.
    7.        }
    8.        steps {
    ```

```
 9.            bat '"C:\\Program Files (x86)\\Android\\android-
      sdk\\build-tools\\28.0.3\\zipalign.exe" -v 4 "app\\build\\
      outputs\\apk\\release\\app-release-signed.apk"        "app\\
      build\\outputs\\apk\\release\\app-release-optimized.apk"'
10.            bat '"C:\\Program Files (x86)\\Android\\android-
      sdk\\build-tools\\28.0.3\\zipalign.exe" -c  -v 4 "app\\
      build\\outputs\\apk\\release\\app-release-optimized.apk"'
11.        }
12.      }
```

We can use the log parser **https://plugins.jenkins.io/log-parser/** plugin to find whether the verification for signing and optimization process is successful or not. Install the Jenkins Parser plugin and create its syntax using the pipeline Syntax or by adding a step on the Blue Ocean dashboard. Create a rule file.

For example,

```
1.  # create a quick access link to lines in the report containing
    'INFO'
2.  info /jar verified./
3.  info /Verification succesful/
```

The pipeline syntax for log parser using the rules file is as follows:

```
1.  logParser(useProjectRule:  true,  projectRulePath:  'C:\\
    Users\\Mitesh\\Desktop\\BPBOnline\\3.Hands-on      Jenkins
    Pipeline  as  Code  using  Blue  Ocean\\FirstDraft\\Chapter
    #4\\JarVerification.rules', parsingRulesPath: 'C:\\Users\\
    Mitesh\\Desktop\\BPBOnline\\3.Hands-on   Jenkins   Pipeline
    as  Code  using  Blue  Ocean\\FirstDraft\\Chapter  #4\\
    JarVerification.rules')
```

26. Add the script in Windows Batch script.

27. **Save and Execute** the pipeline:

Stage View

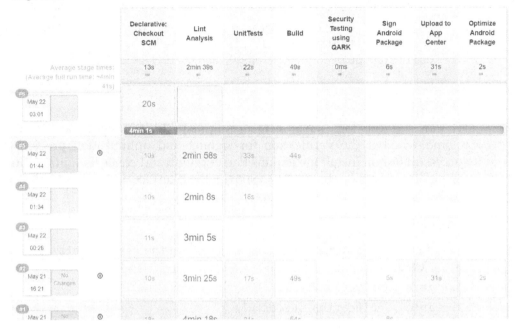

	Declarative: Checkout SCM	Lint Analysis	UnitTests	Build	Security Testing using QARK	Sign Android Package	Upload to App Center	Optimize Android Package
Average stage times: (Average full run time: ~4min 41s)	13s	2min 39s	22s	49s	0ms	6s	31s	2s
#6 May 22 03:01		20s						
4min 1s								
#5 May 22 01:44		10s	2min 58s	33s	44s			
#4 May 22 01:34		10s	2min 8s	18s				
#3 May 22 00:26		11s	3min 5s					
#2 May 21 16:21	No Changes	10s	3min 25s	17s	49s	5s	31s	2s
#1 May 21	No		4min 18s					

Figure 4.51: Pipeline stage view

> # NOTE
>
> Faster time to market, quality of outcome, and productivity gains are essential and drivers for the DevOps movement.

28. Provide the required parameters on whether we want to perform Security Testing: **Do we want to upload app to App Center** and **Do we want to Optimize the App**.

29. Click on **Run**:

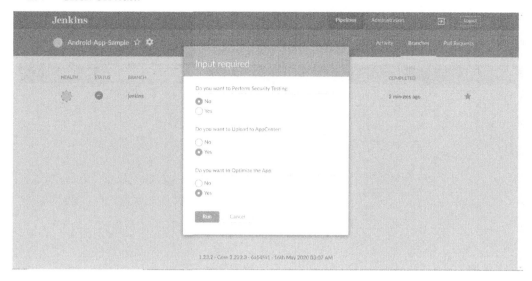

***Figure 4.52:** Parameters for pipeline*

30. Verify the successful pipeline:

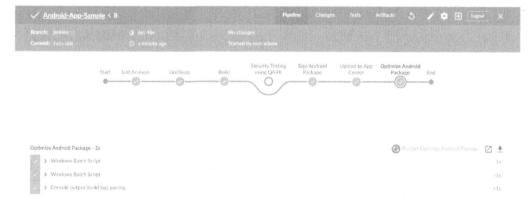

***Figure 4.53:** Pipeline execution in Blue Ocean*

31. Verify the log parser result to find out whether the signing and optimization process worked successfully or not.

32. Go to the Jenkins dashboard and go to the Build History of the last execution. Click on **Console Output (parsed)**:

Figure 4.54: Console Output (parsed)

33. Go to the App Center and verify the **Releases** section. The package will be available for download:

Figure 4.55: App Release

34. Click on the **Groups** tab and select the **Beta Testing** group that we created. The app is available in that section as well:

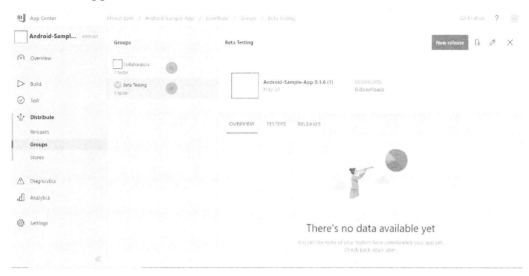

Figure 4.56: *App distribution available for a Group of users*

35. The following is the end-to-end pipeline script – Declarative way using Blue Ocean:

```
1.  pipeline {
2.    agent any
3.    stages {
4.      stage('Lint Analysis') {
5.        steps {
6.          tool 'gradle-5.4.1-all'
7.          tool 'JDK8'
8.          bat 'gradlew.bat lint'
9.          androidLint()
10.        }
11.      }
12.
13.      stage('UnitTests') {
14.        steps {
15.          tool 'gradle-5.4.1-all'
16.          tool 'JDK8'
17.          bat 'gradlew.bat jacocoTestReportDebug'
```

```
18.           junit '**/testDebugUnitTest/*.xml'
19.         publishCoverage(adapters: [jacocoAdapter('app\\build\\
    reports\\jacoco\\debug\\jacoco.xml')], sourceFileResolver:
    sourceFiles('NEVER_STORE'))
20.         }
21.     }
22.
23.     stage('Build') {
24.       steps {
25.         tool 'gradle-5.4.1-all'
26.         tool 'JDK8'
27.         bat 'gradlew.bat assemble'
28.         archiveArtifacts '**/*.apk'
29.       }
30.     }
31.
32.     stage('Security Testing using QARK') {
33.       when {
34.         expression {
35.           params.SecurityTesting == 'Yes'
36.         }
37.
38.       }
39.       steps {
40.         bat 'qark "app\\build\\outputs\\apk\\release\\app-
    debug.apk"'
41.       }
42.     }
43.
44.     stage('Sign Android Package') {
45.       steps {
46.         bat '"jarsigner.exe" -verbose -keystore "C:\\Users\\
    Mitesh\\Desktop\\BPBOnline\\3.Hands-on Jenkins Pipeline as
    Code using Blue Ocean\\FirstDraft\\Chapter #4\\jenkinsbook.
    keystore" -storepass jenkinsbook -signedjar "app\\build\\
    outputs\\apk\\release\\app-release-signed.apk"        "app\\
    build\\outputs\\apk\\release\\app-release-unsigned.apk"
    jenkinsbook'
```

```
47.              bat '"jarsigner.exe" -verify "app\\build\\outputs\\
          apk\\release\\app-release-signed.apk"'
48.          }
49.        }
50.

51.        stage('Upload to App Center') {
52.          when {
53.            expression {
54.              params.Upload2AppCenter == 'Yes'
55.            }
56.

57.          }
58.          steps {
59.              appCenter(apiToken: '*************************',
          ownerName: 'xxxxxxxxxx-outlook.com', appName: 'Android-
          Sample-App',    pathToApp:    'app\\build\\outputs\\apk\\
          release\\app-release-signed.apk',    distributionGroups:
          'Beta Testing', releaseNotes: 'Security Bug Fixed - Ticket
          2020.05.20')
60.          }
61.        }
62.

63.        stage('Optimize Android Package') {
64.          when {
65.            expression {
66.              params.Optimize == 'Yes'
67.            }
68.

69.          }
70.          steps {
71.            bat '"zipalign.exe" -v 4 "app\\build\\outputs\\apk\\
          release\\app-release-signed.apk"    "app\\build\\outputs\\
          apk\\release\\app-release-optimized.apk"'
72.            bat '"zipalign.exe" -c -v 4 "app\\build\\outputs\\
          apk\\release\\app-release-optimized.apk"'
73.              logParser(useProjectRule: true, projectRulePath:
          'C:\\Users\\Mitesh\\Desktop\\BPBOnline\\3.Hands-on Jenkins
          Pipeline as Code using Blue Ocean\\FirstDraft\\Chapter
          #4\\JarVerification.rules', parsingRulesPath: 'C:\\Users\\
```

```
           Mitesh\\Desktop\\BPBOnline\\3.Hands-on  Jenkins  Pipeline
           as   Code   using   Blue   Ocean\\FirstDraft\\Chapter   #4\\
           JarVerification.rules')
74.          }
75.        }
76.
77.      }
78.      environment {
79.          ANDROID_HOME = 'C:\\Program Files (x86)\\Android\\
           android-sdk'
80.          JAVA_HOME = 'C:\\Program Files\\Java\\jdk1.8.0_111'
81.      }
82.      parameters {
83.        choice(name: 'SecurityTesting', choices: ['No', 'Yes'],
           description: 'Do you want to Perform Security Testing:')
84.        choice(name: 'Upload2AppCenter', choices: ['No', 'Yes'],
           description: 'Do you want to Upload to AppCenter:')
85.          choice(name: 'Optimize', choices: ['No', 'Yes'],
           description: 'Do you want to Optimize the App:')
86.      }
87.  }
```

NOTE

DevOps is the **default!**

DevOps is **mainstream!**

DevOps is a new **normal!**

DevOps is **conventional!**

DevOps is a **change!**

DevOps is a **transformation!**

DevOps is just a beginning for most **organizations!**

Done!

TIP

What if I want to wait for the input or approval before executing any stage? The common issue right? None allows us to deploy into specific environments due to governance and security concerns.

Jenkins provides an input step that will pause the pipeline. It provides two options: Proceed and Abort.

submitter/Type: String (optional): Create a user and provide the username(s) permitted to respond to the input, separated by ','. Admin also has the right to provide input.

The following step can be used for input: input id: 'Rollback', message: '**Do you want to Rollback**?', ok: **'Rollback'**, submitter: **'mitesh'**:

The following is the console log on the traditional Jenkins dashboard:

```
1.   [Pipeline] // stage
2.   [Pipeline] withEnv
3.   [Pipeline] {
4.   [Pipeline] withEnv
5.   [Pipeline] {
6.   [Pipeline] stage
7.   [Pipeline] { (Approval)
8.   [Pipeline] input
9.   Do you want to Rollback?
10.  Rollback or Abort
```

The following is the stage view where the input can be given:

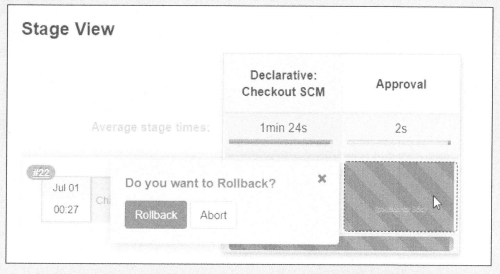

Figure 4.57: Approval in Stage View

The pipeline is paused for input in the Branches section:

Figure 4.58: Pipeline in Pause mode

In the Pipeline view, the submitter can provide input on the Blue Ocean Dashboard:

Figure 4.59: Approval in Blue Ocean

The following is the log after approval by the admin:

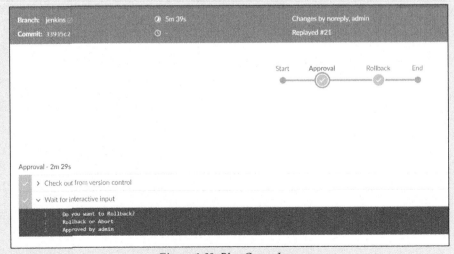

Figure 4.60: Blue Ocean Logs

```
1.   timeout(time:2, unit:'DAYS') {
2.     input message: 'Approve deployment to stage slot?', submitter:
       'mitesh'
3.   }
```

Conclusion

Continuous Integration and Continuous Delivery implementation are more or less similar in mobile and web applications. However, tools and distribution may change. It is essential to have some knowledge of Android, how it is uploaded to the play store, how different environment variables are utilized, which secure files or Keystore files are utilized, and so on.

In the next chapter, we will use Blue Ocean to create a pipeline for iOS applications.

Points to remember

- Code Coverage for an Android app written in Java and Kotlin will have a different configuration.

- Use the Gradle tasks command to find out available tasks for execution.

Multiple choice questions

1. **Tests results are required to calculate code coverage. State true of false.**

   a. True

   b. False

2. **To get code coverage, the following configuration is not required:**

   ```
   debug {
       testCoverageEnabled true
   }
   ```
   a. True

   b. False

Answer

1. a
2. b

Questions

1. What is the purpose of unit tests?

2. An Android app can be developed in how many languages?

3. What is code coverage, and why is it important?

4. Which build tool is generally used for Android applications?

CHAPTER 5

Building CI/CD Pipeline for an iOS App

> **"There is always room for improvement."**
>
> — *Anonymous*

Financial service giants need an effective and faster application lifecycle management to cope up with the competition in the market. Higher management wants to migrate from older technologies to newer technologies. Their major customers are iPhone users and hence they want to focus on faster delivery of iOS apps to end users. The need of the hour is to implement Continuous Integration and Continuous Delivery. The leadership team wants to adopt the phase-wise implementation of DevOps practices to remove friction between development and operations teams. They want to automate manual processes for code analysis, unit testing, build, functional testing, and deployment. In this chapter, we will cover the CI/CD implementation of an iOS application with Jenkins. We will use the Pipeline as Code to create the CI/CD pipeline. Blue Ocean provides a simple way to create a pipeline using a simple user interface as well as a code editor to configure the **Continuous Integration (CI)** and **Continuous Delivery (CD)** pipeline for iOS applications. We will distribute an application to the App Center to a specific group. We will also provide some valuable Notes related to DevOps, culture, challenges, market trends, and so on for a better understanding.

Structure

In this chapter, we will discuss the following topics:

- Introduction
- Blue Ocean Multi-Stage pipeline for an iOS App
    - o Continuous Integration
        - Create a Jenkins connection to the MAC Agent
        - Configure Signing Certificates and Provisioning Profiles to Jenkins
        - Understand how to perform Lint analysis for an iOS application
        - Execute Unit tests
        - Calculate Code coverage
        - Verify Build Quality
        - Create an IPA file
    - o Continuous Delivery
        - Deploy IPA to the App Center
- Conclusion
- Questions and exercises

Objectives

After studying this unit, you should be able to:

- Understand how to perform SwinftLint Analysis for an iOS application
- Execute nit tests
- Calculate Code coverage
- Verify Build quality
- Create an IPA file
- Deploy IPA to the App Center

Introduction

The organization has selected one application as a pilot while there are two other early adopter iOS applications that are waiting in the queue. We have the responsibility to create a CI/CD pipeline using Pipeline as Code in Jenkins in the declarative syntax.

> **NOTE**
>
> Agile, DevOps, and Cloud Computing go hand in hand. Each one is complementary to others and accelerates time to market.

The following is the list of tools and deliverables that will be integrated into the pipeline:

Tools	
Version Control	Git
Code Analysis	SwiftLint
Unit Tests	XCUnit
Code Coverage	XCCov, Slather
Secret File (s)	Certificate and Provisioning Profile
Distribution	App Center
Continuous Integration	Jenkins
Continuous Delivery	Jenkins
Pipeline	Pipeline as Code, Jenkinsfile, Blue Ocean

Expected Deliverables or Features in an Automated Pipeline	
<ul><li>Installation and configuration of Jenkins</li><li>Distributed Architecture/Master Agent Architecture</li><li>Role-based access</li><li>Configuration of the CI/CD pipeline using Pipeline as Code</li><li>Configuration of the CI/CD pipeline that distributes the Android package to the App Center</li><li>Documentation<ul><li>Documentation of defined processes and implementations</li><li>Technical documentation – *How to guides*</li></ul></li><li>Best practices documentation for the usage of Jenkins/Blue Ocean</li><li>Terminology in iOS</li></ul>	
Provisioning Profile	<ul><li>A collection of digital entities.</li><li>It serves as a connection between developers and devices.</li><li>It enables a device to be used for testing.</li><li>It requires a developer account.</li></ul>

Signing Identity	• The signing of an iOS app indicates the integrity aspect of the application.
	• Indication of no modification since it is signed.
	• It consists of asymmetric cryptography (public-private key pair); private key (.p12 file), certificate (.cer file), and provisioning profile that matches the certificate and private key
Xcode IDE	• Xcode is an integrated development environment (IDE) for macOS.
	• A suite of software development tools.
	• Supports application development for Mac, iPhone, iPad, Apple Watch, and Apple TV, and so on.
Xcodebuild	• Command-line utility to build, test, archive, and upload the app to iTunes Connect.
	• Clean the source code using the xcodebuild clean action.
	• Analyze the source code using the xcodebuild analyze action.
	• Build an iOS app using the xcodebuild build action.
	• Test an iOS app using the xcodebuild test action.
XCCov	• Command-line tool to inspect Xcode code coverage reports.
Slather	• Generate test coverage reports for Xcode projects and integrate them into the CI/CD pipeline.
	• Support for HTML and Cobertura reports.

Table 5.1: Tools and deliverables

In the next section, we will create a pipeline for an iOS application using the Blue Ocean interface in a step-by-step manner.

Multi-stage pipeline for an iOS app using Blue Ocean

In this chapter, we will cover CI/CD for a sample iOS application. Following is a big picture that we will try to implement in the rest of the chapter.

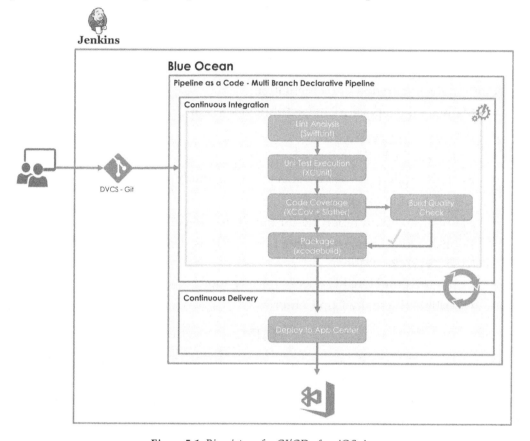

Figure 5.1: *Big picture for CI/CD of an iOS App*

Let's try to create a pipeline for a sample iOS application using Blue Ocean.

Continuous integration – iOS app

Continuous Integration (CI) is a prevalent DevOps practice that requires a development team to commit the iOS app code into a shared distributed version control system several times a day based on a bug fix or feature implementation. Each commit is verified by an automated code analysis, test execution, build, and code coverage, thus allowing teams to detect and locate issues early in the development cycle.

We need to keep in mind the fact about improving the build time as the codebase size increases, the time for Jenkins pipeline execution increases, and hence issues also will take longer to be reported. The following are tasks that can be executed in the Continuous Integration implementation:

- Maintain the repository in Distributed Version Control System (DVCS)
- Automate unit tests
- Automate the build
- Keep the build fast - use parallel jobs using multiple agents
- Calculate code coverage
- Maintain standard reporting for unit tests and code coverage
- Publish artifacts such as Swift Lint Analysis, Unit test results, IPA file(s), Code coverage results
- Configure Build Quality checks for iOS apps
- Distribute IPA to the App Center

Let's understand some prerequisites.

Prerequisites

For building an iOS mobile application, you need the following prerequisite tools installed on the Mac machine you are going to use for the entire CI/CD pipeline:

- Apple Signing Certificate and Provisioning Profiles
- Xcode installed
- Swiftlint installed
- Slather
- App Center CLI

Create a Jenkins connection with the MAC Agent

To connect with the MAC agent using an SSH connection, we first need to enable **Remote Login**. This can be done in two ways. Let's first enable it using the **Sharing** setting from the UI:

1. Go to **Sharing** by searching it in the **Search** option. You will be directed to the following screen. Now, select the **Remote Login** option and enable it as shown in the following screenshot:

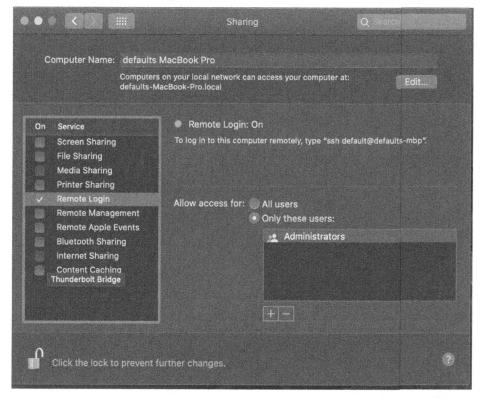

Figure 5.2: Enable Remote Login ON in MAC

Or you can go to the terminal and use the following command to enable remote login:

```
sudo systemsetup -setremotelogin on
```

2. Now, let us log into Jenkins as an **Admin** user and create a Mac Agent by performing the following steps. Go to the Jenkins dashboard and select **Manage Jenkins | Manage Nodes and Clouds**, as shown in the following screenshot:

Figure 5.3: Manage Nodes and Clouds

3. You will be redirected to the following screen. On the left-hand side of this screen, you will find the **New Node** option. Click on this option to create a new node:

Figure 5.4: New Node option

4. Once you click on the **New Node** option, you will be redirected to the screen as shown in the following screenshot. Please enter the name of the agent and select the **Permanent Agent** option and click on the **OK** button:

Figure 5.5: *MAC Node Creation*

NOTE

CALMS – Automation: All or most manual activities involved in **Software Development Lifecycle (SDLC)** can be and should be automated based on a given set of restrictions. Automation is an enabler and not the only thing in this culture transformation initiative. Manual activities are prone to errors due to lack of focus or other limitations. Automation helps to make repetitive activities more effective and errorless with maturity.

5. Then, on the next page, please enter the details of the Mac Agent you want to connect to. You can refer to the following screenshot to create an ssh-agent on MAC:

***Figure 5.6:** MAC Node Creation*

6. Once you save the correct details, your agent will be connected, and you can find the log, as shown in the following screenshot, on successful connection of the MAC agent:

***Figure 5.7:** MAC Agent Connection*

7. On successful connection and creation of the MAC Agent, you can see a new MAC agent in the list of Nodes in Jenkins as shown in the following screenshot:

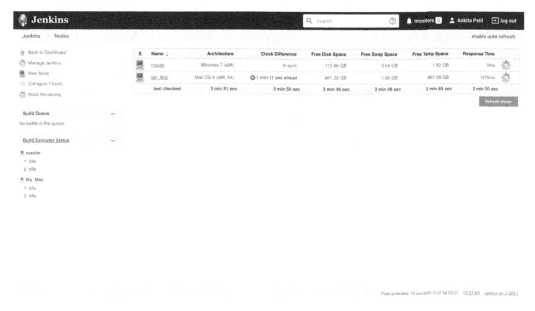

Figure 5.8: MAC Agent Creation

Now, we can start with the CI pipeline for the iOS Native Mobile app on this connected MAC agent. But before this, we should now configure the Signing Certificate and Provisioning Profile required for building an iOS application.

Configure signing certificates and provisioning profiles to Jenkins

Now for this step, you should have either Apple Developer Certificate or Apple Distribution Certificate. You should also have a provisioning profile for the complete setup of this step. But I would like to briefly discuss how to add the Keychain with a sample Apple Developer Certificate. To add the provisioning profile to Jenkins would be your exercise.

NOTE

CALMS – Lean: It is important to eliminate repetitive tasks and unnecessary activities from the SDLC or Sprint activities to become lean and faster.

Before we start, install the following plugins to configure the iOS pipeline:

1. Cobertura plugin

2. HTML Publisher

3. Keychains and Provisioning Profiles Management

4. Xcode integration (optional)

Now, let's start with the following steps to add the keychain to Jenkins:

1. Go to **Manage Jenkins | Keychains and Provisioning Profiles Management.** You will be redirected to the following screen:

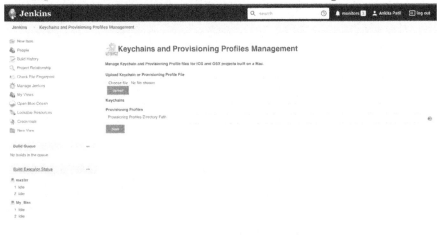

Figure 5.9: Keychain Configuration

2. The Keychain inside which the Developer Certificate is configured is located in a hidden folder Library/Keychains. Now, to upload the keychain, choose the keychain file by navigating to the location and selecting the file to be uploaded (in my case, it is `login.keychain`) as shown in the following screenshot:

Figure 5.10: Keychain upload

3. Once you select the keychain file, click on the **Upload** button as shown in the following screenshot:

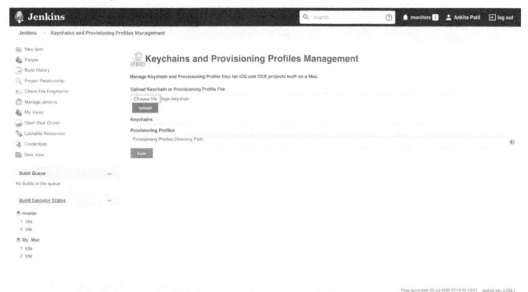

Figure 5.11: Keychain upload

4. Once you upload the keychain file, you can find the entry below and you can enter the details of the certificate's code signing identity:

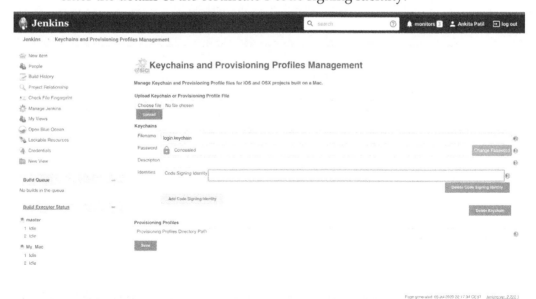

Figure 5.12: Code Signing Identity

5. To find Code Signing Identity, go to **Search** in the MAC agent and search Keychain Access. You can refer to the following screenshot:

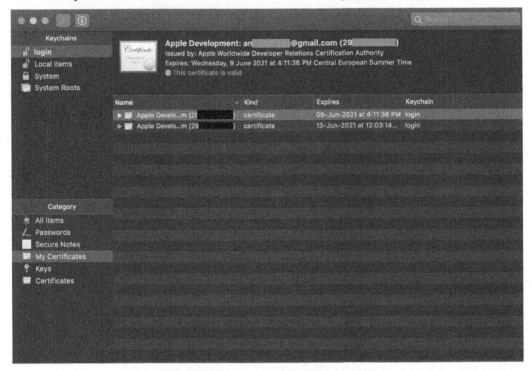

Figure 5.13: Code Signing Identity

NOTE

CALMS – Measure: Measure the AS-IS situation and compare it with situations after DevOps practices implementation. It helps to gain confidence in culture transformation activities as well as convince the higher management on the benefits of DevOps practices implementation.

6. Select the certificate that you are going to use to build the iOS App. Right click on Get Info as shown in the following screenshot:

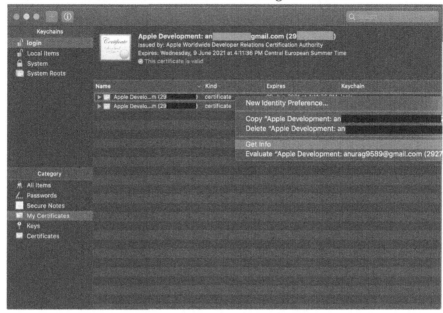

Figure 5.14: Code Signing Identity

7. You can find the Code Signing Identity, as shown in the following screenshot, as **Apple Development: an****** as **Common Name** in the information box about the certificate:

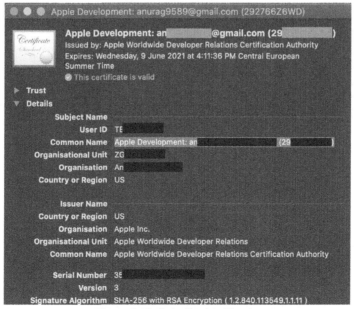

Figure 5.15: Code Signing Identity

8. Enter this Identity in the Jenkins keychain details as shown in the following screenshot:

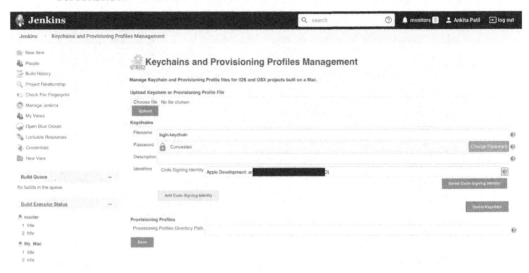

Figure 5.16: Code Signing Identity

9. Now, we need to provide the **Provisioning Profile** details as shown in the following screenshot. The default path is given in the following screenshot, and you can also upload the provisioning profile as we uploaded the keychain:

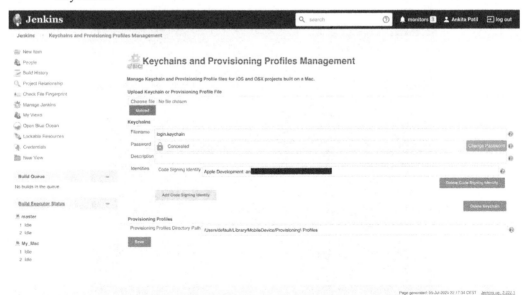

Figure 5.17: Provisioning Profile

Now that we have configured Jenkins to build the iOS application, we can start with Continuous integration first, starting with Swiftlint Analysis.

Understand how to perform Lint Analysis for an iOS application

As mentioned in the prerequisites, to perform this step, you need to install the Swiftlint tool on the MAC agent. Now, first we should create the Blue Ocean project (Refer to the previous chapter to create the Blue Ocean Project) and then select the MAC agent node in the **Pipeline Setting** option as shown in the following screenshot:

Figure 5.18: *Agent selection for Blue Ocean pipeline*

Now, let us start with Swiftlint analysis, and for this, you need to follow the following steps:

1. First, create a `.swiftlint.yml` file in the root directory of your iOS application in GitHub as shown in the following screenshot. This .swiftlint. yml file is the configuration file used for customizing the Swiftlint default

rules. You can enable and disable the rules important for you, or you can change the thresholds values of the limits defined by the Swiftlint rules:

Figure 5.19: .swiftlint.yml

TIP

Disable the rules which are not related to the nature of an IOS app we are working on. Use tools such as SonarQube for a detailed static code analysis to find bugs, vulnerabilities, and code smells.

The following is a sample `.swiftlint.yml` file in the following code snippet:

```
1.   disabled_rules: # rule identifiers to exclude from running
2.     - force_cast
3.     - empty_count
4.     - identifier_name
5.
6.   opt_in_rules: # some rules are only opt-in
7.     - empty_count
8.    # Find all the available rules by running: swiftlint rules
9.
10.  included: # paths to include during linting. `--path` is
     ignored if present.
11.    - XCCov-Demo
12.
13.  # configurable rules can be customized from this configuration file
14.  line_length: 200
15.
```

```
16.    # they can set both implicitly with an array
17.    type_body_length:
18.      - 300 # warning
19.      - 400 # error
20.
21.    # or they can set both explicitly
22.    file_length:
23.      warning: 600
24.      error: 1200
25.
26.    type_name:
27.      allowed_symbols: "_"
28.      min_length: 4 # only warning
29.      max_length: # warning and error
30.        warning: 50
31.        error: 60
32.      excluded: iPhone
33.
34.    cyclomatic_complexity:
35.      warning: 15
36.      error: 20
```

2. Then, add the following shell script in the Blue Ocean pipeline as shown in following screenshot of Swiftlint Analysis:

```
swiftlint --config .swiftlint.yml --reporter html >> report.html
```

Figure 5.20: Swiftlint Analysis

3. The preceding step will generate an HTML report for Swiftlint analysis. So, to publish the `report.html` file result on the Jenkins dashboard, add a new step in the Blue Ocean pipeline **Publish HTML Report** as shown in the following screenshot. Add the following script target in the text box:

```
1.  [
2.     allowMissing: false,
3.     alwaysLinkToLastBuild: false,
4.     keepAll: true,
5.     reportDir: '.',
6.     reportFiles: 'report.html',
7.     reportTitles: "Swiftlint Report",
8.     reportName: "Swiftlint Report"
9.  ]
```

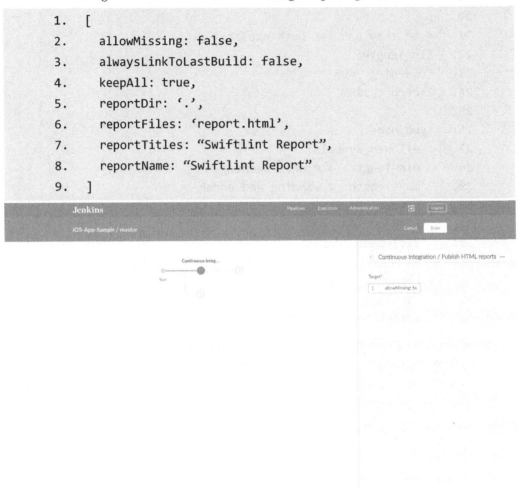

Figure 5.21: Publish HTM Reports: Swiftlint

4. Once you save and run the pipeline, the Swiftlint Analysis will be performed and the report will be published on the Jenkins project main dashboard (Not on the Blue Ocean Dashboard). Please refer to the following screenshot:

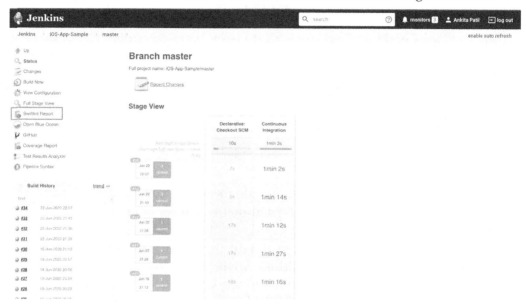

Figure 5.22: Jenkins Project dashboard

5. Once you click on the **Swiftlint Report** button, you will be redirected to the Swiftlint report screen as shown in the following screenshot:

Figure 5.23: Swiftlint HTML report

The pipeline will not proceed if you have single violations. So, you first need to solve all the bugs to make the pipeline proceed for the rest of the CI steps.

> **NOTE**
>
> The DevOps **Center is Excellence (COE)** team helps to nudge the business unit or project to implement DevOps practices and drives culture change initiatives, and hence, it is very important to empower the COE team.

The next step is to execute the unit test cases to verify the code and calculate the code coverage to check whether the code meets the expected standard.

Execute unit tests

Now, the first step is to add a step to execute the Xcode command to run the unit test cases and then convert the result to a format which we can publish the unit test results on the Jenkins dashboard:

1. I have first added a command to edit the signing identity to the project `.pbxproj` so that we can build the application according to the Certificate and Development Team we want to use or change at Build time. For this, refer to the following `sed` command I used as follows. The details of the code signing identity can be fetched from the signing certificate in keychains:

   1.
   ```
   sed -i \'\' \'s/CODE_SIGN_IDENTITY = "iPhone Developer";/
   CODE_SIGN_IDENTITY = "Apple Development: user_email
   (profile_id)";/\' XCCov-Demo.xcodeproj/project.pbxproj
   ```

   The following command is used to run the unit test cases and this command is piped with the `xcpretty` command to convert the unit test results in the Junit format. We can publish this report to the Blue Ocean and Jenkins dashboard:

   1.
   ```
   xcodebuild -project XCCov-Demo.xcodeproj -scheme XCCov-
   Demo -sdk iphonesimulator -destination \'platform=iOS
   Simulator,name=iPhone 8\' -derivedDataPath Build/
   -enableCodeCoverage YES clean test | xcpretty -t -r junit
   && exit ${PIPESTAUTS[0]}
   ```

Now, add both the preceding commands to a new step called execute Shell in the pipeline as shown in the following screenshot:

Figure 5.24: Xcode Unit Test case execution

Now, once the result is generated, the next step is to publish the result using the Junit report publisher.

2. Add the **Archive Junit formatted test result** step to publish the test result junit.xml to view the result. The following screenshot displays how to set up the step:

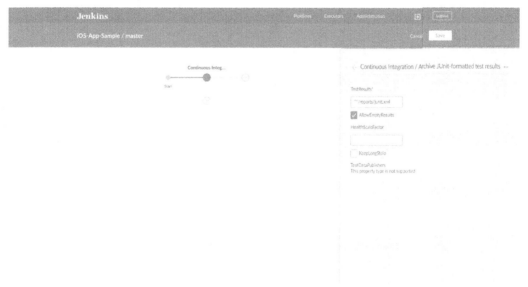

Figure 5.25: Unit Test Result publish

When you save and run the test case, the following result is published on the Blue Ocean dashboard and also on the Blue Ocean dashboard in the **Test** tab:

Figure 5.26: Unit Test result on Blue Ocean

The report and the Jenkins dashboard is shown in the following screenshot:

Figure 5.27: Test result trend on the Jenkins Dashboard

Once the test cases are executed successfully, we can then find the code coverage in the following step.

Calculate the code coverage

To convert the Xcode test result and code coverage result in the Cobertura publishable format, we will use the slather tool in the following command:

```
1.  slather coverage -x --output-directory test-reports --build-
    directory Build --scheme XCCov-Demo --workspace XCCov-Demo.
    xcodeproj/project.xcworkspace  --show "XCCov-Demo.xcodeproj"
```

Add a shell script step with this command, as shown in the following screenshot:

Figure 5.28: Code Coverage report execution

This step we give us the result as shown in the following screenshot:

Figure 5.29: Code Coverage on Build dashboard

> **NOTE**
>
> The DevOps CoE team drives the culture transformation initiative that is uniform and standardized across the organization with a well-defined roadmap and maturity model

Figure 5.30: *Code Coverage Report*

Verify Build quality

For Build Quality check, go to *Chapter 8: Building CI/CD pipeline with Blue Ocean for Hybrid Mobile Application* and refer to the section Verify Build Quality.

In the next section, we will create an IPA file.

Create an IPA file

Now, once the code verification and unit testing are done, we need to first build the iOS application archive file and then export the archive to an IPA file so that we can upload it to the App Center for beta testing.

1. The following command is used to archive the iOS build:

```
1.  xcodebuild -sdk iphoneos -configuration Release -workspace
    XCCov-Demo.xcodeproj/project.xcworkspace  -scheme  XCCov-
    Demo archive -archivePath XCCov-Demo.xcarchive
```

Add a shell script step in the pipeline with the preceding command as shown in the following screenshot:

Figure 5.31: *Xcode archive step*

2. Now, once the archive is successfully done, we get a file with the .xcarchive file which we will use to export to the IPA file. Before this, we need to verify the signing certificate and provisioning profile in a file called `ExportOptions.plist`. These are the settings required to export the archive to the IPA file. Without a proper signing certificate and provisioning profile, we cannot export the IPA file.

A sample `ExportOptions.plist` is as follows:

```
1.  <?xml version="1.0" encoding="UTF-8"?>
2.  <!DOCTYPE plist PUBLIC "-//Apple//DTD PLIST 1.0//EN"
    "http://www.apple.com/DTDs/PropertyList-1.0.dtd">
3.  <plist version="1.0">
4.  <dict>
5.    <key>method</key>
6.    <string>development</string>
7.    <key>teamID</key>
8.    <string>XXXXXXXXX</string>
9.    <key>uploadBitcode</key>
10.   <true/>
```

```
11.    <key>compileBitcode</key>
12.    <true/>
13.    <key>uploadSymbols</key>
14.    <true/>
15.    <key>signingStyle</key>
16.    <string>manual</string>
17.    <key>signingCertificate</key>
18.    <string>iOS Development: email(ID)</string>
19.    <key>provisioningProfiles</key>
20.    <dict>
21.      <key>com.sample.appname</key>
22.        <string>******UUID of provisioning profile*******</string>
23.      <key>com.sample.appname.extension</key>
24.        <string>******UUID of extension provisioning profile*******</string>
25.      </dict>
26.    </dict>
27.  </plist>
```

Please do not forget to compare the bundle id in the Xcode App for an iOS application and the bundle id in the provisioning profile. They both should be the same.

3.   Now, we can use the following command to export it to IPA:

```
1.    xcodebuild -exportArchive -archivePath XCCov-Demo.xcarchive
      -exportOptionsPlist ExportOptions.plist -exportPath .
```

Add a step to execute this command in a shell script as shown in the following screenshot:

Figure 5.32: Export to IPA

4. Now, once this export is successful, we need to archive the IPA file on the Blue Ocean dashboard to maintain the artifacts per build. Add the **Archive the artifacts** step and configure the step as shown in the following screenshot:

Figure 5.33: Archive artifact- IPA

Once these steps are added, save and run the pipeline. Generally, you may face the problem related to signing, which you need to verify in `ExportOptions.plist` and the **Signing Certificate and Provisioning profiles.**

On successful execution, you can find the IPA file archived on the Blue Ocean dashboard on the **Artifacts** tab, as shown in the following screenshot:

Figure 5.34: *Artifacts - Sample-iOS.ipa file*

Now as the build artifact is generated successfully, the next step is to deliver the application for Beta testing. In the next section, let us see how to deliver it to the App Center.

Continuous delivery – iOS app

In this section, we will deliver the Sample-iOS.ipa file to the App Center for testing to a testing team so that they can download this IPA file in an iPhone for testing.

Deploy IPA to the App Center

Before we start the delivery step, we need the following details from the App Center.

1. App center login token (Can be first created from the terminal and reused from the Jenkins shell script by using the `app center login` command as a sudo user. Note: Copy the token generated for future use.)
2. App Name in the App Center
3. Username and Password
4. Tester Group name to whom you need to share the app

Now, we can start with deploying to the App Center from Blue Ocean. To do this, the following commands are used first to login to the App Center and the second command is used for uploading the build to the App Center:

1. The values of **<MAC-user-password>** and **<Use the Copied token>** can be added to Jenkins credentials and can be used by calling parameters (Refer to *Chapter 3: Building Continuous Integration and Continuous Delivery (CI/CD)*

pipeline for Java Web Application to do this from the Credential manager). But I have directly provided these values for POC.

2. To store the App Center credentials in the keychain, we need to use unlock-keychain as shown in the following command:

```
security unlock-keychain -p <MAC-user-password> | appcenter login
--token <Use the Copied token>
```

Now, add a Shell script step in the Blue Ocean pipeline and paste the preceding command in the Shell script as shown in the following screenshot:

Figure 5.35: App Center Login

This step is to be done one time so you can remove the step after login credentials are added to the keychain.

3. Now, once we have successfully logged into to the App Center from the CLI, we can upload the app to the App Center. Use the following command to upload the IPA to a specific app in the App Center to share to a specific group as a Tester, UAT Tester, etc.

```
1.  appcenter distribute release --app appcenter_username/Sample_
    iOS   --file   "Build/Build/Products/Debug-iphonesimulator/
    Sample-iOS.ipa" --group "Sample_iOS_Tester"
```

Add this command to the Shell script new step in the Blue Ocean pipeline as shown in the following screenshot:

Figure 5.36: App Center IPA upload to Release

Once you have added this step, save and run the pipeline. On successful execution of the pipeline, you can find the Blue Ocean dashboard as shown in the following screenshot:

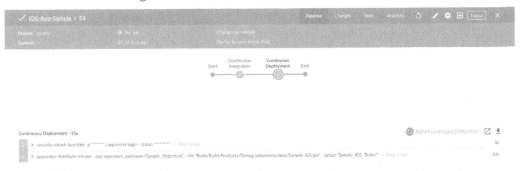

Figure 5.37: Continuous Deployment to App Center

Once this successful execution is done, the iOS application will get uploaded to the App Center. You can find the sample App Center in the following screenshot:

NOTE

The DevOps maturity model should be dynamic and it should improve continuously based on the requirements, evolvement and technology evolution and innovation.

Figure 5.38: App Center Release

This pipeline is only up to Release to the App Center. But this can be extended further to deploy to the App Store. But before that, you need to build the IPA using the distribution certificate and provisioning profiles.

The whole pipeline script is as follows:

```
1.  pipeline {
2.    agent {
3.      node {
4.        label 'My_Mac'
5.      }
6.
7.    }
8.    stages {
```

```
9.        stage('Continuous Integration') {
10.         steps {
11.           sh '''sed -i \'\' \'s/DEVELOPMENT_TEAM = ""';/DEVELOPMENT_
      TEAM = "DEVELOPMENT_TEAM_ID"';/\' XCCov-Demo.xcodeproj/project.
      pbxproj
12.           sed -i \'\' \'s/CODE_SIGN_IDENTITY = "iPhone Developer"';/
      CODE_SIGN_IDENTITY = "Apple Development: email (CODE_SIGN_
      IDENTITY_ID)"';/\' XCCov-Demo.xcodeproj/project.pbxproj
13. xcodebuild -project XCCov-Demo.xcodeproj -scheme XCCov-Demo -sdk
      iphonesimulator -destination \'platform=iOS Simulator,name=iPhone
      8\' -derivedDataPath Build/ -enableCodeCoverage YES clean test |
      xcpretty -t -r junit && exit ${PIPESTAUTS[0]}
14. '''
15.           sh '''slather coverage -x --output-directory test-
      reports --build-directory Build --scheme XCCov-Demo --workspace
      XCCov-Demo.xcodeproj/project.xcworkspace   --show "XCCov-Demo.
      xcodeproj"
16. ls test-reports'''
17.           cobertura(coberturaReportFile: 'test-reports/cobertura.
      xml', classCoverageTargets: 'test-reports')
18.           sh 'swiftlint --config .swiftlint.yml --reporter html >>
      report.html'
19.           publishHTML([
20.                   allowMissing: false,
21.                   alwaysLinkToLastBuild: false,
22.                   keepAll: true,
23.                   reportDir: '.',
24.                   reportFiles: 'report.html',
25.                   reportTitles: "Swiftlint Report",
26.                   reportName: "Swiftlint Report"
27.                   ])
28.     junit(testResults: '**/reports/junit.xml', allowEmptyResults:
      true)
29.           sh '''xcodebuild -sdk iphoneos -configuration Release
      -workspace   XCCov-Demo.xcodeproj/project.xcworkspace   -scheme
      XCCov-Demo archive -archivePath XCCov-Demo.xcarchive'''
30.           sh '''xcodebuild -exportArchive -archivePath XCCov-Demo.
      xcarchive -exportOptionsPlist ExportOptions.plist -exportPath
      .'''
31.           archiveArtifacts 'Build/**/Sample-iOS.ipa'
```

```
32.              }
33.            }
34.        stage('Continuous Deployment') {
35.          steps {
36.              sh '''security unlock-keychain -p ****** | appcenter
       login --token *****token*****'''
37.            sh 'appcenter distribute release --app appcenter_username/
       Sample_iOS --file "Build/Build/Products/Debug-iphonesimulator/
       Sample-iOS.ipa" --group "Sample_iOS_Tester"'
38.              }
39.            }
40.
41.        }
42.        environment {
43.            PATH = '/usr/local/bin:/usr/bin:/bin:/usr/sbin:/sbin:/
       Library/Apple/usr/bin'
44.          }
45.        }
```

Done!

NOTE

Fail Early and Recover Early simulate failures to manage failures in future without high impacts in automation or cloud.

Conclusion

In this chapter, we used XCCov and Slather to generate code coverage and created the coverage report XML in the Cobertura format so that we can publish it on the Azure DevOps dashboard. We need to use the Library (secure files and variables) for secrets used to create an IPA file in XCode apps.

In the next chapter, we will configure CI/CD for Angular applications using Blue Ocean in Jenkins.

Multiple choice questions

1. **To publish code coverage for the xCode app in Azure DevOps, we need to use which two tools?**

    a. XCCov

b. Slather

c. A and b

d. None of these

Answer

1. c

Questions

1. What is the provisioning profile?

2. Explain the use of a certificate and provisioning profile.

3. Explain the App slug in the App Center task.

CHAPTER 6

Building CI/CD Pipeline for an Angular Application

> "The journey is never-ending. There's always gonna be growth, improvement, adversity; you just gotta take it all in and do what's right, continue to grow, continue to live in the moment."
>
> — *Antonio Brown*

Angular 8 is a client-side TypeScript-based framework that is used to create dynamic web applications and mobile applications. Angular has the following features or advantages: such as new compiler - Ivy Rendering Engine, Deep Linking Routing, Restful APIs, Lazy Loading, Builders APIs, and Service Workers and Web Worker building.

A detailed discussion on Angular and its features is beyond the scope of the book. Let's focus on the Blue Ocean pipeline for a sample Angular application.

Blue Ocean provides a simple way to create a pipeline using a simple user interface as well as a code editor to configure the **Continuous Integration (CI)** and **Continuous Delivery (CD)** pipeline for Angular applications. We can deploy an application to Azure Kubernetes Services or in the Microsoft Azure Cloud environment. In this book, we will cover the CI/CD implementation of an Angular application with Jenkins. We will also provide some valuable *notes* related to DevOps, culture, challenges, market trends, and so on for a better understanding.

Structure

In this chapter, we will discuss the following topics:

- Introduction
- Blue Ocean multi-stage pipeline for an Angular app
    - o Continuous Integration
        - Junit and Cobertura configuration in karma.conf.js
        - Lint, Unit tests, and Code coverage configuration in Package.json
        - Configure Unit tests and Code coverage in a Multi-Stage pipeline
        - End-to-End Test Execution
        - NPM Audit
    - o Continuous Delivery
        - Deploy an Angular App to Azure App Services

Objectives

After studying this unit, you should be able to:

- Understand how to perform Lint analysis for an Angular application
- Execute unit tests and calculate code coverage
- Verify Build Quality
- Deploy an Angular application to a Docker container
- Deploy an Angular application to Azure Kubernetes Services (AKS)

Introduction

One of the leading organizations in the manufacturing sector needs to accelerate application delivery with high quality. The leadership of an organization is decisive in the implementation approach. They want the phase-wise implementation of DevOps practices. They want to automate manual processes for code analysis, unit testing, build, functional testing, and deployment. The need of the hour is to implement Continuous Integration and Continuous Delivery. This is an application selected as a pilot while there are 15 early adopter Angular applications, which are waiting in the queue.

The following is the list of tools and deliverables that will be integrated into the pipeline:

Tools	
Version Control	Git
Code Analysis	SonarQube
Unit Tests	Karma, Junit reports
Code Coverage	Cobertura
Build Script	Package.json
Deployment	Docker, Azure Kubernetes Services
Continuous Integration	Jenkins
Continuous Delivery	Jenkins
Pipeline	Pipeline as Code, Jenkinsfile, Blue Ocean
Expected Deliverables or Features in an Automated pipeline	

- Installation and Configuration of Jenkins

- Distributed Architecture/Controller Agent Architecture (Covered in *Chapter 11: Best Practices*)

- Role-based access (Covered in *Chapter 11: Best Practices*)

- Configuration of a CI/CD pipeline using Pipeline as Code

- Configuration of a CI/CD Pipeline that distributes an Angular package to Azure Kubernetes Services (AKS)

- Documentation

    o Documentation of defined processes and implementations

    o Technical documentation – *How* to guides

- Best practices documentation for the usage of Jenkins/Blue Ocean (Covered in *Chapter 11: Best Practices*)

Table 6.1: Tools and deliverables

In the next section, we will create a pipeline for an Angular application using the Blue Ocean interface in a step-by-step manner.

Multi-stage pipeline for an Angular app using Blue Ocean

In this chapter, we will try to cover CI/CD for a sample Angular application. Following is the big picture that we will implement in this chapter using Jenkins.

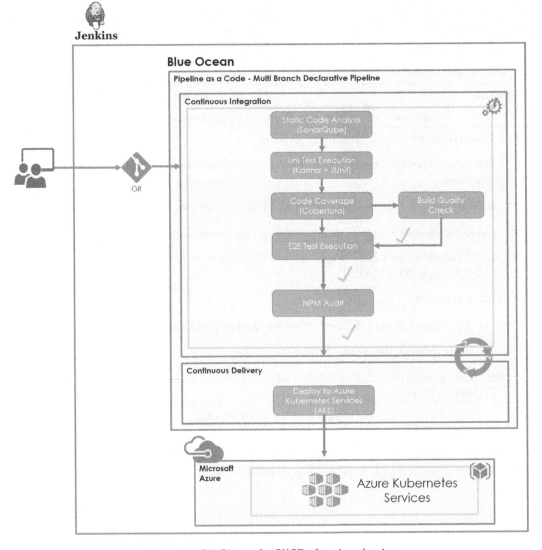

Figure 6.1: Big Picture for CI/CD of an Angular App

Let's create a pipeline for a sample Angular application using Blue Ocean.

1. Install NodeJS from **https://nodejs.org/en/download/**.

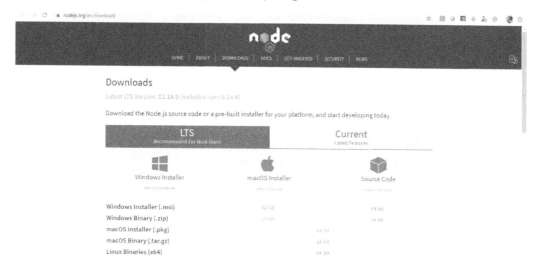

Figure 6.2: Download NodeJS

2. Verify the version of Node and Node Package Manager (NPM) in the Command Prompt:

```
1.    Microsoft Windows [Version 10.0.18362.836]
2.    (c) 2019 Microsoft Corporation. All rights reserved.
3.
4.    C:\Users\Mitesh>npm
5.
6.    Usage: npm <command>
7.
8.    where <command> is one of:
9.        access, adduser, audit, bin, bugs, c, cache, ci, cit,
10.       clean-install, clean-install-test, completion, config,
11.       create, ddp, dedupe, deprecate, dist-tag, docs, doctor,
12.       edit, explore, fund, get, help, help-search, hook, I, init,
13.       install, install-ci-test, install-test, it, link, list, ln,
14.       login, logout, ls, org, outdated, owner, pack, ping, prefix,
15.       profile, prune, publish, rb, rebuild, repo, restart, root,
```

```
16.      run, run-script, s, se, search, set, shrinkwrap, star,

17.      stars, start, stop, t, team, test, token, tst, un,

18.      uninstall, unpublish, unstar, up, update, v, version, view,

19.      whoami

20.

21.   npm <command> -h  quick help on <command>

22.   npm -l            display full usage info

23.   npm help <term>   search for help on <term>

24.   npm help npm      involved overview

25.

26.   Specify configs in the ini-formatted file:

27.        C:\Users\Mitesh\.npmrc

28.   or on the command line via: npm <command> --key value

29.   Config info can be viewed via: npm help config

30.

31.   npm@6.14.4 C:\Program Files\nodejs\node_modules\npm

32.

33.   C:\Users\Mitesh>npm -version

34.   6.14.4

35.

36.   C:\Users\Mitesh>node --version

37.   v12.18.0
```

In the next section, we will create a Continuous Integration pipeline using Blue Ocean.

Continuous Integration – Angular Application

In this section, we will create a pipeline for a sample angular application by using the sample code available in the Git repository:

1. Open the Blue Ocean Dashboard and click on **Create Pipeline**:

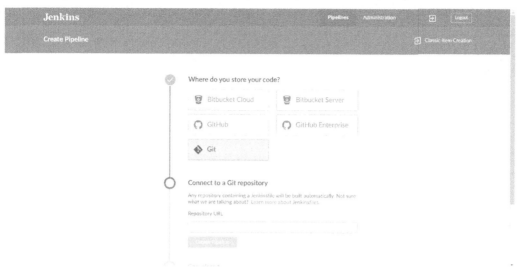

Figure 6.3: *Connect to Git Repo*

2. Provide a Git repository's URL and provide credentials. Click on **Create Pipeline**:

Figure 6.4: *Git Repo and Credentials*

3. The sample application doesn't have any Jenkinsfile in the repository in any branch. Hence, we need to create one. Click on **Create Pipeline**:

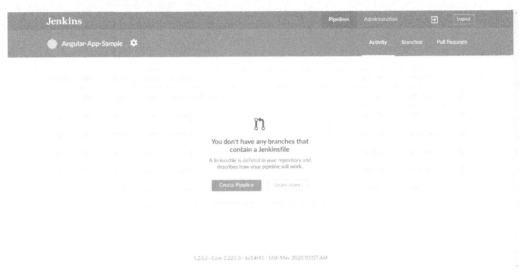

Figure 6.5: Create pipeline in Blue Ocean

4. Create the following three stages:

    • Continuous Integration
    • Deploy to Dev (Deploy to Docker container)
    • Deploy to Azure Kubernetes Services

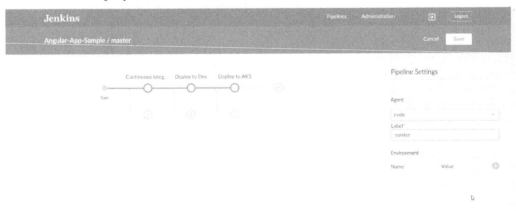

Figure 6.6: Pipeline Editor

In the next section, we will configure Junit and code coverage-related settings in the package.

Junit and the Cobertura configuration in karma.conf.js

In this section, we will configure Lint analysis, unit test execution, and code coverage, build quality checks, execute end-to-end tests, and execute the audit command. Perform the following steps:

1. Import a sample Angular application code from GitHub with unit tests.

2. Let's do a few configurations in the `karma.conf.js` file.

3. Add the required plugins for the Junit (unit testing) and Cobertura (code coverage) output:

```
1.    plugins: [
2.            require('karma-jasmine'),
3.            require('karma-chrome-launcher'),
4.            require('karma-mocha-reporter'),
5.            require('karma-coverage-istanbul-reporter'),
6.            require('karma-junit-reporter'),
7.          require('@angular-devkit/build-angular/plugins/karma')
8.        ],
```

4. Add Cobertura in the reports key section to `karma.conf.js`:

```
1.        coverageIstanbulReporter: {
2.          dir: require('path').join(__dirname, './coverage'),
3.          reports: ['html', 'lcovonly','cobertura'],
4.          fixWebpackSourcePaths: true
5.        },
6.        reporters: ['progress', 'mocha', 'junit'],
```

5. Add JunitReporter configuration details in `karma.conf.js` if it is not available in the file:

```
1.        junitReporter: {
2.          outputDir: '',
3.          outputFile: undefined,
4.          suite: '',
5.          useBrowserName: true,
6.          nameFormatter: undefined,
7.          classNameFormatter: undefined,
8.          properties: {}
9.        },
```

6. Configure the Headless Browser so that test cases can be executed:

```
1.    autoWatch: true,
2.    singleRun: false,
3.    browsers: ['ChromeHeadlessNoSandbox'],
4.
5.    customLaunchers: {
6.      ChromeHeadlessNoSandbox: {
7.        base: 'ChromeHeadless',
8.        flags: ['--no-sandbox']
9.      }
10.   },
```

In the next section, we will configure scripts in package.json.

Lint, Unit tests, and Code coverage configuration in package.json

Let's configure scripts in `package.json`:

1. Configure `package.json` with scripts:

```
1.    "lint": "tslint --project tslint.json",
2.    "test": "ng test angular-sample-app --code-coverage --no-
      watch",
3.    "e2e": "ng e2e",
```

2. To execute lint analysis, the following command needs to be executed: `npm install && npm install --save-dev tslint-angular`:

```
1.  Linting "angular-sample-app"...
2.  All files pass linting.
3.  Linting "ngx-example-library"...
4.  All files pass linting.
```

Once we have configured the required settings, we need to configure it in the Jenkinsfile using Blue Ocean.

Configure unit tests and code coverage in a multi-stage pipeline

Let's configure unit tests and code coverage in declarative pipeline using Blue Ocean.

1. Go to the Blue Ocean dashboard and open the pipeline editor for the Project:

Figure 6.7: Continuous Integration stage

2. Add Windows Batch Script tasks to execute NPM-related tasks, archive Junit formatted XML results, and publish code coverage reports:

```
1.   pipeline {
2.     agent {
3.       node {
4.         label 'master'
5.       }
6.     }
7.     stages {
8.       stage('Continuous Integration') {
9.         steps {
10.          bat 'npm install'
11.          bat 'npm run lint > lint.txt'
12.          bat 'npm install karma-junit-reporter --save-dev &&
     npm run test'
13.          junit 'TESTS-*.xml'
```

```
14.        publishCoverage(adapters: [coberturaAdapter('coverage\\
       cobertura-coverage.xml')],                    sourceFileResolver:
       sourceFiles('NEVER_STORE'))
15.            bat 'npm run build:prod:en'
16.            zip(dir: 'dist\\browser', zipFile: 'browser.zip')
17.            stash(includes: 'browser.zip', name: 'dist')
18.        }
19.      }
20.    }
21.  }
```

We will also execute the command to create a build/distribution directory and ZIP for deploying it in a Docker container.

3. Lint analysis is successful based on the logs:

```
1.    Linting "angularexampleapp"...
2.    All files pass linting.
3.    Linting "ngx-example-library"...
4.    All files pass linting
```

4. Let's verify different task executions on the Blue Ocean dashboard:

Figure 6.8: *Continuous Integration stage in Blue ocean*

The following are some important logs for unit tests execution:

```
1.   F:\1.DevOps>npm  install  karma-junit-reporter  --save-dev
     && npm run test

2.

3.   + karma-junit-reporter@2.0.1

4.   added 2 packages from 43 contributors and audited 1921
     packages in 19.337s

5.   found 838 vulnerabilities (799 low, 11 moderate, 28 high)

6.     run `npm audit fix` to fix them, or `npm audit` for details

7.   .

8.   .

9.   .

10.  START:

11.

12.  08 06 2020 17:07:08.115:INFO [karma-server]: Karma v4.1.0
     server started at http://0.0.0.0:9876/

13.  08 06 2020 17:07:08.119:INFO [launcher]: Launching browsers
     ChromeHeadlessNoSandbox with concurrency unlimited

14.  08 06 2020 17:07:08.125:INFO [launcher]: Starting browser
     ChromeHeadless

15.  08  06  2020  17:07:24.840:INFO  [HeadlessChrome  83.0.4103
     (Windows 10.0.0)]: Connected on socket cCcCUYh8DF_cHWzPAAAA
     with id 53786348

16.  HeadlessChrome 83.0.4103 (Windows 10.0.0): Executed 0 of 43
     SUCCESS (0 secs / 0 secs)

17.  HeadlessChrome 83.0.4103 (Windows 10.0.0): Executed 1 of 43
     SUCCESS (0 secs / 0.371 secs)

18.  HeadlessChrome 83.0.4103 (Windows 10.0.0) SLOW 0.371 secs:
     SearchBarComponent should create hero search component

19.  HeadlessChrome 83.0.4103 (Windows 10.0.0): Executed 1 of 43
     SUCCESS (0 secs / 0.371 secs)

20.  .

21.  .

22.  HeadlessChrome 83.0.4103 (Windows 10.0.0): Executed 42 of
     43 SUCCESS (0 secs / 0.76 secs)

23.  HeadlessChrome 83.0.4103 (Windows 10.0.0): Executed 43 of
     43 SUCCESS (0 secs / 0.761 secs)

24.  HeadlessChrome 83.0.4103 (Windows 10.0.0): Executed 43 of
     43 SUCCESS (2.032 secs / 0.761 secs)
```

```
25.

26.    TOTAL: 43 SUCCESS

27.    TOTAL: 43 SUCCESS

28.

29.    Finished in 2.032 secs / 0.761 secs @ 17:07:37 GMT+0530
       (India Standard Time)

30.

31.    SUMMARY:

32.

33.    âˆš 43 tests completed

34.    â€¼ 1 test slow
```

5.   Click on the **Test** link to verify unit test results on the Blue Ocean dashboard:

Figure 6.9: Unit test results

NOTE

Continuous Improvement and Continuous Innovation are the main priorities of all organizations to remain competitive in a dynamic market. DevOps practices are enablers of digital transformation as they enable high quality and faster time to market by complementing Agile principles and cloud resources.

6. The following are the important logs for the build command execution:

```
1.  F:\1.DevOps\2020\Jenkins_Home\workspace\Angular-App-Sample_
    master>npm run build:prod:en

2.

3.

4.  > angular-example-app@8.0.0 build:prod:en F:\1.DevOps\2020\
    Jenkins_Home\workspace\Angular-App-Sample_master

5.  > ng build --configuration=production-en

6.  Browserslist: caniuse-lite is outdated. Please run next
    command `npm update`

7.

8.  Date: 2020-06-08T11:39:33.990Z

9.  Hash: d35de1b5dd1eccb596b2

10. Time: 98032ms

11.

12. chunk  {0}  runtime-es5.0b3e38ccfd1dee6a14a6.js  (runtime)
    2.15 kB [entry] [rendered]

13. chunk {1} main-es5.4d3d4e78f4efda3a64a8.js (main) 1.43 MB
    [initial] [rendered]

14. chunk  {2}  polyfills-es5.a17668551f01d2e249e3.js  (polyfills)
    133 kB [initial] [rendered]

15. chunk {3} styles.b27e958b28dbe09adf6c.css (styles) 66.5 kB
    [initial] [rendered]

16. chunk {4} 4-es5.da246c5a78614f62b17d.js () 48.5 kB [rendered]

17. chunk  {scripts}  scripts.4dfa083dee6d8a0bb97f.js  (scripts)
    1.95 kB [entry] [rendered]

18. Date: 2020-06-08T11:40:54.426Z

19. Hash: 24aae5ce7f050b117e37

20. Time: 80231ms

21.

22. chunk  {0}  runtime-es2015.57596d6713f936f5ca33.js  (runtime)
    2.15 kB [entry] [rendered]

23. chunk {1} main-es2015.061e67488e270ccedd27.js (main) 1.32 MB
    [initial] [rendered]

24. chunk {2} polyfills-es2015.79f2a6adf0a40ba9e09f.js (polyfills)
    58.5 kB [initial] [rendered]

25. chunk {3} styles.b27e958b28dbe09adf6c.css (styles) 66.5 kB
    [initial] [rendered]

26. chunk {4} 4-es2015.8fc24ffa3a6fee6ad1df.js () 48.1 kB [rendered]

27. chunk  {scripts}  scripts.4dfa083dee6d8a0bb97f.js  (scripts)
    1.95 kB [entry] [rendered]
```

Our idea is to transfer distribution files to an agent where Docker is installed. We will create a Docker image with the use of *distribution files*. We will not archive the distribution directory, but we will use stash and unstash tasks available in Jenkins. We have not archived any directory as of now. Hence, there are no artifacts available in the Artifacts section:

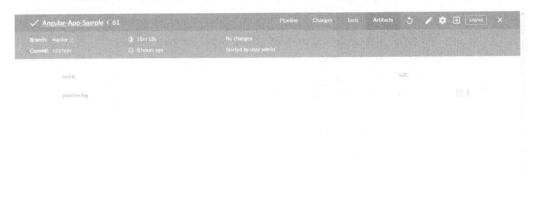

Figure 6.10: Artifacts

7. The following are tasks in the pipeline to ZIP (compress) the `dist` folder and stash it:

```
1.          zip(dir: 'dist\\browser', zipFile: 'browser.zip')
2.          stash(includes: 'browser.zip', name: 'dist')
```

8. Let's verify the status on the traditional Jenkins dashboard for a sample Angular application pipeline:

Figure 6.11: Multi-branch pipeline

9. Verify coverage reports available here:

Figure 6.12: Pipeline Status

10. Click on **Test Results** to get more details on **History of Test Results**:

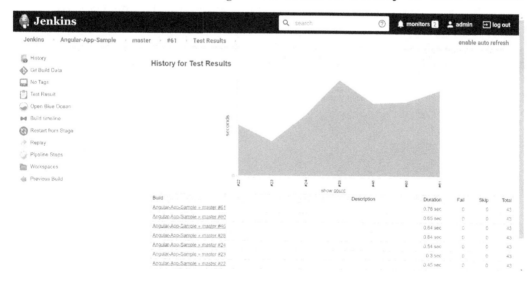

Figure 6.13: History of Test results

11. Click on the available package to get a more granular level of details for the unit test execution:

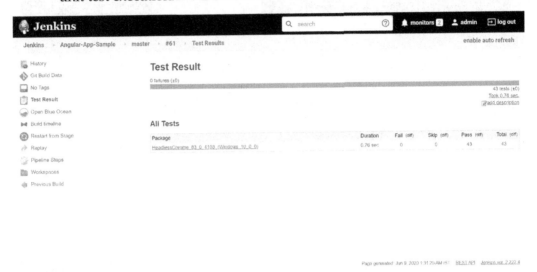

Figure 6.14: Details for unit test execution

12. In the Project status section, you will get test results and code coverage charts:

Figure 6.15: Test results and Code Coverage charts

13. Verify the Code Coverage and Stage view on the Jenkins dashboard:

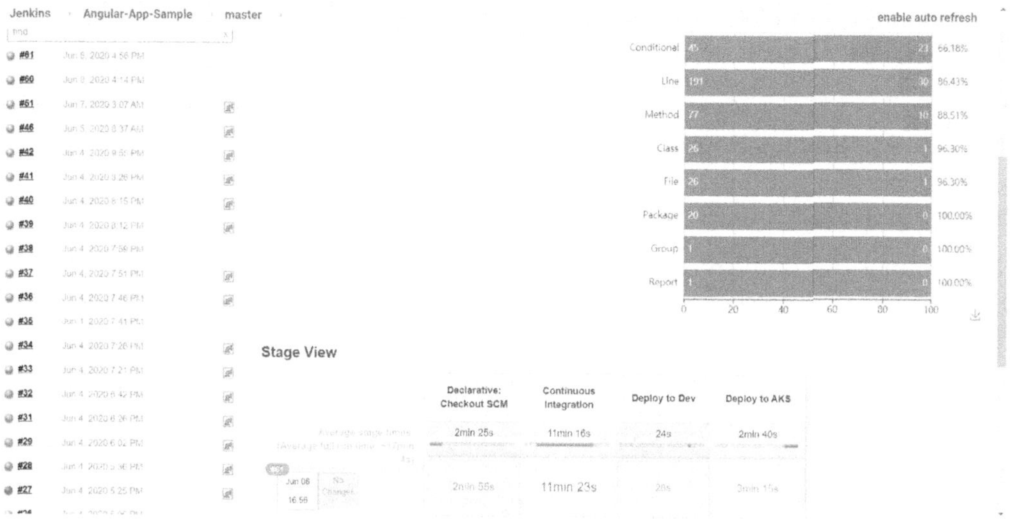

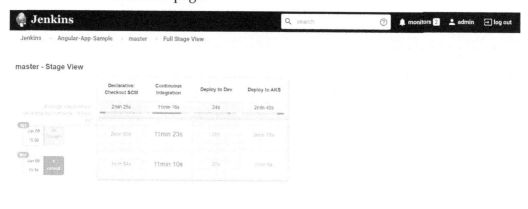

Figure 6.16: Code Coverage

NOTE

Agile and DevOps are not the same. Agile and DevOps complement each other. The Agile approach is a driver for DevOps practices implementation.

14. Click on the **`Full Stage View`** to get more details on the pipeline stages and to see it on the full page:

Figure 6.17: Full Stage View

In the next section, we will provide a command for an end-to-end test execution.

End-to-end test execution

Add Windows Batch Script to execute the command npm run e2e. Publish the results in Continuous Integration as an exercise.

NPM audit

NPM audit is one of the most significant features that was introduced with npm@6. It provides the facility to perform a security review of dependencies. The Npm audit report provides details regarding security vulnerabilities:

```
1.  F:\1.DevOps\2020\Jenkins_Home\workspace\Angular-App-Sample_
    master>npm audit
2.  [90m                                                     [39m
3.  [90m [39m                  === npm audit security report ===
    [90m [39m
4.  [90m                                                     [39m
5.
6.  # Run  npm install firebase@7.15.0  to resolve 3 vulnerabilities
7.  SERVER  WARNING: Recommended action  is  a  potentially  breaking
    change
8.  [90m                  [39m[90m                               [39m
9.  [90m [39m Low       [90m [39m Prototype Pollution              [90m
    [39m
10. [90m                  [39m[90m                               [39m
11. [90m [39m Package      [90m [39m minimist                     [90m
    [39m
12. [90m                  [39m[90m                               [39m
13. [90m [39m Dependency of [90m [39m firebase                    [90m
    [39m
14. [90m                  [39m[90m                               [39m
15. [90m [39m Path         [90m [39m firebase > @firebase/firestore >
    grpc > node-pre-gyp >      [90m [39m
16. [90m [39m                          [90m [39m mkdirp > minimist
    [90m [39m
17. [90m                  [39m[90m                               [39m
18. [90m [39m More info  [90m [39m https://npmjs.com/advisories/1179
    [90m [39m
19. [90m                  [39m[90m                               [39m
20. .
21. .
```

```
22.  .
23.
24.  found 838 vulnerabilities (799 low, 11 moderates, 28 high) in
     1920 scanned packages
25.    run `npm audit fix` to fix 805 of them.
26.    11 vulnerabilities require server-major dependency updates.
27.    22 vulnerabilities require manual review. See the full report
     for details.
```

The npm   audit   fix command scans project dependencies for vulnerabilities and automatically installs any compatible updates to fix vulnerabilities in the dependencies:

```
1.   F:\1.DevOps\2020\Jenkins_Home\workspace\Angular-App-Sample_
     master>npm audit fix
2.   npm WARN deprecated chokidar@2.1.8: Chokidar 2 will break on
     node v14+. Upgrade to chokidar 3 with 15x less dependencies.
3.
4.   > grpc@1.24.3 install F:\1.DevOps\2020\Jenkins_Home\workspace\
     Angular-App-Sample_master\node_modules\grpc
5.   > node-pre-gyp install --fallback-to-build --library=static_
     library
6.
7.   node-pre-gyp WARN Using request for node-pre-gyp https download
8.   [grpc]    Success:    "F:\1.DevOps\2020\Jenkins_Home\workspace\
     Angular-App-Sample_master\node_modules\grpc\src\node\exte
9.   nsion_binary\node-v72-win32-x64-unknown\grpc_node.node"        is
     installed via remote
10.  .
11.  .
12.  .
13.  .
14.  .
15.  npm WARN optional SKIPPING OPTIONAL DEPENDENCY: fsevents@1.2.9
     (node_modules\fsevents):
16.  npm WARN notsup SKIPPING OPTIONAL DEPENDENCY: Unsupported
     platform for fsevents@1.2.9: wanted {"os":"darwin","arch":"any"}
     (current: {"os":"win32","arch":"x64"})
17.
18.  + helmet@3.22.0
19.  + http-server@0.12.3
20.  + @angular-devkit/build-angular@0.901.7
```

```
21.  + grpc@1.24.3
22.  added 600 packages from 182 contributors, removed 104 packages,
     updated 125 packages and moved 12 packages in 484.281s
23.
24.  43 packages are looking for funding
25.    run `npm fund` for details
26.
27.  fixed 805 of 838 vulnerabilities in 1920 scanned packages
28.     22 vulnerabilities required manual review and could not be
     updated
29.     4 package updates for 11 vulnerabilities involved breaking
     changes
30.     (use `npm audit fix --force` to install breaking changes; or
     refer to `npm audit` for steps to fix these manually)
```

In the next section, we will discuss how to create a Docker image with the use of a dist folder that we created using the Continuous Integration stage. We will create a Docker instance and then deploy a Docker image to Azure Kubernetes Services.

TIP

Manage the Jenkins section that has a new look and feel in Jenkins 2.235.1. It is more user friendly with Categories. Following is the new UI for configuration.

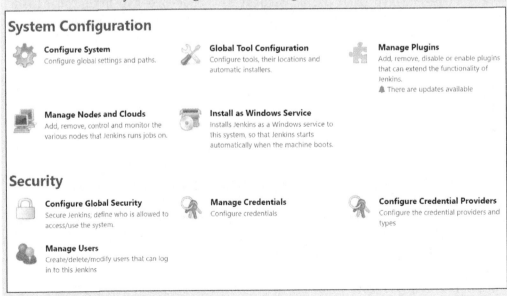

System Configuration

Configure System
Configure global settings and paths.

Global Tool Configuration
Configure tools, their locations and automatic installers.

Manage Plugins
Add, remove, disable or enable plugins that can extend the functionality of Jenkins.
⚠ There are updates available

Manage Nodes and Clouds
Add, remove, control and monitor the various nodes that Jenkins runs jobs on.

Install as Windows Service
Installs Jenkins as a Windows service to this system, so that Jenkins starts automatically when the machine boots.

Security

Configure Global Security
Secure Jenkins; define who is allowed to access/use the system.

Manage Credentials
Configure credentials

Configure Credential Providers
Configure the credential providers and types

Manage Users
Create/delete/modify users that can log in to this Jenkins

Figure 6.18: Jenkins 2.235.1

Continuous Delivery – Angular App

We are assuming that Docker is available on the agent. Controller agent-related details are available in *Chapter 11: Best Practices*. We will create a docker image and create instance to verify application deployment.

1. We need to unstash the `dist` folder and create a Docker image using it.

2. Verify the Docker version in the pipeline using the `docker version` command:

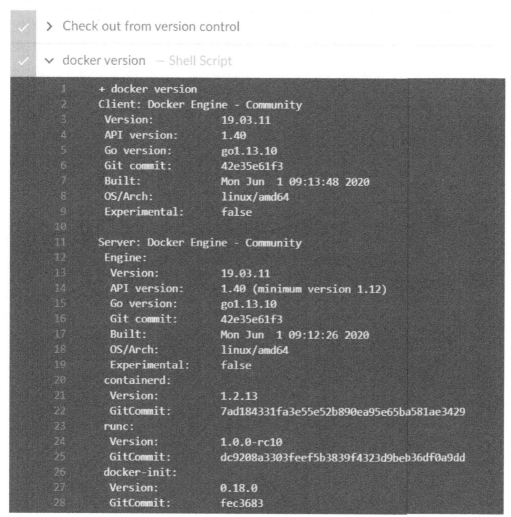

Figure 6.19: Docker version

3. `Dist` — Restore files previously stashed, change access rights, and extract files:

Figure 6.20: Distribution folder operations

4. The next task is to create a Docker image using the dockerfile. We have a simple Docker file available:

```
1.  FROM nginx:1-alpine
2.  COPY dist/browser/ /usr/share/nginx/html
3.  EXPOSE 80
```

5. Execute Docker build `. -t test/angular-sample` to build a docker image.

6. The following is the log of the command execution:

```
1.  + docker build . -t test/angular-sample
2.  Sending build context to Docker daemon   9.655MB
3.
4.  Step 1/3 : FROM nginx:1-alpine
5.   ---> 7d0cdcc60a96
6.
7.  Step 2/3 : COPY dist/browser/ /usr/share/nginx/html
8.   ---> 88322dff3cc3
9.
10. Step 3/3 : EXPOSE 80
11.  ---> Running in ef457fd989e4
```

```
12.
13.    Removing intermediate container ef457fd989e4
14.    ---> b4d8a5a66b4c
15.
16.    Successfully built b4d8a5a66b4c
17.    Successfully tagged test/angular-sample:latest
```

7. The next task is to create a Docker instance using the docker run -p command:

   8080:80 --detach test/angular-sample:

   + docker run -p 8080:80 --detach test/angular-sample

   01ac269f6b7aa8a4a2315fc42b6df1503e8b9469221a0b7a7546ee8a231b1a79

8. The following is the Deploy to Dev Stage on the Blue Ocean dashboard – pipeline editor with steps:

Figure 6.21: *Deploy using Docker instance*

9. The following is the successful execution of a stage to create a Docker image and running an instance:

Figure 6.22: Stage execution

10. The following is the Jenkinsfile stage block to create an image and run a Docker instance:

```
1.   stage('Deploy to Dev') {
2.        agent {
3.           node {
4.              label 'centos'
5.           }
6.
7.        }
8.        steps {
9.           sh 'docker version'
10.          unstash 'dist'
11.          sh 'chmod 755 browser.zip'
12.          unzip(dir: 'dist/browser', zipFile: 'browser.zip')
13.          sh 'docker build . -t test/angular-sample'
14.         sh 'docker run -p 8080:80 --detach test/angular-sample'
15.        }
16.     }
```

TIP

Cron expression consists of five fields separated by *Tab* or whitespace:

MINUTE HOUR DOM MONTH DOW

MINUTE	Minutes within the hour (0–59)
HOUR	The hour of the day (0–23)
DOM	The day of the month (1–31)
MONTH	The month (1–12)
DOW	The day of the week (0–7) where 0 and 7 are Sundays

Examples:

* * * * *	Execute after every minute
H/30 * * * *	Every 30 Minutes
H(0-29)/10 * * * *	Every ten minutes in the first half of every hour

@yearly, @annually, @monthly, @weekly, @daily, @midnight, and @ hourly can be used.

```
1.  triggers {
2.      cron '@midnight'
3.  }
```

In the next section, we will discuss pushing the Docker image into the Azure Container Registry and then deploying instances into Azure Kubernetes Services.

Deploy Angular App to Azure Kubernetes Services (AKS)

Before we integrate commands for Azure Kubernetes Services operations in the Jenkinsfile, let's install Azure CLI in the agent so we can perform various operations.

NOTE

Automation doesn't imply DevOps. Automation is one enabler. People, processes, and tools are critical for culture transformation.

1. Import the Microsoft repository key using: `sudo rpm --import https://packages.microsoft.com/keys/microsoft.asc`

2. Create the `local azure-cli repository` information using: `sudo sh -c 'echo -e "[azure-cli]:`

```
1.  [root@localhost Downloads]# sudo rpm --import https://
    packages.microsoft.com/keys/microsoft.asc
2.  [root@localhost Downloads]# sudo sh -c 'echo -e "[azure-cli]
3.  > name=Azure CLI
4.  > baseurl=https://packages.microsoft.com/yumrepos/azure-cli
5.  > enabled=1
6.  > gpgcheck=1
7.  > gpgkey=https://packages.microsoft.com/keys/microsoft.asc"
    > /etc/yum.repos.d/azure-cli.repo'
```

3. Install the Azure CLI using yum install.

NOTE

To install the Azure CLI on a different operating system, go to **https://docs. microsoft.com/en-us/cli/azure/install-azure-cli?view=azure-cli-latest**.

```
1.  [root@localhost /]# sudo yum install azure-cli
2.  Loaded plugins: fastestmirror, langpacks
3.  Loading mirror speeds from cached hostfile
4.  epel/x86_64/metalink                                          |
    8.2 kB  00:00:00
5.   * base: mirrors.piconets.webwerks.in
6.   * epel: mirror.xeonbd.com
7.   * extras: mirrors.piconets.webwerks.in
8.   * updates: mirrors.piconets.webwerks.in
9.  azure-cli                                                     |
    3.0 kB  00:00:00
10. base                                                          |
    3.6 kB  00:00:00
11. docker-ce-stable                                              |
    3.5 kB  00:00:00
12. epel                                                          |
    4.7 kB  00:00:00
13. extras                                                        |
    2.9 kB  00:00:00
14. updates                                                       |
    2.9 kB  00:00:00
15. (1/4): azure-cli/primary_db                                   |
    53 kB  00:00:04
```

```
16.  (2/4): epel/x86_64/updateinfo                          |
     1.0 MB  00:00:09
17.  (3/4): updates/7/x86_64/primary_db                     |
     2.1 MB  00:00:10
18.  (4/4): epel/x86_64/primary_db                          |
     6.8 MB  00:00:34
19.  Resolving Dependencies
20.  --> Running transaction check
21.  ---> Package azure-cli.x86_64 0:2.7.0-1.el7 will be
     installed
22.  --> Processing Dependency: python3 for package: azure-
     cli-2.7.0-1.el7.x86_64
23.  --> Processing Dependency: libpython3.6m.so.1.0()(64bit)
     for package: azure-cli-2.7.0-1.el7.x86_64
24.  --> Running transaction check
25.  ---> Package python3.x86_64 0:3.6.8-13.el7 will be installed
26.  --> Processing Dependency: python3-setuptools for package:
     python3-3.6.8-13.el7.x86_64
27.  --> Processing Dependency: python3-pip for package:
     python3-3.6.8-13.el7.x86_64
28.  ---> Package python3-libs.x86_64 0:3.6.8-13.el7 will be
     installed
29.  --> Running transaction check
30.  ---> Package python3-pip.noarch 0:9.0.3-7.el7_7 will be
     installed
31.  ---> Package python3-setuptools.noarch 0:39.2.0-10.el7
     will be installed
32.  --> Finished Dependency Resolution
33.
34.  Dependencies Resolved
35.
36.  ================================================================
37.   Package                          Arch              Version
     Repository       Size
38.  ================================================================
39.  Installing:
40.   azure-cli              x86_64     2.7.0-1.el7          azure-
     cli      44 M
41.  Installing for dependencies:
42.   python3                x86_64     3.6.8-13.el7          base
```

```
           69 k
43.    python3-libs          x86_64      3.6.8-13.el7        base
       7.0 M
44.    python3-pip           noarch      9.0.3-7.el7_7     updates
       1.8 M
45.    python3-setuptools    noarch      39.2.0-10.el7       base
       629 k
46.
47.  Transaction Summary
48.  ==============================================================
     ================
49.  Install  1 Package (+4 Dependent packages)
50.
51.  Total download size: 54 M
52.  Installed size: 502 M
53.  Is this ok [y/d/N]: y
54.  Downloading packages:
55.  (1/5): python3-3.6.8-13.el7.x86_64.rpm                     |
       69 kB   00:00:00
56.  (2/5): python3-setuptools-39.2.0-10.el7.noarch.rpm         |
       629 kB   00:00:01
57.  (3/5): python3-pip-9.0.3-7.el7_7.noarch.rpm                |
       1.8 MB   00:00:03
58.  (4/5): python3-libs-3.6.8-13.el7.x86_64.rpm                |
       7.0 MB   00:00:12
59.  (5/5): azure-cli-2.7.0-1.el7.x86_64.rpm                    |
       44 MB   00:00:44
60.  -------------------------------------------------------------
     ------------------------------
61.  Total                                           1.2 MB/s |
       54 MB   00:44
62.  Running transaction check
63.  Running transaction test
64.  Transaction test succeeded
65.  Running transaction
66.        Installing   :   python3-pip-9.0.3-7.el7_7.noarch
       1/5
67.      Installing  :  python3-setuptools-39.2.0-10.el7.noarch
       2/5
```

```
68.    Installing : python3-libs-3.6.8-13.el7.x86_64          3/5
69.    Installing : python3-3.6.8-13.el7.x86_64               4/5
70.    Installing : azure-cli-2.7.0-1.el7.x86_64              5/5
71.    Verifying  : azure-cli-2.7.0-1.el7.x86_64              1/5
72.    Verifying  : python3-3.6.8-13.el7.x86_64               2/5
73.    Verifying  : python3-pip-9.0.3-7.el7_7.noarch          3/5
74.    Verifying  :        python3-setuptools-39.2.0-10.el7.noarch
       4/5
75.    Verifying  : python3-libs-3.6.8-13.el7.x86_64          5/5
76.
77.    Installed:
78.      azure-cli.x86_64 0:2.7.0-1.el7
79.
80.    Dependency Installed:
81.      python3.x86_64 0:3.6.8-13.el7          python3-libs.x86_64
       0:3.6.8-13.el7
82.      python3-pip.noarch 0:9.0.3-7.el7_7     python3-setuptools.
       noarch 0:39.2.0-10.el7
83.
84.    Complete!
```

4. We can execute the Azure CLI with the `az` command. Use the `az` login command to sign in:

```
1.    [root@localhost /]# az login
2.
3.    START   /bin/firefox   "https://login.microsoftonline.com/
      common/oauth2/authorize?response_type=code&client_
      id=04b07795-8ddb-461a-bbee-02f9e1bf7b46&redirect_
      uri=http://localhost:8400&state=ktqdattw4hsxlyvaoo
      we&resource=https://management.core.windows.
      net/&prompt=select_account"
4.    Running without a11y support!
5.
6.    You have logged in.
```

5. A successful login will open a browser window with a message in the CentOS Agent.

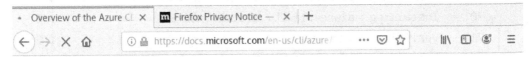

You have logged into Microsoft Azure!

You can close this window, or we will redirect you to the Azure CLI documents in 10 seconds.

Figure 6.23: Azure CLI redirection

6. We can create the Azure Container Registry using the `az acr create` command.

7. We have already created a resource group named `aks-jenkins` in the Microsoft Azure:

```
1.  [root@localhost /]# az acr create -n sampleImages -g aks-
    jenkins --sku Basic
2.  {- Finished ..
3.    "adminUserEnabled": false,
4.    "creationDate": "2020-06-05T21:29:27.273877+00:00",
5.    "dataEndpointEnabled": false,
6.    "dataEndpointHostNames": [],
7.    "encryption": {
8.      "keyVaultProperties": null,
9.      "status": "disabled"
10.   },
11.   "id": "/subscriptions/<subscription_id>/resourceGroups/
      aks-jenkins/providers/Microsoft.ContainerRegistry/
      registries/sampleImages",
12.   "identity": null,
```

```
13.     "location": "eastus",
14.     "loginServer": "sampleimages.azurecr.io",
15.     "name": "sampleImages",
16.     "networkRuleSet": null,
17.     "policies": {
18.       "quarantinePolicy": {
19.         "status": "disabled"
20.       },
21.       "retentionPolicy": {
22.         "days": 7,
23.       "lastUpdatedTime": "2020-06-05T21:29:28.045851+00:00",
24.         "status": "disabled"
25.       },
26.       "trustPolicy": {
27.         "status": "disabled",
28.         "type": "Notary"
29.       }
30.     },
31.     "privateEndpointConnections": [],
32.     "provisioningState": "Succeeded",
33.     "publicNetworkAccess": "Enabled",
34.     "resourceGroup": "aks-jenkins",
35.     "sku": {
36.       "name": "Basic",
37.       "tier": "Basic"
38.     },
39.     "status": null,
40.     "storageAccount": null,
41.     "tags": {},
42.     "type": "Microsoft.ContainerRegistry/registries"
43.   }
```

8. Let's verify the creation of the Container Registry in the Azure portal:

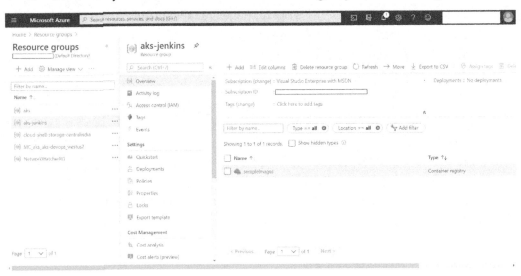

Figure 6.24: Container Registry

9. Click on the **Container Registry** and verify the **Usage** section:

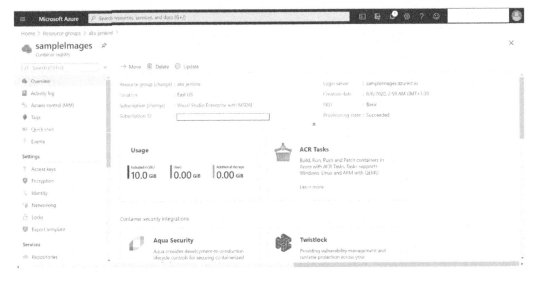

Figure 6.25: Container Registry Overview

10. Log in to an Azure Container Registry through the Azure CLI using the `az acr login` command:

```
1.  [root@localhost /]# az acr login --name sampleImages
2.  Uppercase characters are detected in the registry name.
    When using its server url in docker commands, to avoid
    authentication errors, use all lowercase.
3.  Login Succeeded
```

11. Before we push an image to the Container Registry, we must tag it with the fully qualified name of the ACR login server. The login server name is in the format `<registry-name>.azurecr.io` (all lowercase); for example, `sampleimages.azurecr.io`.

12. Verify Docker images:

```
1.  [root@localhost  /]#  docker  tag  test/angular-sample
    sampleimages.azurecr.io/angular-sample:v1
2.  [root@localhost /]# docker images
3.  REPOSITORY            TAG        IMAGE ID        CREATED       SIZE
4.  test/angular-sample         latest       93a9abd31747      19
    hours ago    25.7MB
5.  sampleimages.azurecr.io/angular-sample   v1    93a9abd31747
    19 hours ago    25.7MB
6.  <none>                    <none>         52205811804e      19
    hours ago    793MB
7.  nginx                  1-alpine     7d0cdcc60a96     3 days
    ago      21.3MB
8.  node                  11-alpine     f18da2f58c3d      12
    months ago   75.5MB
```

13. The next step is to push the image to ACR:

```
1.  [root@localhost /]# docker push sampleimages.azurecr.io/
    angular-sample
2.  The push refers to repository [sampleimages.azurecr.io/
    angular-sample]
3.  dc0cf0d0ca6e: Pushed
4.  a181cbf898a0: Pushed
5.  570fc47f2558: Pushed
6.  5d17421f1571: Pushed
7.  7bb2a9d37337: Pushed
8.  3e207b409db3: Pushed
9.  v1:digest:       sha256:e4a882e5702d63feede4e56d245153782d
    018ff761c3d28 size: 1571
```

14. Go to the Microsoft Azure Portal and verify the **Usage** section and observe the changes in the **Used** column:

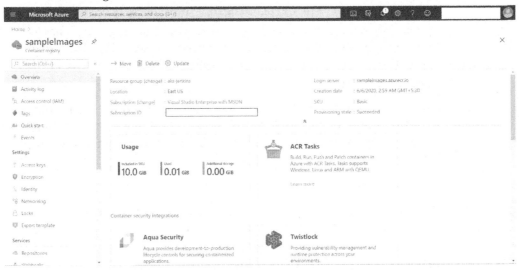

Figure 6.26: ACR Usage section

NOTE

DevOps is useful to all kinds of organizations and is applicable to most of the applications. However, a detailed assessment is required before DevOps practices implementation.

15. Click on the **Repositories** section to verify the available repository – the one we pushed recently:

Figure 6.27: ACR Repositories

16. If you push the image again, then you may get the following message:

```
1.  [root@localhost /]# docker push sampleimages.azurecr.io/
    angular-sample

2.  The push refers to repository [sampleimages.azurecr.io/
    angular-sample]

3.  dc0cf0d0ca6e: Layer already exists

4.  a181cbf898a0: Layer already exists

5.  570fc47f2558: Layer already exists

6.  5d17421f1571: Layer already exists

7.  7bb2a9d37337: Layer already exists

8.  3e207b409db3: Layer already exists
```

17. Use the `az acr repository list` command to list all available repositories in ACR using the Azure CLI:

```
1.  [root@localhost /]# az acr repository list --name
    sampleImages --output table

2.  Result

3.  --------------

4.  angular-sample
```

18. A Docker image is available in ACR. The next task is to perform the Azure Kubernetes Services operation from the agent.

19. Install the AKS CLI using the `az aks install-cli` command:

```
1.  [mitesh@localhost /]$ sudo az aks install-cli

2.  [sudo] password for mitesh:

3.  Downloading client to "/usr/local/bin/kubectl" from
    "https://storage.googleapis.com/kubernetes-release/
    release/v1.18.3/bin/linux/amd64/kubectl"

4.  Please ensure that /usr/local/bin is in your search PATH,
    so the `kubectl` command can be found.
```

20. Create a Kubernetes cluster using the `az aks create` command:

```
1.  [mitesh@localhost /]$ az aks create -g aks-jenkins -n
    AngularCluster

2.  An RSA key file or key value must be supplied to SSH Key
    Value. You can use --generate-ssh-keys to let CLI generate
    one for you
```

21. Verify the AKS cluster in the Microsoft Azure Portal:

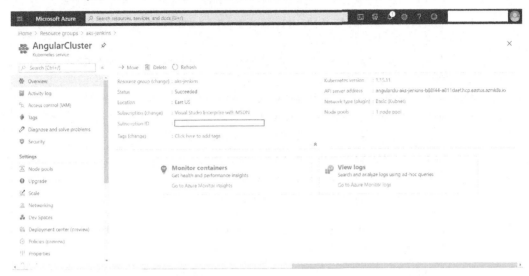

Figure 6.28: AKS Cluster in the Microsoft Azure Portal

22. Click on **Node pools** to verify existing Nodes available in the AKS Cluster.

23. Observe the Node count available in the **Node pool**:

Figure 6.29: Node Pools

24. Click on the Node count link.

25. We can configure the scaling operation with **Manual** or **Autoscale** methods.

26. Let's change it to 1. Click on **Apply**:

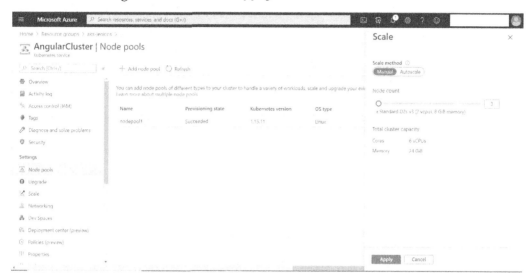

Figure 6.30: *Scale Method in AKS Node pools*

27. Verify the Node count again after the modification:

Figure 6.31: *Node Count*

28. Use `--generate-ssh-keys` to generate SSH key files '/home/mitesh/.ssh/id_rsa' and '/home/mitesh/.ssh/id_rsa.pub' under ~/.ssh to allow SSH access to the VM:

    1. ```
       [mitesh@localhost /]$ az aks create -g aks-jenkins -n
       AngularCluster --generate-ssh-keys
       ```

    2. ```
       SSH key files '/home/mitesh/.ssh/id_rsa' and '/home/mitesh/.
       ssh/id_rsa.pub' have been generated under ~/.ssh to allow
       SSH access to the VM. If using machines without permanent
       storage like Azure Cloud Shell without an attached file
       share, back up your keys to a safe location
       ```

    3. ```
       Finished service principal creation [#####################
       #############]  100.0000%
       ```

29. Use `az aks get-credentials` to get access credentials for a managed Kubernetes cluster (Azure Kubernetes Services). Once the context is merged in the current context, we can operate `kubectl` commands directly from the terminal and get details on the AKS cluster:

    1. ```
       [mitesh@localhost /]$ az aks get-credentials --resource-
       group aks-jenkins --name AngularCluster
       ```

    2. ```
       Merged "AngularCluster" as current context in /home/mitesh/.
       kube/config
       ```

    We have already created the Azure Container Registry and Azure Kubernetes Services. When we would like to use **Azure Container Registry (ACR)** with **Azure Kubernetes Service (AKS),** we need some kind of authentication. The authentication mechanism helps to integrate ACR and AKS seamlessly.

30. Let's try to integrate an existing ACR (`sampleimages`) with existing AKS clusters (`AngularCluster`) by providing `acr-name` or `acr-resource-id` as follows:

    1. ```
       az aks update -g aks-jenkins -n AngularCluster --attach-acr
       sampleimages
       ```

    2. ```
       az aks update -g aks-jenkins -n AngularCluster --attach-acr
       <acr-id>
       ```

    3. ```
       [mitesh@localhost Desktop]$ az aks update -g aks-jenkins -n
       AngularCluster --attach-acr sampleimages
       ```

31. The following are commands to detach to an existing ACR (`sampleimages`) with existing AKS clusters (`AngularCluster`) by providing `acr-name` or `acr-resource-id` as follows:

    1. ```
       az aks update -g aks-jenkins -n AngularCluster --detach-acr
       sampleimages
       ```

    2. ```
       az aks update -g aks-jenkins -n AngularCluster --detach-acr
       <acr-id>
       ```

32. The following is the YAML that we have used to deploy the Docker image stored in ACR to AKS. We have used Deployment and Service kind for this deployment:

```
1.    apiVersion: apps/v1
2.    kind: Deployment
3.    metadata:
4.     name: myangularapp-deployment
5.     labels:
6.        app: myapp
7.        type: front-end
8.    spec:
9.     template:
10.       metadata:
11.        name: myapp-pod
12.        labels:
13.           app: myapp
14.       spec:
15.        containers:
16.           - name: angular-app-container
17.             image: sampleimages.azurecr.io/angular-sample:v1
18.    replicas: 1
19.
20.    selector:
21.       matchLabels:
22.           app: myapp
23.    ---
24.    apiVersion: v1
25.    kind: Service
26.    metadata:
27.     name: myangularapp-service
28.     labels:
29.        app: myapp
30.        type: front-end
31.    spec:
32.     selector:
33.        app: myapp
```

```
34.    ports:
35.     - protocol: TCP
36.       port: 80
37.       targetPort: 80
38.    type: LoadBalancer
```

33. Execute `kubectl apply -f angular-deployment.yaml`.

34. The `kubectl` apply command is used to manage applications with the use of files. These files define Kubernetes resources. It helps to create and update resources in a Kubernetes cluster by running `kubectl` apply. This is one of the most used ways of managing Kubernetes applications in a production environment.

35. We have already merged the context so let's execute `kubectl` get services to get details on Services available in the cluster. In the preceding YAML, one deployment and one service are available:

```
1.  [root@localhost Angular-App-Sample_master_2]# /usr/local/
    bin/kubectl get services
2.  NAME      TYPE        CLUSTER-IP   EXTERNAL-IP   PORT(S)   AGE
3.  kubernetes ClusterIP  10.0.0.1     <none>        443/TCP   40h
```

36. Only the `kuberneted` service is available as of now. Try after some time and we will get a service created using YAML.

37. External IP is still not available for Service. Once the external IP address is available, we can verify whether the Application is available and working or not:

```
1.  [root@localhost Angular-App-Sample_master_2]# /usr/local/
    bin/kubectl get services
2.  NAME                    TYPE          CLUSTER-IP     EXTERNAL-IP
    PORT(S)      AGE
3.  kubernetes              ClusterIP     10.0.0.1       <none>        443/
    TCP       40h
4.  myangularapp-service    LoadBalancer  10.0.16.245    <pending>
    80:31158/TCP    8s
```

38. Verify the deployment using kubectl get deployment:

```
1.  [root@localhost Angular-App-Sample_master_2]# /usr/local/
    bin/kubectl get deployment
2.  NAME                    READY   UP-TO-DATE   AVAILABLE    AGE
3.  myangularapp-deployment 1/1     1            1            86s
```

39. Let's try to see if the external IP address is available now or not. Use the `kubectl` get services command:

1. ```
   [root@localhost Angular-App-Sample_master_2]# /usr/local/
   bin/kubectl get services
   ```
2. ```
   NAME                    TYPE          CLUSTER-IP    EXTERNAL-IP
   PORT(S)      AGE
   ```
3. ```
   kubernetes              ClusterIP     10.0.0.1      <none>
   443/TCP      40h
   ```
4. ```
   myangularapp-service    LoadBalancer  10.0.16.245
   52.186.99.205   80:31158/TCP    93s
   ```

40. To get details on pods, execute the `kubectl get pods` command:

1. ```
   [root@localhost Angular-App-Sample_master_2]# /usr/local/
   bin/kubectl get pods
   ```
2. ```
   NAME                                      READY    STATUS
   RESTARTS    AGE
   ```
3. ```
   myangularapp-deployment-7dccdbcc46-thrxq   1/1      Running
   0          43h
   ```
4. ```
   [root@localhost Angular-App-Sample_master_2]#
   ```

41. Add commands related to the ACR login such as tagging for ACR, pushing Docker image to ACR, setting AKS cluster context, and applying YAML file for deployment in the stage as shown in the following screenshot:

Figure 6.32: Deploy to AKS stage

42. The following is the pipeline code for the stage:

```
1.      stage('Deploy to AKS') {
2.         agent {
3.            node {
4.               label 'centos'
5.            }
6.
7.         }
8.         steps {
9.            echo 'AKS'
10.               sh 'az acr login --name sampleImages && docker
         tag test/angular-sample sampleimages.azurecr.io/angular-
         sample:v1 && docker push sampleimages.azurecr.io/angular-
         sample'
11.               sh 'az aks get-credentials --resource-group aks-
         jenkins --name AngularCluster && /usr/local/bin/kubectl
         apply -f angular-deployment.yaml'
12.         }
13.      }
```

43. Execute the entire pipeline and verify Deploy to the AKS stage in the pipeline view:

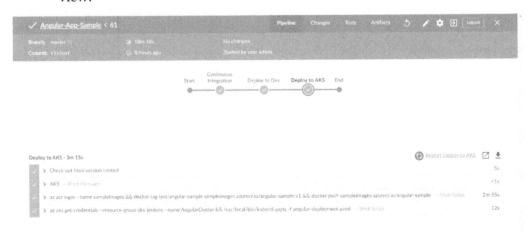

Figure 6.33: Deploy to AKS stage logs

44. Let's verify logs for pushing the Docker image to ACR:

Deploy to AKS - 3m 15s

> Check out from version control 5s

> AKS — Print Message <1s

> az acr login --name sampleimages && docker tag test/angular-sample sampleimages.azurecr.io/angular-sample:v1 && docker push sampleimages.azurecr.io/angular-sample — Shell Script 2m 55s

```
+ az acr login --name sampleimages
Uppercase characters are detected in the registry name. When using its server url in docker commands, to avoid authentication errors, use all lowercase.
Login Succeeded
+ docker tag test/angular-sample sampleimages.azurecr.io/angular-sample:v1
+ docker push sampleimages.azurecr.io/angular-sample
The push refers to repository [sampleimages.azurecr.io/angular-sample]
7bf99e4e46b3: Preparing
a181cbf898a0: Preparing
570fc47f2558: Preparing
5d17421f1571: Preparing
7bb2a9d37337: Preparing
3e207b400db3: Preparing
3e207b400db3: Waiting
a181cbf898a0: Pushed
570fc47f2558: Pushed
5d17421f1571: Pushed
7bf99e4e46b3: Pushed
3e207b400db3: Pushed
7bb2a9d37337: Pushed
v1: digest: sha256:d9de9f7d8b185465c9820ba46557b44262594f5ddee9a1639c847221a592594  size: 1571
```

> az aks get-credentials --resource-group aks-jenkins --name AngularCluster && /usr/local/bin/kubectl apply -f angular-deployment.yaml — Shell Script 12s

Figure 6.34: *Docker Image push to ACR*

NOTE

SCM: Git, SVN, CVS, BitBucket

CI: Azure DevOps, Jenkins, TeamCity, Atlassian Bamboo, TFS

Infrastructure Automation: Public Cloud, Private Cloud, Docker, Kubernetes

Configuration Management: Chef, Puppet, Salt, Ansible

Testing: Appium, Selenium, Apache JMeter, Load Runner

Monitoring: New Relic, Nagios, Zabbix

App Server: Tomcat, Apache, IIS, Ngnix, Weblogic, Websphere, JBoss

Artifact Repository: Artifactory, Nexus

Build Tools: Maven, Ant, Gradle, MS Build

45. Let's verify logs for the `kubectl apply` command in the Jenkins pipeline.

46. Deployment and Service are created:

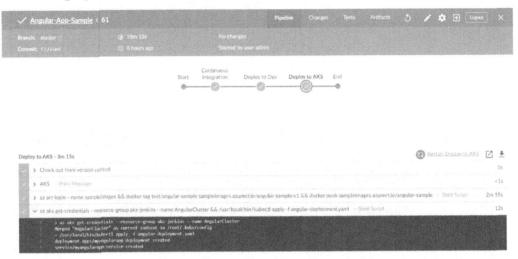

Figure 6.35: AKS Service and Deployment

47. As mentioned earlier, use `kubectl` commands to get details of services, deployments, and pods. Service details will provide an external IP address. Use the external IP address of service to access an application.

Done.

TIP

Environment variables in Jenkins are available in the pipeline directly and not as steps. Visit **http://JENKINS_URL/env-vars.html/**.

Conclusion

In this chapter, we configured Continuous Integration and Continuous Delivery for an Angular app. We covered Lint analysis, Unit test Execution, Code coverage, Build Quality check, and deployment to Azure Kubernetes Services. It helps to create an end-to-end pipeline and maintain quality in a big development team as everything is visible. Code quality and coverage helps to find issues at an early stage and hence it is less costly in terms of rework.

In the next chapter, we will talk about building the CI/CD pipeline.

Multiple choice questions

1. To fix the vulnerabilities identified by the npm audit command, use npm audit fix based on the console log. State true or false.

   a. True

   b. False

2. AKS is a Kubernetes service provided by Microsoft Azure. State true or false.

   a. True

   b. False

Answer

1. a

2. a

Questions

1. What is the objective of using Angular?

2. Explain the significance of scripts in `package.json`.

3. Explain the significance of `karma-conf.js` for unit tests and code coverage calculation.

CHAPTER 7

Building CI/CD Pipeline for a NodeJS Application

> "The more a person learns how to use the forces of nature for his own purposes, by means of perfecting the sciences and the invention and improvement of machines, the more he will produce.
>
> —*Friedrich List*

An electronic manufacturing giant conducted an exercise of value stream mapping for its application lifecycle management activities. Based on the exercise, the leadership team realized that there are issues in the existing processes and these issues result in the delay of the delivery of applications. They have a major portfolio of applications based on the Express framework and NodeJS. Express.js or Express is a minimal and flexible Node.js framework used to develop web and mobile applications. Some important features or advantages of the Express framework are open-source and rapid development. The program manager wants to accelerate application delivery with high quality. The need of the hour is to implement Continuous Integration and Continuous Delivery.

The program manager wants to automate manual processes for code analysis, unit testing, build, functional testing, and deployment. In this chapter, we will cover the CI/CD implementation of Express and NodeJS applications with Jenkins. We will use the Pipeline as Code to create a CI/CD Pipeline. Blue Ocean provides a simple way to create a pipeline using a simple user interface as well as a code editor to configure the **Continuous Integration (CI)** and **Continuous Delivery (CD)** pipeline for Express and NodeJS applications. We will also provide some valuable *Notes* related to DevOps culture, challenges, market trends, and so on for a better understanding.

Structure

In this chapter, we will discuss the following topics:

- Introduction
- Multi-Stage Pipeline for a NodeJS Express app
  - o Continuous Integration
    - Lint, Unit tests, and code coverage configuration in Package.json
    - Express a web app to Linux on Azure
    - Create Azure app service to deploy the Express App
    - Configure Unit tests and Code coverage using Jest
    - Configure the build quality plugin
  - o Continuous Delivery
- Multi-Stage Pipeline for a NodeJS Application
  - o Continuous Integration
    - Lint, Unit tests, and code coverage configuration in Package.json
    - Multi-stage pipeline using the Node.js Template
    - Configure Unit Tests and code coverage using Mocha
    - Configure the build quality plugin
  - o Continuous Delivery
    - Deploy the Node.js app to Azure App Services
- Conclusion
- Questions and exercises

Objectives

After studying this section, you should be able to:

- Understand how to perform static code analysis for a NodeJS application
- Execute unit tests
- Calculate code coverage
- Verify build quality

Introduction

The organization has selected one application as a pilot while there are three other early adopter NodeJS applications that are waiting in the queue. We have the responsibility to create a CI/CD pipeline using Pipeline as Code in Jenkins in the Declarative syntax. The following is the list of tools and deliverables that will be integrated into the pipeline:

Tools	
Version Control	Git
Code Analysis	SonarQube
Unit Tests	Jest, mocha, Junit reports
Code Coverage	Cobertura
Build Script	Package.json
Continuous Integration	Jenkins
Continuous Delivery	Jenkins
Pipeline	Pipeline as Code, Jenkinsfile, Blue Ocean
Expected Deliverables or Features in an Automated Pipeline	

- Installation and Configuration of Jenkins
- Distributed Architecture/Master Agent Architecture (Covered in *Chapter 11: Best Practices*)
- Role-based access (Covered in *Chapter 11: Best Practices*)
- Configuration of a CI/CD Pipeline using Pipeline as Code
- Documentation
    - o Documentation of defined processes and implementations
    - o Technical documentation – How to guides
- Best practices documentation for the usage of Jenkins/Blue Ocean (Covered in *Chapter 11: Best Practices*)

Table 7.1: Tools and deliverables

Before we start configuring a CI/CD pipeline, let's understand Jest and Mocha testing frameworks in brief:

	Jest	**Mocha**
Open Source	Yes	Yes
Developed By	Facebook	
Maturity Level	Getting popular	Higher

Features	Simplicity, faster and easier to write unit tests, snapshot testing, built-in mocking and assertion	Flexible, asynchronous testing, assertion, mocking, and spy libraries, better control on configuration
Support for Programming Languages	Babel, TypeScript, Node.js, React, Angular, Vue.js	Node.js

Table 7.2

In the next section, we will create a pipeline for a NodeJS application using the Blue Ocean interface in a step-by-step manner.

Multi-stage pipeline for a NodeJS Express App using Blue Ocean

What is an Express framework? It is a Node.js web application framework that provides an extensive set of features for web and mobile applications.

We will configure options from a DevOps engineer's perspective, and hence, it might not include end-to-end technical aspects for all the configurations. As a DevOps engineer, we need to have enough knowledge to configure the CI/CD pipeline while we may not be experts in all the programming languages.

In this chapter, we will try to cover CI/CD for a sample Express application. Following is a big picture we will try to implement in this chapter using Jenkins.

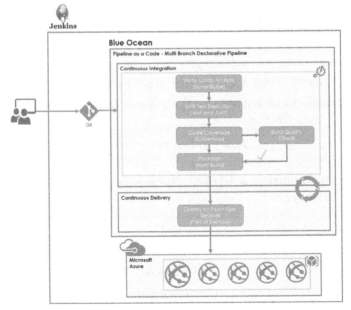

Figure 7.1: Big Picture for CI/CD of Sample Express App

Let's create a pipeline for a sample Express application using Blue Ocean. We will create two stages in the Jenkins pipeline with names Continuous Integration and Continuous Delivery:

Figure 7.2: *Blue Ocean pipeline Editor*

In the next section, we will configure the unit test and code coverage execution using the Jenkins pipeline.

Continuous Integration – Express application

In the Continuous Integration stage, configure tasks related to Static Code Analysis using SonarQube, execute unit test using Jest, archive test results, and publish the code coverage report:

Figure 7.3: *Continuous integration stage*

In the next section, we will configure the different settings in package.json and other files to enable unit tests execution and code coverage calculation.

Lint, unit tests, and code coverage configuration in package.json

Let's configure lint, unit tests, and code coverage configuration in `Package.json` available in the source code if it is not already available:

1. Note the following statement:

```
1.  jest  --ci  --testResultsProcessor=jest-junit  --coverage
    --coverageReporters=cobertura --coverageReporters=html
2.  This is important for executing and getting the code coverage
    report:
3.   "scripts": {
4.      "start": "nodemon app/server.js",
5.      "test": "npm run lint && npm run jest",
6.      "test:e2e": "jest --runInBand e2e_tests/*.test.js",
7.         "jest": "jest  --ci  --testResultsProcessor=jest-
    junit        --coverage        --coverageReporters=cobertura
    --coverageReporters=html",
8.      "lint": "eslint app/** e2e_tests/*",
9.        "prettier":  "prettier  --write  app/*.js  app/__
    {tests,mocks}__/*.js e2e_tests/*.js"
10.    },
```

2. Configure dependencies in the `devDependencies` section for `eslint` and `jest`:

```
1.  "devDependencies": {
2.      "eslint": "^4.12.1",
3.      "jest": "^21.2.1",
4.      "nodemon": "^1.12.5",
5.      "prettier": "^1.9.1",
6.      "supertest": "~3.0.0"
7.    },
```

3. Configure `jest` and junit key-value pairs in Package.json:

```
1.    "jest": {
2.       "testEnvironment": "node",
3.          "testResultsProcessor":  "./node_modules/jest-junit-
```

```
     reporter",
4.        "verbose": true
5.     },
```

4. Use any sample Express application available on GitHub for Proof of Concept.

NOTE

Nudge theory is more helpful in DevOps transformation activities rather than forcing project teams or units to implement DevOps practices. For a full-fledged DevOps practices implementation, it is necessary to have a skilled CoE team as well-trained resources understand the power of change and DevOps practices.

5. Verify the pipeline execution and its steps:

Figure 7.4: Pipeline execution

6. Go to the Blue Ocean dashboard and sample Express pipeline. Click on the **Tests** tab to see all the results of the unit test execution:

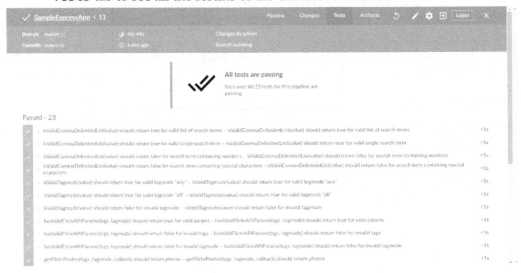

Figure 7.5: Blue Ocean Tests

7. Go to the URL given in the logs or open SonarQube to get more details on Static Code Analysis performed using SonarQube. Verify the Sonar way profile for the sample app and make changes as per your requirements:

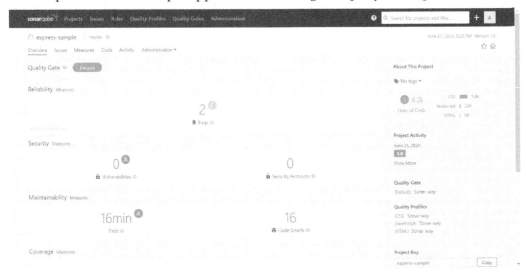

Figure 7.6: SonarQube Dashboard

8. Click on the Test results chart to get more details related to the unit test execution:

Figure 7.7: *Test Result*

9. Click on the Code coverage chart to get more details on Code coverage based on individual units:

Figure 7.8: *Code Coverage breakdown*

10. In the branch status view, we can get charts for Unit test reports and Code coverage reports:

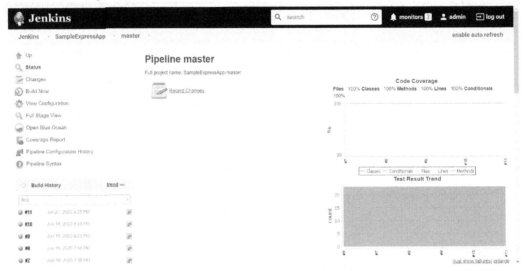

Figure 7.9: Branch Status

NOTE

To remain competitive in the dynamic market, it is essential to empower the ops team or DevOps team for Continuous Delivery and Continuous Deployment to automate manual tasks with the consistent, repeatable pipeline.

11. Verify the status for a specific run of a pipeline:

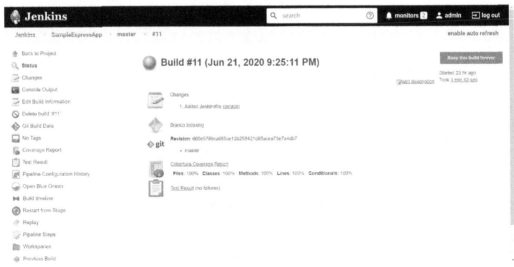

Figure 7.10: Pipeline status

12. Verify the Full Stage View for the entire pipeline:

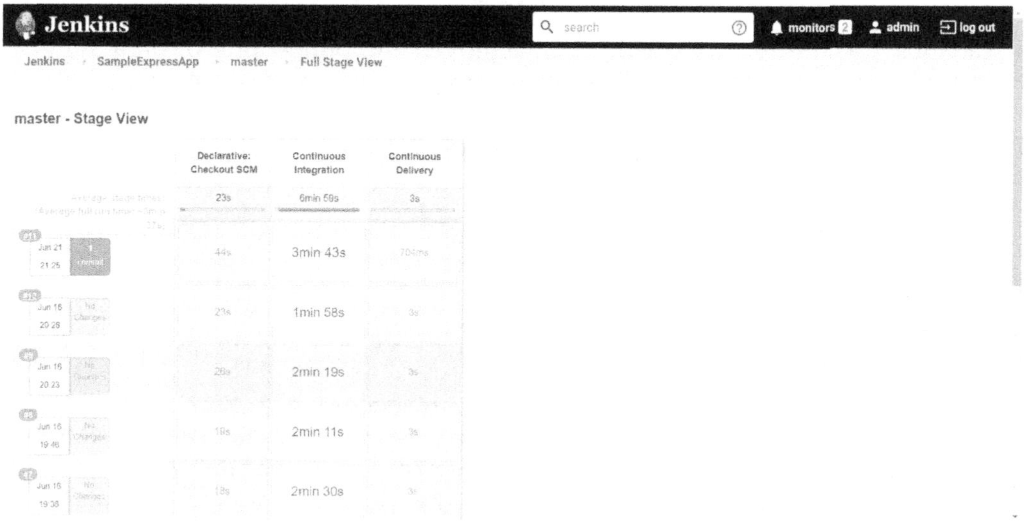

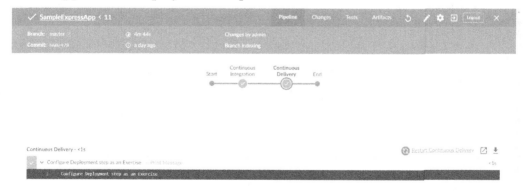

Figure 7.11: Full stage view

The next section will include some details related to Continuous Delivery.

Continuous Delivery – Express Application

We have already created a stage for Continuous Delivery. The CD part for a sample express application is for an exercise. We have previously covered how to create Azure App Service. Deployment is a part of an exercise:

Figure 7.12: CI/CD pipeline

NOTE

DevOps is a culture, movement, change movement, philosophy, or paradigm shift for culture transformation and better communication and collaboration.

The following is the CI/CD pipeline for a sample express app:

```
1.   pipeline {
2.     agent any
3.     stages {
4.   stage('Continuous Integration') {
5.         steps {
6.         bat 'F:\\1.DevOps\\2020\\sonar-scanner-3.2.0.1227-windows\\
     bin\\sonar-scanner.bat  -Dsonar.host.url=http://localhost:9000/
     -Dsonar.login=cba67104bb4f4ef081b55e7ef43168a40b49d6b9 -Dsonar.
     projectVersion=1.0  -Dsonar.projectKey=express-sample  -Dsonar.
     sources=app'
7.           bat 'npm -v'
8.           bat 'npm install &&npm install jest-junit&&npm audit fix'
9.           bat 'npm run lint > lint.txt &npm run jest'
10.  cobertura(coberturaReportFile:  'coverage\\cobertura-coverage.
     xml', conditionalCoverageTargets: '70, 0, 0', lineCoverageTargets:
     '80, 0, 0', methodCoverageTargets: '80, 0, 0', sourceEncoding:
     'ASCII')
11.  junit '**/junit.xml'
12.         }
13.       }
14.
15.  stage('Continuous Delivery') {
16.       steps {
17.           echo 'Configure Deployment step as an Exercise'
18.         }
19.       }
20.
21.     }
22.  }
```

In the next section, we will create a pipeline using Blue Ocean for a sample NodeJS application.

Multi-stage pipeline for a NodeJS application using Blue Ocean

Node.js is a JavaScript runtime built on Chrome's V8 JavaScript engine developed by *Ryan Dahl* in 2009. Some of the important applications of NodeJS are Data Streaming Applications, Data-Intensive Real-time Applications, JSON APIs based applications, and so on. The following are some important features or advantages of Node.js:

- Open-source
- Asynchronous event-driven
- Server-side platform
- Cross-platform runtime environment
- Rich library of various JavaScript modules
- Single-threaded

In this section, we will discuss the following topics:

- Multi-stage pipeline for a NodeJS application
  - o Continuous Integration
    - Lint, unit tests, and code coverage configuration in Package.json
    - Multi-stage pipeline using the Node.js template
    - Configure unit tests and code coverage using Mocha
    - Configure the build quality plugin
  - o Continuous Delivery
    - Deploy the Node.js app to Microsoft Azure PaaS service - Azure App Services

In this chapter, we will try to cover CI/CD for a sample NodeJS application. Following is a big picture we will try to implement in this chapter using Jenkins.

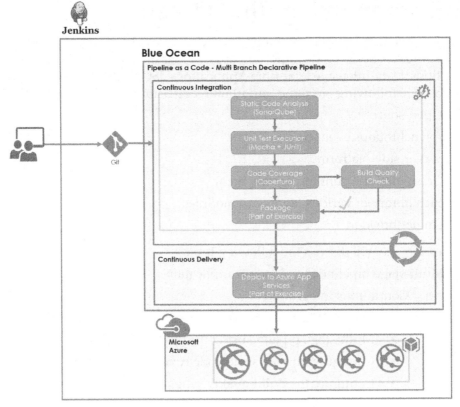

Figure 7.13: Big Picture for CI/CD of Node JS App

Let's create a pipeline for a sample NodeJS application using Blue Ocean. We will create two stages in the Jenkins pipeline with continuous integration and continuous delivery:

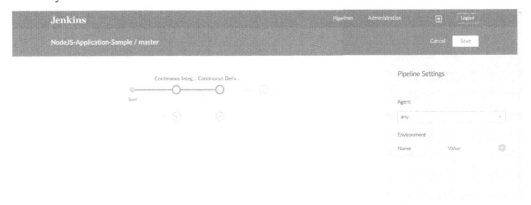

Figure 7.14: Blue Ocean pipeline Editor

TIP

Archive artifacts with each build using the step: `archiveArtifacts` artifacts: '**/*.war', onlyIfSuccessful: true

How to archive artifacts when the pipeline fails?

```
1.  pipeline {
2.      agent any
3.      stages {
4.          stage('SCA') {
5.              ...
6.          }
7.          stage('Test') {
8.              ...
9.          }
10.         stage('Build') {
11.             ...
12.         }
13.     }
14.     post {
15.         always {
16.             archive '**/*.war', fingerprint: true, onlyIfSuccessful:
    true
17. junit 'reports/**/*.xml'
18.         }
19.     }20.     }
```

In the next section, we will configure the unit test and code coverage execution using the Jenkins pipeline.

Continuous integration – NodeJS application

In the Continuous Integration stage, we will configure tasks related to Static Code Analysis using SonarQube, execute unit tests using a NodeJS application, archive test results, and publish the code coverage report.

TIP

How to verify if the file exists in the workspace or not: fileExists 'package-lock.json'

Lint, unit tests, and code coverage configuration in Package.json

We will configure unit tests and code coverage in the script section in `package.json` so that we can get the test and code coverage execution and reports generation:

1. Configure mocha and `nyc` in the `devDependencies` section. Configure more details in the `nyc` section as well:

```
1.  {
2.    "name": "NodeJS-Test",
3.    "version": "1.0.0",
4.    "main": "index.js",
5.    "scripts": {
6.      "test": "npm run test-unit",
7.      "test-unit": "mocha --require babel-polyfill --compilers
   js:babel-register **/*.spec.js --reporter mocha-junit-
   reporter --reporter-options mochaFile=./TestResults/TEST-
   RESULT.xml",
8.      "coverage": "nyc npm test --repoter=cobertura mocha",
9.      "report": "nyc report",
10.       "coveralls": "nyc report --reporter=text-lcov |
   coveralls"
11.   },
12.   "license": "MIT",
13.   "dependencies": {
14.     "bluebird": "^3.5.0",
15.     "express": "^4.16.0",
16.     "mongoose": "^5.7.5",
17.     "request": "^2.84.0"
18.   },
19.   "devDependencies": {
20.     .
21.     .
22.     .
23.     .
24.
25.     "mocha": "^3.4.2",
26.     "mocha-junit-reporter": "^1.17.0",
27.     "nyc": "^11.2.1",
```

```
28.        .
29.        .
30.      },
31.      "nyc": {
32.        "check-coverage": false,
33.        "per-file": true,
34.        "lines": 99,
35.        "statements": 99,
36.        "functions": 99,
37.        "branches": 99,
38.        "include": [
39.          "app/*.js"
40.        ],
41.        "reporter": [
42.          "text",
43.          "cobertura",
44.          "html"
45.        ],
46.        "report-dir": "./.test_output/coverage"
47.      }
48.    }
```

2. Create different steps to execute commands to perform `npm install`, unit test execution, archive results or tests, and code coverage:

Figure 7.15: Continuous Integration Stage

TIP

To configure Security in Jenkins, go to **Manage Jenkins | Security.**

1. Configure Global Security.

   a. Configure Authentication using the Azure Active Directory or Jenkins' user database or LDAP.

   b. Configure Authorization Strategy using the Azure Active Directory, Matrix-based security or Matrix-based security or Project-based Matrix Authorization Strategy.

   c. Enable Agent ---> Master Access Control

2. **Credentials:** Configure credentials.

3. **Users:** Manage users.

3. The following is a Declarative pipeline script:

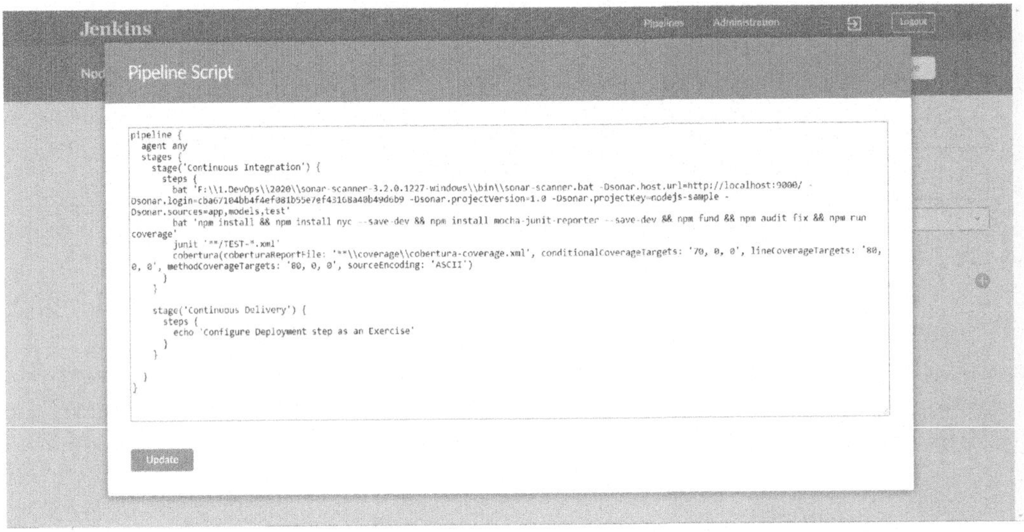

Figure 7.16: Pipeline Script

4. Verify the pipeline execution and its steps:

Figure 7.17: *Pipeline execution*

5. Go to the Blue Ocean dashboard and NodeJS app pipeline. Click on the **Tests** tab to see all the results of the unit test execution:

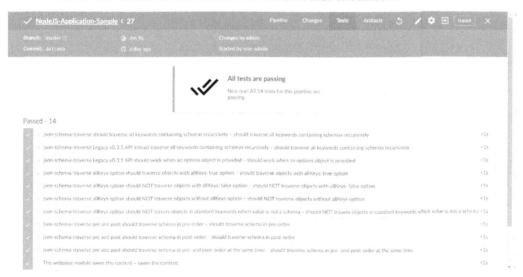

Figure 7.18: *Blue Ocean Tests*

TIP

The agent directive suggests where the pipeline or a specific stage must run:

Name	Unique identifier of an agent within this Jenkins
Description	Easy to read the description of an agent.
# of executors	If a number of executors are more than one, then parallel builds can be executed on an agent machine.
	Minimum one executor has to be available on each agent for execution.
Remote root directory	Provide the path of a directory where the Jenkins workspace can reside. All the data of jobs or pipelines execution on the agent will be stored in this directory.
	Note: Job configurations, build logs, and artifacts are stored on the master.
Labels	Tags
	Useful to group multiple agents logically.
	Examples:
	Docker
	Windows
	JDK8
	JDK11
	Web
	DB
	Windows10
	More than one label can be assigned to the agent. Multiple labels must be separated by a space.
Usage	**Default:** Use this node as much as possible.
	Only build jobs with label expressions matching this node: Use these settings so only specific jobs that are assigned a specific agent wait for the availability of an executor.
Launch method	**Launch an agent by connecting it to the master:** Allows an agent to be connected to the Jenkins master whenever it is ready.
	Launch an agent via the execution of a command on the master.
	Launch agents via SSH.
	Let Jenkins control this Windows agent as a Windows service.

Availability	Keep this agent online as much as possible.
	Bring this agent online and offline at specific times.
	Bring this agent online when in demand and take it offline when idle.
Node properties	Disable deferred wipeout on this node.
	Enable node-based security.
	Configure Environment variables.
	Configure Tool locations.

6. Go to the URL given in the logs or open SonarQube to get more details on Static Code Analysis performed using SonarQube:

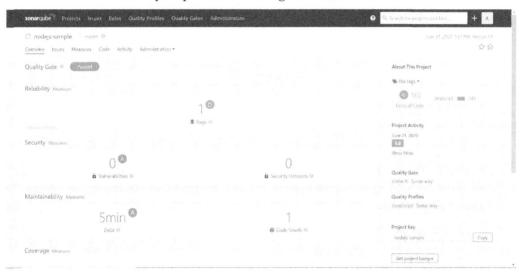

Figure 7.19: SonarQube Dashboard

7. Click on the Test results chart to get more details related to the unit test execution:

Figure 7.20: *Test Result*

NOTE

Tools: IDE with Code verification plugins, Distributed Version Control System, Build tools, Static Code Analysis Tools, Continuous Integration Tools, Unit test tools or packages, Functional test tool, Performance, and Security testing tool, Automated Deployment tools, scripts, Configuration Management tools, Artifact Repository, Cloud Services Providers, and Monitoring tools

8. Click on the Code Coverage chart to get more details on Code coverage based on individual units:

Figure 7.21: *Code Coverage breakdown*

TIP

How to specify the agent in the Declarative pipeline?

1. Run the pipeline on any agent:

   ```
   1.  agent any
   ```

2. Run the pipeline on the agent that is matching the label:

   ```
   1.  agent {
   2.    label 'master'
   3.  }
   ```

3. Run the agent inside a docker container:

   ```
   1.  agent {
   2.    docker {
   3.        image 'nginx:1-alpine'
   4.    }
   5.  }
   ```

4. Build a Dockerfile and run it in a container using the same image:

   ```
   1.  agent {
   2.  dockerfile {
   3.        filename 'Dockerfile'
   4.    }
   5.  }
   ```

5. Don't run on an agent:

   ```
   1.  agent none
   ```

9. In the branch status view, we can get charts for Unit test reports and Code coverage reports:

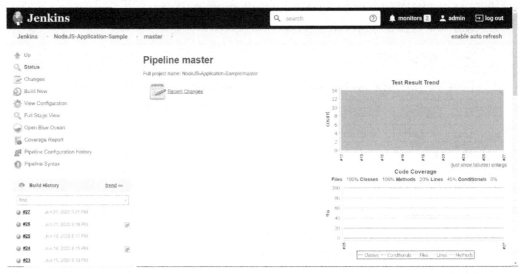

Figure 7.22: Branch Status

10. Verify the status for a specific run of a pipeline.

Figure 7.23: Pipeline status

TIP

Set the global timeout after which Jenkins should abort the pipeline:

```
1.  options {
2.     timeout(time: 10, unit: 'MINUTES')
3.  }
```

Build Quality Check

For Build Quality check, go to *Chapter 8: Building a CI/CD pipeline with Blue Ocean for a Hybrid Mobile Application and refer to the section Verify Build Quality.*

In the next section, we will discuss Continuous Delivery.

Continuous Delivery – NodeJS application

We have already created a stage for Continuous Delivery. The CD part for NodeJS is for an exercise. We have previously covered how to create Azure App Service. Deployment is a part of the exercise. Let's create a stage in Jenkins for deployment automation.

1. The following is the stage on the Blue Ocean dashboard for Continuous Delivery:

Figure 7.24: Continuous Delivery stage

2. Verify the Full stage view for the entire pipeline:

Figure 7.25: Full stage view

NOTE

Culture transformation requires a combination of people, processes, and tools. Training and skill building help to cultivate change in the mindset of people. **Proof of Concept (PoC)** and pilot execution helps to bring confidence in automation and other activities. Implementation roadmap, maturity model, quality gates, governance, and review and approval processes, and so on should be identified, documented, and communicated to stakeholders for transparency.

TIPS

The Options directive can be used to specify properties for settings that should be applied across the pipeline. The following are some of the options we can add in the pipeline:

*   The `skipDefaultCheckout` option disables the standard, automatic checkout **Source Code Management (SCM)** before the first stage. If it is specified and the SCM checkout is desired, it will need to be explicitly included.

*   Enables project-based security.

*   This determines when, if ever, build records for this project should be discarded. Build records include the console output, archived artifacts, and any other metadata related to a particular build.

*   If specified, any stage after the build that has become `UNSTABLE` will be skipped, as if the build had failed.

- Executes the code inside the block with a determined time out limit.
- Adds timestamps to the Console Output.

The following is a Declarative script block for the preceding options::

```
1.   options {
2.   skipDefaultCheckout true
3.   authorizationMatrix(['hudson.model.Item.Build:mitesh',
     'hudson.model.Item.Cancel:mitesh',      'hudson.model.Item.
     Configure:mitesh',         'hudson.model.Item.Delete:mitesh',
     'hudson.model.Item.Discover:mitesh',          'hudson.model.
     Item.Move:mitesh',          'hudson.model.Item.Read:mitesh',
     'hudson.model.Item.Workspace:mitesh',   'hudson.model.Run.
     Delete:mitesh', 'hudson.model.Run.Replay:mitesh', 'hudson.
     model.Run.Update:mitesh', 'hudson.scm.SCM.Tag:mitesh'])
4.
5.   buildDiscarderlogRotator(artifactDaysToKeepStr:        '',
     artifactNumToKeepStr: '', daysToKeepStr: '', numToKeepStr:
     '10')
6.
7.   skipStagesAfterUnstable()
8.
9.   timeout(10)
10.
11.  timestamps
12.  }
```

3. The following is the CI/CD pipeline for a NodeJS application:

```
1.   pipeline {
2.     agent any
3.     stages {
4.   stage('Continuous Integration') {
5.       steps {
6.                 bat  'F:\\1.DevOps\\2020\\sonar-scanner-
     3.2.0.1227-windows\\bin\\sonar-scanner.bat
     -Dsonar.host.url=http://localhost:9000/       -Dsonar.
     login=cba67104bb4f4ef081b55e7ef43168a40b49d6b9   -Dsonar.
     projectVersion=1.0      -Dsonar.projectKey=nodejs-sample
     -Dsonar.sources=app,models,test'
7.        bat 'npm install &&npm install nyc --save-dev &&npm
     install mocha-junit-reporter --save-dev &&npm fund &&npm
     audit fix &&npm run coverage'
8.   junit '**/TEST-*.xml'
```

```
9.    cobertura(coberturaReportFile:    '**\\coverage\\cobertura-
      coverage.xml', conditionalCoverageTargets: '70, 0, 0',
      lineCoverageTargets: '80, 0, 0', methodCoverageTargets:
      '80, 0, 0', sourceEncoding: 'ASCII')
10.        }
11.      }
12.
13.    stage('Continuous Delivery') {
14.        steps {
15.          echo 'Configure Deployment step as an Exercise'
16.        }
17.      }
18.
19.    }
20.  }
```

Done!

TIP

The Parallel block helps us to execute steps/stages in parallel.

```
1.    stage("Testing") {
2.          parallel {
3.    stage("Functional Tests") {
4.            steps {
5.            ...
6.          }
7.        }
8.    stage("Security Tests") {
9.            steps {
10.           ...
11.         }
12.       }
13.       }14.   }
```

Conclusion

In this chapter, we created the CI pipeline for a sample application written in NodeJS where we covered code analysis using SonarQube, unit test execution, code coverage calculation, and publishing results of unit tests and code coverage. There are different test runners and reporters that can be used to generate XML results such as mocha (`mocha-junit-reporter`), jasmine (`jasmine-reporters`), jest (`jest-junit`, `jest-junit-reporter`), and karma (`karma-junit-reporter`).

We covered Jest and Mocha only in this chapter. We tried to create a multi-stage pipeline for other test runners. Thus, we should be able to publish code coverage results in Azure DevOps, as we have done in this chapter for specific test runners and reporters.

In the next chapter, we will configure CI/CD for an Angular application.

Multiple-choice questions

1. **Which are the following test runners for a Node.js application?**

    a. mocha

    b. jest

    c. jasmine

    d. karma

    e. All of the above

2. **State True or False: cobertura step can be used to publish Code coverage reports in Declarative pipeline syntax:**

    a. True

    b. False

Answer

1. e
2. a

Questions

1. Explain the various test runners and reporters to generate XML reports for a Node.js application.

2. How to create a build, archive, and deploy distribution files to Azure App Services?

Building CI/CD Pipeline for Hybrid Mobile Apps

> "Almost all quality improvement comes via simplification of design, manufacturing... layout, processes, and procedures."
>
> — *Tom Peters*

An Indian multinational software organization makes applications for the edutainment and media industries. The marketing team decides to promote mobile apps for end-users and principle architects suggest hybrid Apps rather than native apps. Project teams decide to use Ionic and Flutter for edutainment and media industries related apps. Ionic provides robust UI components for building a hybrid mobile application. The following are some important features or advantages of the Ionic framework such as open-source, the library of mobile-optimized UI components, gestures, reusable, components, write once, run anywhere, and it has a MIT License. Flutter is a UI toolkit used to create beautiful, natively compiled applications for mobiles, websites, and desktops from a single codebase for faster time to market. The management needs to automate manual processes in the application lifecycle management and increase productivity with frequent deployments by implementing Continuous Integration and Continuous Delivery. In this chapter, we will cover the CI/CD implementation of Hybrid applications with Jenkins. We will use the Pipeline as Code to create the CI/CD pipeline. Blue Ocean provides a simple way to create a pipeline using a simple user interface as well as a code editor to configure **Continuous Integration (CI)** and **Continuous Delivery (CD)** pipeline for Ionic and Flutter Applications. We will distribute an application to the App Center to a specific group. We will also provide some valuable notes related to DevOps and its culture, challenges, market trends, and so on for a better understanding.

Structure

In this chapter, we will discuss the following topics:

- Introduction
- Blue Ocean multi-stage pipeline for the Ionic app
    - o Continuous Integration for Ionic – Android app
    - o Continuous Delivery for Ionic – Android app
- Blue Ocean multi-stage pipeline for the Flutter app
    - o Continuous Integration for Ionic – Flutter app
    - o Continuous Delivery for Ionic – Flutter app

Objectives

After studying this section, you should be able to:

- Understand how to perform static code analysis for the Ionic Cordova application
- Execute unit tests
- Calculate code coverage
- Verify build quality

Introduction

The organization has selected one application as a pilot while there are 10 early adopter hybrid applications that are waiting in the queue. We have the responsibility to create a CI/CD pipeline using Pipeline as Code in Jenkins in the declarative syntax.

The following is the list of tools and deliverables that will be integrated into the pipeline:

Tools	
Version Control	Git
Code Analysis	SonarQube
Unit Tests	Karma, Junit reports
Code Coverage	Cobertura
Build Script	Package.json
Continuous Integration	Jenkins
Continuous Delivery	App Center
Pipeline	Pipeline as Code. Jenkinsfile, Blue Ocean
Expected Deliverables or Features in an Automated pipeline	

- Installation and Configuration of Jenkins
- Distributed Architecture/Master Agent Architecture (Covered in *Chapter 11: Best Practices)*
- Role-based access (Covered in *Chapter 11: Best Practices*)
- Configuration of the CI/CD pipeline using Pipeline as Code
- Documentation
    - o   Documentation of defined processes and implementations
    - o   Technical documentation – How to guides
- Best practices documentation for the usage of Jenkins / Blue Ocean (Covered in *Chapter 11: Best Practices)*

Table 8.1: *Tools and deliverables*

In the next section, we will create a pipeline for the Ionic Cordova application using the Blue Ocean interface in a step-by-step manner.

Multi-stage pipeline for an Ionic app using Blue Ocean

In this chapter, we will cover CI/CD for a sample Ionic Cordova application. Following is the big picture that we will try to implement in Jenkins pipeline

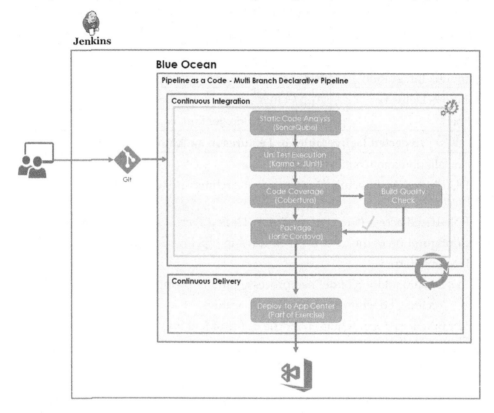

Figure 8.1: Big picture for CI/CD of the Ionic Cordova app

Let's create a pipeline for a sample Ionic Cordova application using Blue Ocean.

1. We will configure static code analysis using SonarQube, unit test execution, and code coverage calculation and report for a sample Ionic Cordova application.

2. We will create two stages in the Jenkins pipeline with the names: Continuous Integration and Continuous Delivery.

3. We will configure environment variables. We need to provide **Name** and **Value** in the Environment section:

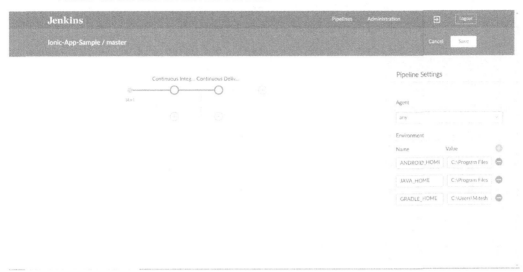

Figure 8.2: *Blue Ocean Pipeline Editor*

4. The following is the snippet generated by the configuration:

```
1.   environment {
2.       ANDROID_HOME = 'C:\\Program Files (x86)\\Android\\
     android-sdk'
3.       JAVA_HOME = 'C:\\Program Files\\Java\\jdk1.8.0_111'
4.   }
```

In the next section, we will configure the unit test and code coverage execution using the Jenkins pipeline.

Continuous Integration for the Ionic – Android app

Let's configure plugins and other blocks related to Junit and coverage.

1. Let's do a few configurations in the karma.conf.js file.

2. Add the required plugins for the Junit (unit testing) and Cobertura (code coverage) output:

```
1.   plugins: [
2.       require('karma-jasmine'),
3.       require('karma-chrome-launcher'),
```

```
4.        require('karma-mocha-reporter'),
5.        require('karma-coverage-istanbul-reporter'),
6.        require('karma-junit-reporter'),
7.        require('@angular-devkit/build-angular/plugins/karma')
8.      ],
```

3. Add Cobertura in the reports key section to `karma.conf.js`:

```
1.    coverageIstanbulReporter: {
2.        dir: require('path').join(__dirname, './coverage'),
3.        reports: ['html', 'lcovonly','cobertura'],
4.        fixWebpackSourcePaths: true
5.    },
6.    reporters: ['progress', ' kjhtml', 'junit'],
```

4. Add the `JunitReporter` configuration details in `karma.conf.js` if it is not available in the file:

```
1.  junitReporter: {
2.      outputDir: '',
3.      outputFile: undefined,
4.      suite: '',
5.      useBrowserName: true,
6.      nameFormatter: undefined,
7.      classNameFormatter: undefined,
8.      properties: {}
9.    },
```

5. Configure the Headless Browser so test cases can be executed:

```
1.    autoWatch: true,
2.    singleRun: true,
3.    browsers: ['ChromeHeadlessNoSandbox'],
4.
5.    customLaunchers: {
6.      ChromeHeadlessNoSandbox: {
7.        base: 'ChromeHeadless',
8.        flags: ['--no-sandbox']
9.      }
10.   },
```

6. Configure `package.json` with scripts:

```
1.  "scripts": {
2.      "ng": "ng",
3.      "start": "ng serve",
4.      "build": "ng build",
5.      "test": "ng test --code-coverage",
6.      "lint": "ng lint",
7.      "e2e": "ng e2e",
8.      "postinstall": "webdriver-manager update --standalone
    false --gecko false"
9.  },
10.  "devDependencies": {
11.  .
12.  .
13.      "karma-junit-reporter": "2.0.1",
14.  .
15.  .
16.  },
```

NOTE

`npm install` installs the dependencies in the local `node_modules` folder. If we use `-g` or `--global`, then it installs the current working directory as a global package. The important thing to note is that the `npm install` execution will install all the modules available as dependencies in `package.json`. To skip the installation of modules available in the `devDependencies` section, we need to provide `--production` flag.

For more details, visit: **https://docs.npmjs.com/cli/install**.

7. In the Continuous Integration stage, configure tasks related to Static Code Analysis using SonarQube, NPM Module installation, update, text execution, and publish unit tests and code coverage results. The following are commands to perform few operations:

```
1.  // SonarQube Analysis command
2.  sonar-scanner.bat  -Dsonar.host.url=http://localhost:9000/
    -Dsonar.login=cba67104bb4f4ef081b55e7ef43168a40b49d6b9
    -Dsonar.projectVersion=1.0 -Dsonar.projectKey=ionic-sample
    -Dsonar.sources=src
3.
```

```
4.    // -Dsonar.login will have sonarqube token as its value.
      Generate token in Sonarqube.

5.    // -Dsonar.sources will have a name of the directory in which
      your source code resides so that can be analyzed using SonarQube

6.

7.    // Node Modules installation

8.    npm install && ng update && npm install karma-junit-reporter
      --save-dev && npm audit fix && npm i @angular-devkit/build-
      angular@0.803.25

9.

10.   // Test execution

11.   npm run test

12.

13.   // Ionic cordova commands

14.   npm i @angular-devkit/build-angular@0.803.25 && ionic cordova
      platform add android . & ionic cordova build android --prod'
```

Figure 8.3: Continuous Integration Stage

While executing the preceding commands in the Jenkins pipeline, we encountered few issues, and hence, we have listed them down with a solution which will help to resolve them here:

- **Issue 1: Vulnerabilities**

```
1.    found 6 low severity vulnerabilities

2.

3.      run `npm audit fix` to fix them, or `npm audit` for details
```

```
4.
5.       at getTargetPackageSpecFromNpmInstallOutput (C:\Users\
         Tempuser\AppData\Roaming\npm\node_modules\cordova\node_
         modules\cordova-fetch\index.js:104:11)
6.
7.        at processTicksAndRejections (internal/process/task_
         queues.js:97:5) {
8.
9.     code: 0,
10.
11.    context: undefined
12.
13.  }
```

Solution: npm audit fix

- **Issue 2: Job name "..getProjectMetadata" does not exist.**

```
1.   An unhandled exception occurred: Job name "..getProjectMetadata"
     does not exist.
2.
3.   See "C:\Users\Tempuser\AppData\Local\Temp\ng-QlctEV\angular-
     errors.log" for further details.
4.
5.   npm ERR! code ELIFECYCLE
6.   npm ERR! syscall spawn
7.   npm ERR! file C:\WINDOWS\system32\cmd.exe
8.   npm ERR! errno ENOENT
9.   npm ERR! ionic-conference-app@0.0.0 test: `ng test --code-
     coverage`
10.  npm ERR! spawn ENOENT
11.  npm ERR!
12.  npm ERR! Failed at the ionic-conference-app@0.0.0 test script.
13.  npm ERR! This is probably not a problem with npm. There is
     likely additional logging output above.
14.  npm ERR! A complete log of this run can be found in:
15.  npm ERR!        C:\Users\Tempuser\AppData\Roaming\npm-cache\_
     logs\2020-06-17T07_13_00_542Z-debug.log
16.
17.  script returned exit code 1
```

Solution: It looks like a problem with @angular-devkit/build-angular. The npm audit command reported vulnerabilities in the version of @angular-devkit/build-angular. After executing npm audit fix, we found the error: An unhandled exception occurred: Job name "..getProjectMetadata" does not exist.

Execute npm i @angular-devkit/build-angular or downgrade it by specifying a previous version such as 0.803.25 with the command: npm i @angular-devkit/build-angular@0.803.25.

- **Issue 3:** stderr: warning: failed to remove

```
1.  stderr:    warning:    failed    to    remove    platforms/
    android/CordovaLib/build/intermediates/javac/debug/
    compileDebugJavaWithJavac/classes/org/apache/cordova/
    NativeToJsMessageQueue$OnlineEventsBridgeMode$OnlineEvents
    BridgeModeDelegate.class: Filename too long

2.

3.  at           org.jenkinsci.plugins.gitclient.CliGitAPIImpl.
    launchCommandIn (CliGitAPIImpl.java:2430)

4.  at           org.jenkinsci.plugins.gitclient.CliGitAPIImpl.
    launchCommandIn (CliGitAPIImpl.java:2360)

5.  at           org.jenkinsci.plugins.gitclient.CliGitAPIImpl.
    launchCommandIn (CliGitAPIImpl.java:2356)

6.  at           org.jenkinsci.plugins.gitclient.CliGitAPIImpl.
    launchCommand (CliGitAPIImpl.java:1916)

7.  at           org.jenkinsci.plugins.gitclient.CliGitAPIImpl.
    launchCommand (CliGitAPIImpl.java:1928)

8.  at        org.jenkinsci.plugins.gitclient.CliGitAPIImpl.clean(
    CliGitAPIImpl.java:1010)

9.  at    hudson.plugins.git.extensions.impl.CleanBeforeCheckout.
    decorateFetchCommand(CleanBeforeCheckout.java:44)

10. at            hudson.plugins.git.extensions.GitSCMExtension.
    decorateFetchCommand(GitSCMExtension.java:288)

11. at hudson.plugins.git.GitSCM.fetchFrom(GitSCM.java:905)

12.

13. ... 11 more

14.

15. Error fetching remote repo 'origin'
```

Solution: Remove the platform directory from the workspace and execute the pipeline again.

- **Issue 4: stderr: warning: failed to remove platforms/: Directory not empty**

  Solution: Probably, you are using the folder or you have opened it in Explorer and so when the pipeline is getting executed, it is not able to remove all directories at the time of checkout.

- **Issue 5: Could not find an installed version of Gradle**

  ```
  Could not find an installed version of Gradle either in Android
  Studio, or on your system to install the Gradle wrapper. Please
  include Gradle in your path, or install Android Studio script
  returned exit code 1
  ```

  Solution: `Set Gradle Path (SET Path=%PATH%;C:\\gradle-4.6-all\\ gradle-4.6\\bin)`

- **Issue 6: Could not find plugin "proposal-numeric-separator" in angular app**

  Solution: Add `@babel/compat-data": "7.8.0 in the devDependencies section in package.json.`

The following is the configuration script for the Continuous Integration stage in the Jenkinsfile:

Figure 8.4: Pipeline Script

The ng update command execution updates your application and its dependencies. For more details, visit **https://angular.io/cli/**update. Execute `npm install karma-junit-reporter --save-dev` to keep `karma-junit-reporter` as a `devDependency in package.json`. It results in npm automatically adding it in `package.json`.

The following is a declarative pipeline script for Ionic Cordova based sample application:

```
1.   pipeline {
2.     agent any
3.     stages {
4.       stage('Continuous Integration') {
5.         steps {
6.             bat 'SET Path=%PATH%;C:\\Users\\Tempuser\\.gradle\\
     wrapper\\dists\\gradle-4.6-all\\bcst21l2brirad8k2ben1letg\\
     gradle-4.6\\bin'
7.             bat 'F:\\1.DevOps\\2020\\sonar-scanner-3.2.0.1227-windows\\
     bin\\sonar-scanner.bat  -Dsonar.host.url=http://localhost:9000/
     -Dsonar.login=cba67104bb4f4ef081b55e7ef43168a40b49d6b9 -Dsonar.
     projectVersion=1.0   -Dsonar.projectKey=ionic-sample   -Dsonar.
     sources=src'
8.             bat 'npm install && ng update && npm install karma-junit-
     reporter --save-dev && npm audit fix && npm i @angular-devkit/
     build-angular@0.803.25 && npm run test'
9.               cobertura(coberturaReportFile: '*\\coverage\\cobertura-
     coverage.xml', sourceEncoding: 'ASCII')
10.            junit '**/TESTS-*.xml'
11.              bat 'npm i @angular-devkit/build-angular@0.803.25 &&
     ionic cordova platform add android . & ionic cordova build
     android --prod'
12.            archiveArtifacts '**/*.apk'
13.        }
14.      }
15.
16.      stage('Continuous Delivery') {
17.        steps {
18.          echo 'Configure Deployment step as an Exercise'
19.        }
20.      }
21.
22.    }
23.    environment {
24.      ANDROID_HOME = 'C:\\Program Files (x86)\\Android\\android-
     sdk'
```

```
25.        JAVA_HOME = 'C:\\Program Files\\Java\\jdk1.8.0_111'
26.          GRADLE_HOME = 'C:\\Users\\Tempuser\\.gradle\\wrapper\\
    dists\\gradle-4.6-all\\bcst21l2brirad8k2ben1letg\\gradle-4.6'
27.    }
28. }
```

Let's verify the execution of Continuous Integration stage.

1. Execute the pipeline.

2. Verify the logs of all the tasks available in the stage. In case of issues, follow the issues and solution list given earlier:

Figure 8.5: *Pipeline and Logs*

NOTE

DevOps practices implementation and culture transformation is at its best when test automation is enabled and incorporated in the CI/CD pipeline.

3. Click on the **Tests** link to get results of the unit test execution:

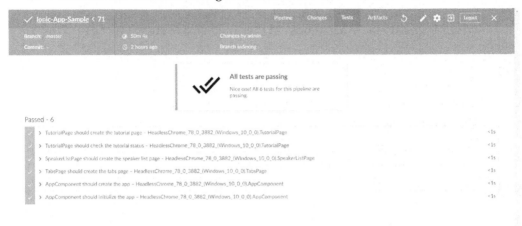

Figure 8.6: *Test results in Blue Ocean*

The following are some important logs from the console:

1. 21 06 2020 18:26:34.528:INFO [karma-server]: Karma v4.4.1 server started at http://0.0.0.0:9876/

2. 21 06 2020 18:26:34.533:INFO [launcher]: Launching browsers ChromeHeadlessNoSandbox with concurrency unlimited

3. 21 06 2020 18:26:34.549:INFO [launcher]: Starting browser ChromeHeadless

4. 21 06 2020 18:26:46.624:INFO [HeadlessChrome 78.0.3882 (Windows 10.0.0)]: Connected on socket tHQcfXYvbXtMnX2VAAAA with id 65866748

5.

6. HeadlessChrome 78.0.3882 (Windows 10.0.0): Executed 0 of 6 SUCCESS (0 secs / 0 secs)

7. HeadlessChrome 78.0.3882 (Windows 10.0.0): Executed 1 of 6 SUCCESS (0 secs / 0.086 secs)

8. INFO: 'Redefining LocalForage driver: cordovaSQLiteDriver'

9. HeadlessChrome 78.0.3882 (Windows 10.0.0): Executed 1 of 6 SUCCESS (0 secs / 0.086 secs)

10. INFO: 'Redefining LocalForage driver: cordovaSQLiteDriver'

11. .

12. .

13. .

```
14.
15.   INFO: 'Redefining LocalForage driver: cordovaSQLiteDriver'
16.   HeadlessChrome 78.0.3882 (Windows 10.0.0): Executed 6 of 6
      SUCCESS (0.648 secs / 0.604 secs)
17.
18.   TOTAL: 6 SUCCESS
```

4. Click on the **Artifacts** link to get all the artifacts that are generated or archived during the successful execution of the pipeline:

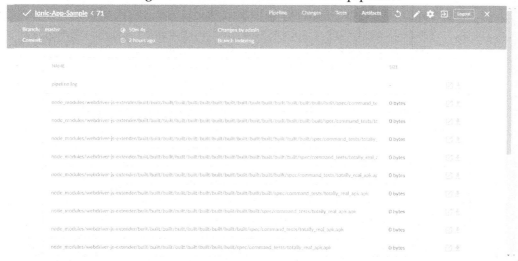

Figure 8.7: *Artifacts in Blue Ocean*

5. Let's verify the SonarQube results as well:

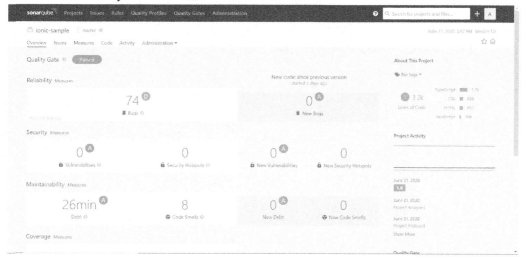

Figure 8.8: *SonarQube Dashboard*

The following are some important logs from the console for the SonarQube command execution:

```
 1.   .
 2.   .
 3.   .
 4.   INFO: Analysis report generated in 306ms, dir size=292 KB
 5.   INFO: Analysis report compressed in 624ms, zip size=177 KB
 6.
 7.   INFO: Analysis report uploaded in 119ms
 8.   INFO: ANALYSIS SUCCESSFUL, you can browse http://
      localhost:9000/dashboard?id=ionic-sample
 9.
10.   INFO: Note that you will be able to access the updated
      dashboard once the server has processed the submitted
      analysis report
11.
12.   INFO: More about the report processing at http://
      localhost:9000/api/ce/task?id=AXLW0XyK1bLJkFupmwk1
13.
14.   INFO: Analysis total time: 1:29.941 s
15.   INFO: ---------------------------------------------------------
      --------------------
16.   INFO: EXECUTION SUCCESS
17.   INFO: ---------------------------------------------------------
      --------------------
18.   INFO: Total time: 1:44.591s
19.   INFO: Final Memory: 16M/260M
```

6. Go to the traditional Jenkins dashboard. Then, verify the status of the pipeline execution for a build number:

Figure 8.9: Jenkins Dashboard Status

7. Verify **Project Status** and we can see **Test results** and **Code Coverage Charts** on the screen:

Figure 8.10: Pipeline Status

NOTE

Automation not only increases the speed of operations, but also eliminates errors due to manual activities. So, it is a win-win situation.

8. Click on the **Test Result** link available on the status page to get more details of test results:

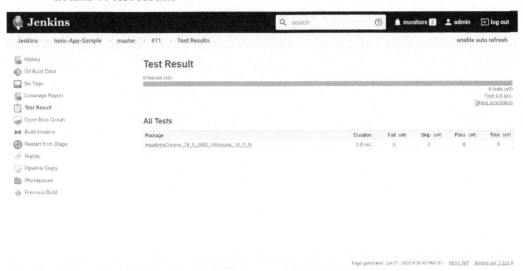

Figure 8.11: Test Results

9. Click on the Code coverage chart available on the status page to get more details with coverage based on packages, classes, files, methods, lines, and conditionals:

Figure 8.12: Cobertura coverage report

10. Click on a specific package to get more details on the Code coverage data:

Figure 8.13: *Directory-wise code coverage data*

11. Verify the logs of adding the Android platform:

```
1.   Using cordova-fetch for cordova-android@^8.1.0
2.   Adding android project...
3.
4.   Creating Cordova project for the Android platform:
5.       Path: platforms\android
6.       Package: com.ionicframework.conferenceapp
7.       Name: Ionic_Conference_App
8.       Activity: MainActivity
9.       Android target: android-28
10.  Subproject Path: CordovaLib
11.  Subproject Path: app
12.  Android project created with cordova-android@8.1.0
13.  Discovered saved plugin "cordova-plugin-device". Adding it
     to the project
14.  Installing "cordova-plugin-device" for android
15.  .
16.  .
17.  .
18.  Installing "cordova-plugin-ionic-keyboard" for android
19.  Adding cordova-plugin-ionic-keyboard to package.json
```

12. Verify the logs of the build execution:

```
1.   Generating ES5 bundles for differential loading...
2.
3.   ES5 bundle generation complete.
4.
5.   chunk {1} runtime-es2015.5674373d5ac9cf64b203.js (runtime)
     4.87 kB [entry] [rendered]
6.   chunk {1}  runtime-es5.5674373d5ac9cf64b203.js  (runtime)
     4.86 kB [entry] [rendered]
7.   .
8.   .
9.   .
10.  Date: 2020-06-21T13:00:53.368Z - Hash: 3dca68df9b7bd898ac55
     - Time: 118526ms
11.
12.  > cordova.cmd build android
13.  Checking Java JDK and Android SDK versions
14.  ANDROID_HOME=C:\Program  Files  (x86)\Android\android-sdk
     (DEPRECATED)
15.
16.  Starting a Gradle Daemon, 4 incompatible and 1 stopped
     Daemons could not be reused, use --status for details
17.  :wrapper
18.
19.  BUILD SUCCESSFUL in 30s
20.
21.  1 actionable task: 1 executed
22.  Picked up _JAVA_OPTIONS: -Xmx512M
23.  Subproject Path: CordovaLib
24.  Subproject Path: app
25.  Starting a Gradle Daemon, 1 incompatible and 1 stopped
     Daemons could not be reused, use --status for details
26.
27.  > Configure project :app
28.
29.  > Task :app:preBuild UP-TO-DATE
30.  > Task :CordovaLib:preBuild UP-TO-DATE
```

```
31.   > Task :CordovaLib:preDebugBuild UP-TO-DATE
32.   > Task :CordovaLib:checkDebugManifest
33.   .
34.   .
35.   > Task :app:assembleDebug
36.   > Task :app:cdvBuildDebug
37.
38.
39.   BUILD SUCCESSFUL in 1m 23s
40.
41.   42 actionable tasks: 42 executed
42.   Built the following apk(s):
43.
44.         F:\1.DevOps\2020\Jenkins_Home\workspace\Ionic-App-
      Sample_master\platforms\android\app\build\outputs\apk\
      debug\app-debug.apk
```

13.   Verify the archived artifact on the Jenkins dashboard:

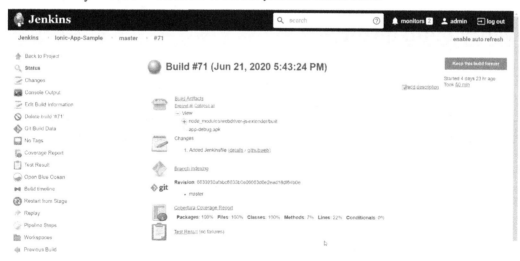

Figure 8.14: Build artifacts

14. Verify the Jenkins workspace. The platform and "www" directory is created after the pipeline execution:

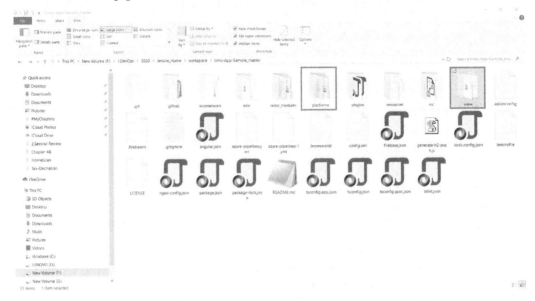

Figure 8.15: Workspace

Verify build quality

To verify the quality, perform the following steps:

1. Click on the **Pipeline Syntax** link available in the pipeline and configure thresholds for the coverage:

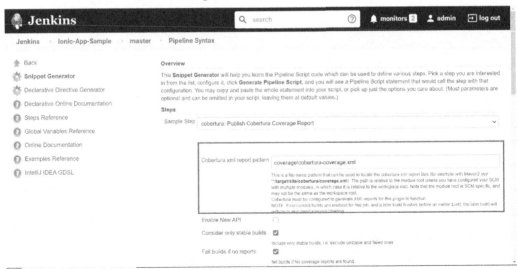

Figure 8.16: Cobertura pipeline syntax

2. Configure **Coverage Metric Targets**:

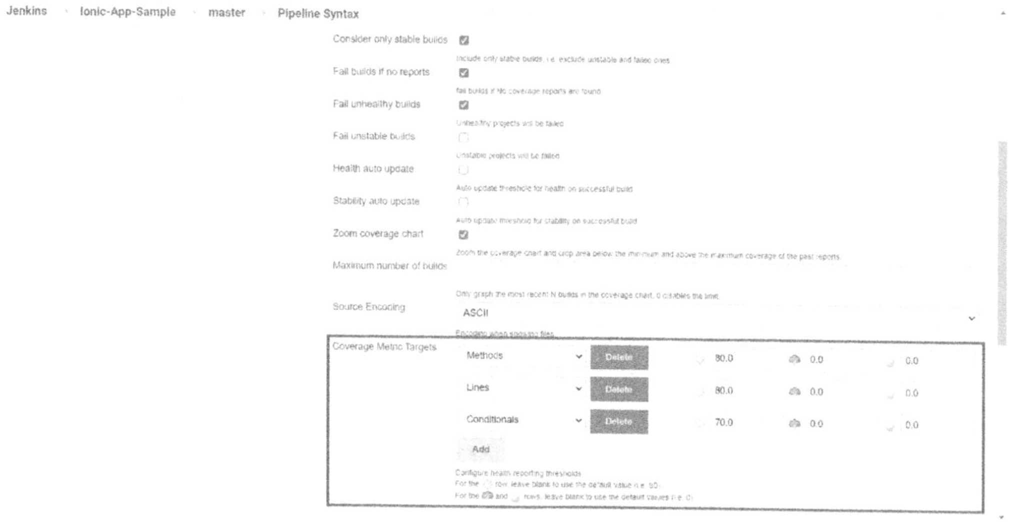

Figure 8.17: *Advance Configuration*

3. The following is the script generated using the pipeline syntax:

```
1.  cobertura autoUpdateHealth: false, autoUpdateStability:
    false, coberturaReportFile: 'coverage\\cobertura-coverage.
    xml', conditionalCoverageTargets: '70, 0, 0', failUnstable:
    false, lineCoverageTargets: '80, 0, 0', maxNumberOfBuilds:
    0, methodCoverageTargets: '80, 0, 0', sourceEncoding:
    'ASCII'
```

In the next section, we will discuss the Continuous Delivery part.

Continuous Delivery for the Ionic – Android app

In *Chapter 4: Building a CI/CD pipeline for an Android App*, we configured the task to distribute it to the App Center. We will configure it as a part of the exercise by performing the following scripts:

1. Create a Keystore with the Java Keytool utility that is available with the JDK distribution.

   The Keytool prompts to provide passwords for the Keystore and other details. It generates the Keystore as a file called jenkinsbook.keystore in the current directory. The Keystore and key are protected by the passwords. The Keystore contains a single key, which is valid for 10000 days. The alias is a name used to refer to this jenkinsbook.keystore when signing the application.

1. C:\Users\Tempuser\Desktop\BPBOnline\3.Hands-on   Jenkins
   PipelinePipeline as Code using Blue Ocean\FirstDraft\
   Chapter #8>"C:\Program Files (x86)\Java\jdk1.8.0_192\jre\
   bin\keytool" -genkey -v -keystore jenkinsbook.keystore
   -alias jenkinsbook -keyalg RSA -keysize 2048 -validity
   10000

2. Picked up _JAVA_OPTIONS: -Xmx512M

3. Enter keystore password:

4. Re-enter new password:

5. What is your first and last name?

6.   [Unknown]: Tempuser

7. What is the name of your organizational unit?

8.   [Unknown]: RainyClouds

9. What is the name of your organization?

10.   [Unknown]: Clouds

11. What is the name of your City or Locality?

12.   [Unknown]: Kochi

13. What is the name of your State or Province?

14.   [Unknown]: Kerala

15. What is the two-letter country code for this unit?

16.   [Unknown]: IN

17. Is CN=Tempuser, OU=RainyClouds, O=Clouds, L=Kochi,
    ST=Kerala, C=IN correct?

18.   [no]: yes

19.

20. Generating 2,048 bit RSA key pair and self-signed certificate
    (SHA256withRSA) with a validity of 10,000 days

21.   for: CN=Tempuser, OU=RainyClouds, O=Clouds, L=Kochi,
    ST=Kerala, C=IN

22. Enter key password for <jenkinsbook>

23.   (RETURN if same as keystore password):

24. [Storing jenkinsbook.keystore]

25.

26. Warning:

27. The JKS keystore uses a proprietary format. It is recommended
    to migrate to PKCS12 which is an industry standard format
    using "keytool -importkeystore -srckeystore jenkinsbook.
    keystore -destkeystore jenkinsbook.keystore -deststoretype
    pkcs12".

2. Sign the Android package using the `jarsigner` tool available in JDK.

3. Use the following command structure to create a signed JAR file:

```
1.    <JDK   path>\bin\jarsigner  -verbose  -keystore  <Directory
      path>/jenkinsbook.keystore -storepass jenkinsbook -signedjar
      <path for signed apk>  <path for unsigned apk> jenkinsbook
```

4. Verify the signed jar file using the `-verify` attribute:

   `<JDK path>\bin\jarsigner -verify <path for signed apk>`

   For example:

```
1.    stage('Sign Android Package') {
2.        steps {
3.            bat '"C:\\Program Files (x86)\\Java\\jdk1.8.0_192\\
      bin\\jarsigner.exe"   -verbose   -keystore   "C:\\Users\\
      Tempuser\\Desktop\\BPBOnline\\3.Hands-on Jenkins Pipeline
      as  Code  using  Blue  Ocean\\FirstDraft\\Chapter  #8\\
      jenkinsbook.keystore" -storepass jenkinsbook -signedjar
      "PATH-to--signed.apk" "PATH-to-unsigned.apk" jenkinsbook'
4.            bat '"C:\\Program Files (x86)\\Java\\jdk1.8.0_192\\
      bin\\jarsigner.exe" -verify "<PATH-to-APK>"'
5.        }
6.    }
```

In the next section, we will discuss deploying the package to the App Center.

Deploy package / APK to app center

App Center is used to distribute mobile applications to the QA team. It is also used to build, test, and distribute Android, iOS, and Windows applications. Let's configure App Center and deploy a package using Jenkins pipeline:

1. Go to **https://appcenter.ms/**.

2. Log in with the appropriate method. Provide **Username** to log in.

3. Let's add a new App in App Center by clicking on **Add new**.

4. Select **App Type, OS**, and **Platform**.

5. Click on **Add new app**.

6. As of now, there is no distribution group available in the Android app we have created.

7. Distribution groups help to organize testers and manage who can have access to the application.

8. Click on **Add Group**.

9. Provide **Group name** and click on **Create Group.**

10. A new Group is available. We will configure this group when we try to upload the Android Package from Jenkins.

11. To integrate the App center in Jenkins, we will need an API token. Let's create it first.

12. Let's go to **Account Settings** of App Center.

13. Scroll down on the **Account Settings** page.

14. Click on **New API token**.

15. Provide **Description** and **Access**.

16. Click on **Add** new **API token**.

17. Copy the API token.

18. Go to **Jenkins** and open the **Pipeline Syntax** section of the sample pipeline project.

19. Select the **Upload to App Center** step in the **Sample** step.

20. Provide the values such as API Token that we created earlier, Owner name from App Center, App Name, Path to the APK file, and Distribution group that we created.

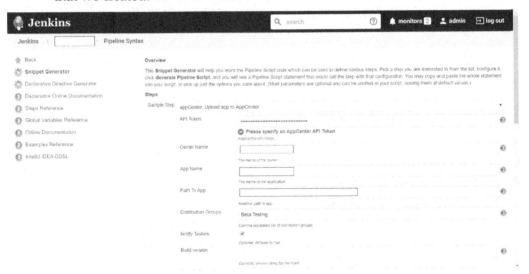

Figure 8.18: App Center - pipeline Syntax

21. Click on **Generate Pipeline Script**.

22. We can directly copy this script into the Pipeline Editor or we can add the Blue Ocean step and provide data here as well:

```
1.  stage('Upload to App Center') {
2.      steps {
3.          appCenter(apiToken: '*************************',
    ownerName: tempuser-outlook.com', appName: 'Ionic-Sample-App',
    pathToApp: 'xxxxxxxx.apk', distributionGroups: 'Beta Testing',
    releaseNotes: 'Security Bug Fixed - Ticket 2020.05.20')
4.      }
5.  }
```

23. Configure the App center distribution task based on the preceding instructions:

Figure 8.19: *Continuous Delivery Stage*

The following is the full stage view of all pipeline stages available in the Jenkinsfile:

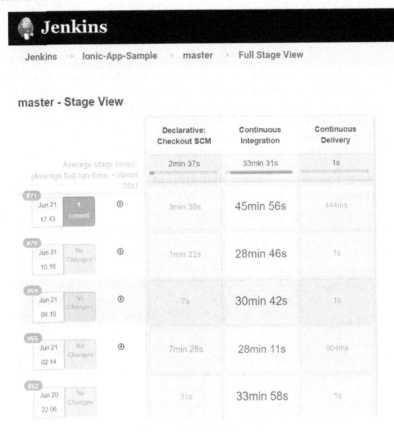

Figure 8.20: Full stage view

Done!

In the next section, we will cover the Blue Ocean pipeline for a sample Flutter application.

Multi-stage pipeline for the Flutter app using Blue Ocean

In this chapter, we will cover CI/CD for a sample Flutter application. Before moving ahead, let's discuss the installation of Flutter on the Windows operating system:

1. Download the installation bundle to get the latest stable release of the Flutter SDK from **https://storage.googleapis.com/flutter_infra/releases/stable/windows/flutter_windows_1.17.5-stable.zip**.

2. Extract the ZIP file.

3. Put the directory into a directory that doesn't require high privileges.

4. Click on the search bar, enter env or edit and select **Edit environment variables** for your account.

5. Configure `<FLUTTER_INSTALLATION_DIRECTORY>\.pub-cache\bin` and `<FLUTTER_INSTALLATION_DIRECTORY>\bin\cache\dart-sdk\bin` as well.

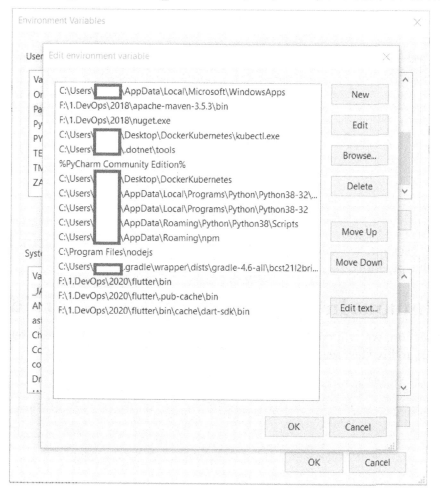

Figure 8.21: Environment Variables

NOTE

For more details on the Flutter installation on Windows, visit **https://flutter. dev/docs/get-started/install/windows**.

Let's create a pipeline for a sample Flutter application using Blue Ocean. We will configure code analysis, unit test execution, and code coverage calculation and report for a sample Flutter application.

6. Create multiple stages in the Jenkins pipeline to create a pipeline for Flutter based on the tasks we want to perform:

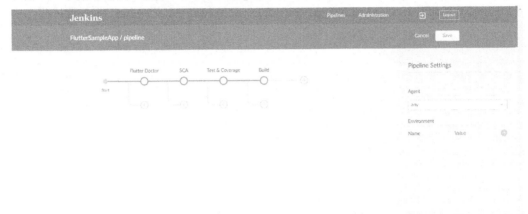

Figure 8.22: Pipeline editor

In the next section, we will configure the unit test and code coverage execution using the Jenkins pipeline.

Continuous Integration for Flutter – Android app

In this section, we will configure tasks related to Static Code Analysis, execute the unit tests, archive test results, and publish the code coverage report:

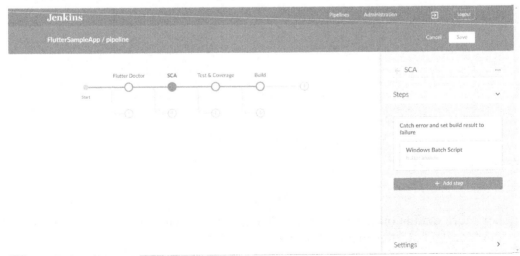

Figure 8.23: Pipeline steps

Let's go through Declarative pipeline script:

1. The following is a declarative pipeline script. Press *Ctrl + S* to get the pipeline script in the Blue Ocean pipeline editor:

```
1.  pipeline {
2.    agent any
3.    stages {
4.      stage('Flutter Doctor') {
5.        steps {
6.          bat 'flutter doctor'
7.        }
8.      }
9.
10.     stage('SCA') {
11.       steps {
12.            catchError(buildResult: 'SUCCESS', stageResult:
    'FAILURE') {
13.             bat 'flutter analyze'
14.           }
15.
16.       }
17.     }
18.
19.     stage('Test & Coverage') {
20.       steps {
21.         bat 'flutter pub get && flutter pub global activate
    junitreport && flutter test --machine | tojunit --output
    test.xml'
22.           junit 'test.xml'
23.         bat 'flutter test --coverage &&  python C:\\Python38\\
    Lib\\site-packages\\lcov_cobertura.py coverage\\lcov.info'
24.         publishCoverage(adapters: [coberturaAdapter('coverage.
    xml')], sourceFileResolver: sourceFiles('NEVER_STORE'))
25.       }
26.     }
27.
28.     stage('Build') {
29.       steps {
```

```
30.            bat 'flutter build apk --%BUILD_TYPE%'
31.            archiveArtifacts '**/*.apk'
32.        }
33.      }
34.
35.    }
36.    parameters {
37.      choice(name: 'BUILD_TYPE', choices: ['debug', 'release'],
       description: 'Build Type for APK')
38.    }
39. }
```

2. Update and save the pipeline to execute it.

3. The command flutter doctor verifies the environment and displays your Flutter installation status:

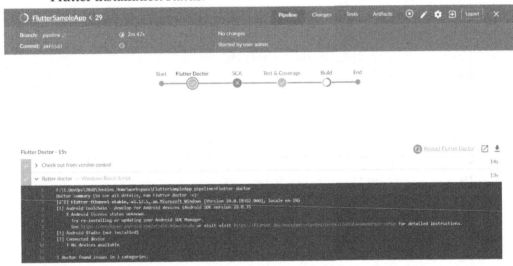

Figure 8.24: Pipeline execution result

4. The command flutter analysis verifies the code quality and standard. It fails if the pipeline finds issues in the code.

   We will use the following block to continue the pipeline even after failure:

```
1. catchError(buildResult: 'SUCCESS', stageResult: 'FAILURE')
   {
2. }
```

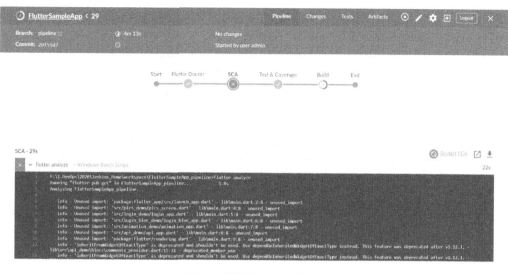

Figure 8.25: flutter analyze

5.   Execute flutter pubs get to add a package dependency to an app. To get details such as the number of tests executed and the tests that are passed or failed, execute flutter test `--machine`. The JUnit report (**https://pub.dev/ packages/junitreport**) is a Dart package that allows you to convert the JSON output of the `--machine` argument to produce a JUnit test report. It helps to publish a report in Jenkins. To use the JUnit report (Dart package), add Dart DK and other packages available to the path. Use the following commands:

```
1.  // Unit test execution and converting test results into a
    Junit test report
2.  flutter pub get && flutter pub global activate junitreport &&
    flutter test --machine | tojunit --output test.xml
3.
4.  // Execute unit tests, calculate code coverage, and convert
    lcov report into cobertura report format
5.  flutter test --coverage &&  python C:\\Python38\\Lib\\site-
    packages\\lcov_cobertura.py coverage\\lcov.info
```

lcov to Cobertura XML converter converts code coverage report files from lcov to Cobertura's XML report. It helps to publish the report in Jenkins.

Install `lcov_cobertura` in Windows:

```
1.  C:\Users\Tempuser>pip install lcov_cobertura
2.  Collecting lcov_cobertura
3.    Downloading lcov_cobertura-1.6.tar.gz (6.3 kB)
```

4. Using legacy setup.py install for lcov-Cobertura, since package 'wheel' is not installed.

5. Installing collected packages: lcov-Cobertura

6.   Running setup.py install for lcov-cobertura ... done

7. Successfully installed lcov-cobertura-1.6

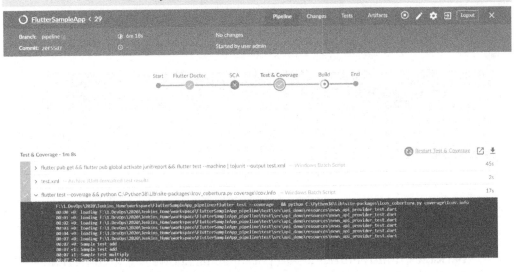

Figure 8.26: Test coverage stage

6. Verify the **Build** stage where the APK file is created:

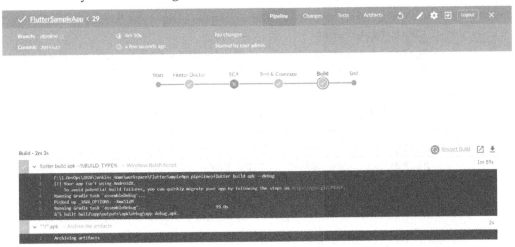

Figure 8.27: Build stage

7. Go to the Blue Ocean dashboard and Flutter pipeline. Click on the **Tests** tab to see all the results of the unit test execution:

Figure 8.28: *Test Results in Blue Ocean*

8. Click on the **Artifacts** tab to download the Android package:

Figure 8.29: *Artifacts in Blue Ocean*

9. If you want to keep the build type as a parameter, then use the following block:

```
1.  parameters {
2.    choice(name: 'BUILD_TYPE', choices: ['debug', 'release'],
      description: 'Build Type for APK')
3.  }
```

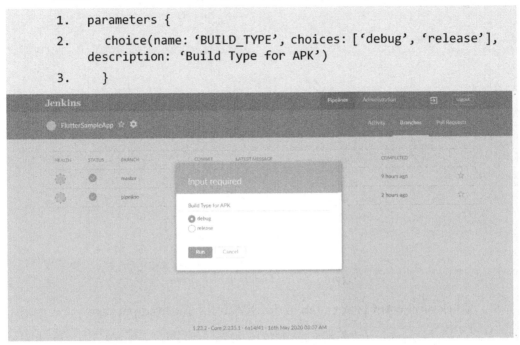

Figure 8.30: Parameters in Blue Ocean

10. Go to the traditional Jenkins dashboard and verify the status of the pipeline execution:

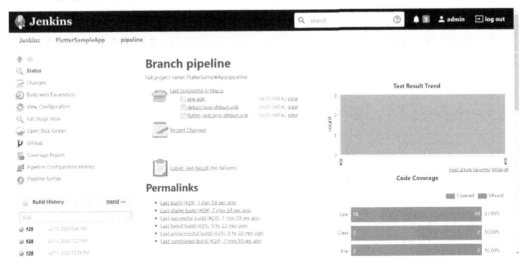

Figure 8.31: Pipeline Status on the traditional Jenkins dashboard

11.	Click on the Code coverage link available on the left-hand side bar:

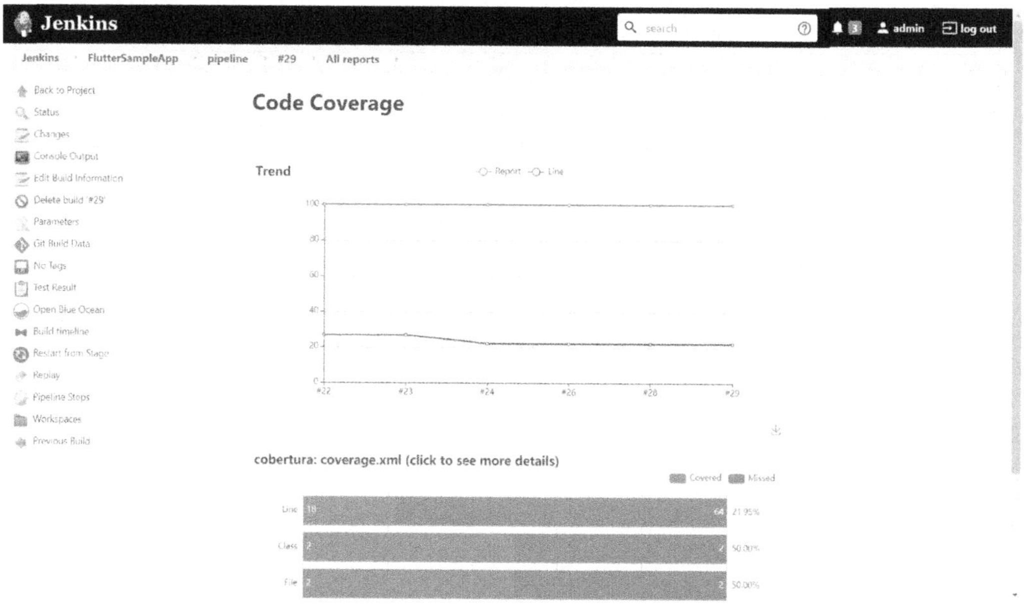

Figure 8.32: *Code Coverage results*

12.	To distribute the Android package to the App center, use the steps given in the available in the section - Ionic Cordova package distribution to the App Center.

TIP

The post section provides one or more additional steps that need to be executed for cleanup or notifications or other activities after the pipeline's or stage's execution.

Always	Execute the steps available in the post section irrespective of the completion status of the pipeline's or stage's run.
Unstable	Execute the steps available in the post if the current pipeline's or stage's run has an "unstable" status. The cause of unstable builds is test failures, code violations, etc.
notBuilt	Execute the steps available in the post if the build status is "Not Built".
Cleanup	Execute the steps available in the post after every other post condition has been evaluated, irrespective of the pipeline or stage's status.
Regression	Execute the steps available in the post if: 1. The current pipeline's or stage's run's status is a failure, unstable, or aborted. 2. The previous run was successful.

Aborted	Execute the steps available in the post if the current pipeline's or stage's run has an aborted status.
Success	Execute the steps available in the post if the current pipeline's or stage's run has a success status.
Failure	Execute the steps available in the post if the current pipeline's or stage's run has a "failed" status.
	Execute the steps available in the post if the current pipeline's or stage's run has not a success status.
Fixed	Execute the steps available in the post if: 1. The current pipeline's or stage's run is successful. 2. The previous run failed or was unstable.
changed	Execute the steps available in the post if the current pipeline's or stage's run has a changed completion status from its previous execution.

Syntax:

```
1.  post {
2.    always {
3.        // One or more steps need to be included within each
      condition's block.
4.    }
5.    unstable {
6.        // One or more steps need to be included within each
      condition's block.
7.    }
8.    notBuilt {
9.        // One or more steps need to be included within each
      condition's block.
10.   }
11.   cleanup {
12.       // One or more steps need to be included within each
      condition's block.
13.   }
14.   regression {
15.       // One or more steps need to be included within each
      condition's block.
16.   }
17.   aborted {
18.       // One or more steps need to be included within each
      condition's block.
19.   }
```

```
20.    success {
21.    mail body: Pipeline Successful', subject: Pipeline Succeeded!',
22.               to: 'jenkinsstatus@etutorialworlds.com'  }
23.    failure {
24.       mail body: Pipeline Failed', subject: Pipeline Failed'!',
25.               to: 'jenkinsstatus@etutorialworlds.com'  }
26.    }
27.    unsuccessful {
28.       // One or more steps need to be included within each
       condition's block.
29.     }
30.    fixed {
31.       // One or more steps need to be included within each
       condition's block.
32.     }
33.    changed {
34.       // One or more steps need to be included within each
       condition's block.
35.     }
36.  }
```

Done!

Conclusion

In this chapter, we created the CI/CD pipeline for a sample application written in Ionic Cordova and Flutter. It covers Continuous Integration that includes code analysis, unit test execution, code coverage, and build creation. We also covered app distribution using the App center.

In the next chapter, we will cover DevOps practices implementation for Python applications. We will configure CI/CD for Python applications.

Multiple choice questions

1. **The code Coverage tab provides the following details:**

    a.   Covered Lines

    b.   Uncovered Lines

    c.   Line Coverage

    d.   All of these

2. **State True or False: We can configure step to fail the pipeline if Code coverage threshold doesn't meet:**

   a. True

   b. False

Answer

1. **d**
2. **a**

Questions

1. What is the difference between the App Center and App Services?

2. How to configure the Headless Browser so that test cases can be executed?

3. Which `JunitReporter` configuration details needs to be included in `karma.conf.js`?

4. What `coverageIstanbulReporter` configuration is required in karma.conf.js?

5. Which Plugins are required plugins for Junit (unit testing) and Cobertura (code coverage) output?

6. How to fix vulnerabilities in node modules?

7. How to solve the following error: `..getProjectMetadata` does not exist?

8. What can be the cause of the error that indicates a failure to remove the platform directory?

9. How to solve the issue: Could not find an installed version of Gradle

10. What is the solution of the issue: Could not find plugin `proposal-numeric-separator` in an angular app?

CHAPTER 9

Building CI/CD Pipeline for a Python Application

> "Excellence is not a destination; it is a continuous journey that never ends."
>
> —*Brian Tracy*

Ahealthcare services organization wants to focus on building high-quality applications with faster time to market and improved security. A **Chief Technology Office (CTO)** wants to evolve the platform and technology stack to manage user- requests efficiently. In the time of the pandemic, they want to roll out more features without compromising on security, compliance, and quality. Technical experts decide to migrate to Python for its popularity in AI and Machine Learning based areas. Python is a general-purpose dynamic programming language founded in 1991 by developer Guido Van Rossum. that focuses on code readability. The following are some important features or advantages of Python: Object-oriented (not fully), Open source and community development, Readability, Interpreted, Interactive, Automatic memory management, Dynamic - Dynamically typed language, Modular, Portable across Operating systems, High level, Easy to learn, Extensible in C++ & C, and Extensive support libraries. A CTO wants to accelerate application delivery with high quality using a phase-wise implementation of DevOps practices. The need of the hour is to implement Continuous Integration and Continuous Delivery. In this chapter, we will cover the CI/CD implementation of a Python application with Jenkins. We will use the Pipeline as Code to create a CI/CD pipeline. Blue Ocean provides a simple way to create a pipeline using a simple user interface as well as a code editor to configure **Continuous Integration (CI)** and **Continuous Delivery (CD)** pipeline for Python applications. We will also provide some valuable notes related to DevOps and its culture, challenges, market trends, and so on for a better understanding.

Structure

In this chapter, we will discuss the following topics:

- Introduction
- Blue Ocean multi-stage pipeline for the Python app
  - o Continuous Integration
- Static code analysis using SonarQube
- Unit test execution and Code coverage
- Build quality check
- Conclusion
- Questions and exercises

Objectives

After studying this section, you should be able to:

- Understand how to perform static code analysis for a Python application
- Execute unit tests
- Calculate code coverage
- Verify build quality

Introduction

The organization has selected one application as a pilot while there are other 5 early adopter Python applications that are waiting in the queue. We have the responsibility to create a CI/CD pipeline using Pipeline as Code in Jenkins in the declarative syntax.

The following is the list of tools and deliverables that will be integrated into the pipeline:

Tools	
Version Control	Git
Code Analysis	SonarQube
Unit Tests	PYTest
Code Coverage	Cobertura
Continuous Integration	Jenkins
Continuous Delivery	Jenkins
Pipeline	Pipeline as Code, Jenkinsfile, Blue Ocean
Expected Deliverables or Features in an Automated pipeline	
<ul><li>Installation and Configuration of Jenkins</li><li>Distributed Architecture/Master Agent Architecture (Covered in *Chapter 11: Best Practices*)</li><li>Role-based access (Covered in *Chapter 11: Best Practices*)</li><li>Configuration of the CI/CD pipeline using Pipeline as Code</li><li>Documentation<ul><li>Documentation of defined processes and implementations</li><li>Technical documentation – How to guides</li></ul></li><li>Best practices documentation for the usage of Jenkins/Blue Ocean (Covered in *Chapter 11: Best Practices*)</li></ul>	

Table 9.1: Tools and deliverables

In the next section, we will create a pipeline for Python application using the Blue Ocean interface in a step-by-step manner.

Multi-stage pipeline for the Python app using Blue Ocean

In this chapter, we will try to cover CI/CD for a sample Python application. Followinf image is a big picture that we will cover in this chapter for CI/CD pipeline implementation.

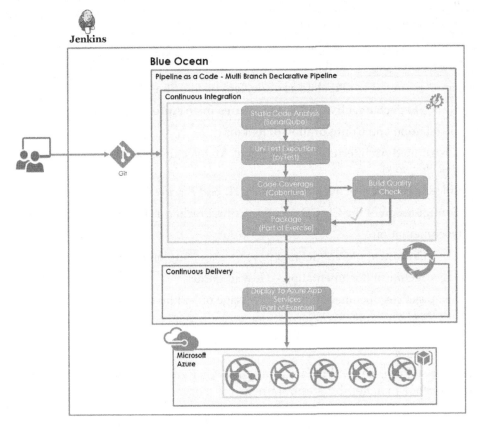

Figure 9.1: *Big Picture for CI/CD of the Python app*

Let's create a pipeline for a sample Python application using Blue Ocean.

1. We will configure static code analysis using SonarQube, unit test execution, and code coverage calculation and report for a sample Python application.

2. We will create two stages in the Jenkins pipeline with the names: Continuous Integration and Continuous Delivery:

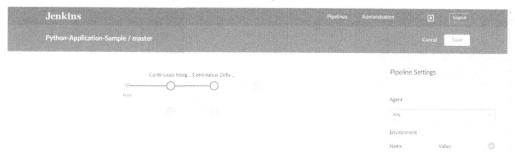

Figure 9.2: *Blue Ocean pipeline Editor*

NOTE

Use Continuous Integration and Continuous Delivery for all the environments, including production.

In the next section, we will configure the unit test and code coverage execution using the Jenkins pipeline.

Continuous Integration – Python application

In the Continuous Integration stage, configure tasks related to static code analysis using SonarQube, execute unit tests using PyTest, archive test results, and publish the code coverage report:

Figure 9.3: *Continuous Integration Stage*

1. The following is a declarative pipeline script:

```
1.   pipeline {
2.     agent any
3.     stages {
4.     stage('Continuous Integration') {
5.         steps {
6.             bat 'F:\\1.DevOps\\2020\\sonar-scanner-3.2.0.1227-
    windows\\bin\\sonar-scanner.bat   -Dsonar.host.url=http://
    localhost:9000/  -Dsonar.login=<SONARQUBE_TOKEN>  -Dsonar.
    projectVersion=1.0        -Dsonar.projectKey=python-sample
    -Dsonar.sources=example-py-pytest'
7.             bat 'pip install pytestpytest-azurepipelinespytest-
    cov&& python -m pytest example-py-pytest/tests/ --cov=com
    --cov-report=xml --cov-report=html'
8.     junit 'test-output.xml'
9.     cobertura(coberturaReportFile:               'coverage.xml',
    sourceEncoding: 'ASCII')
10.        }
```

```
11.        }
12.      }
13.   }
```

2. Press *Ctrl + S* to get the pipeline script in the Blue Ocean pipeline editor:

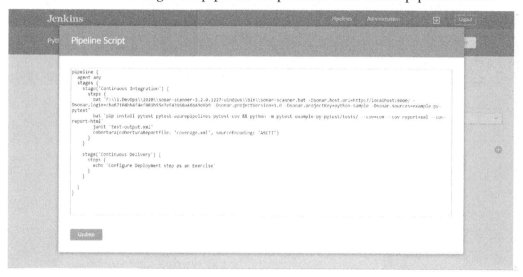

Figure 9.4: Pipeline Script

3. Update and save the pipeline to execute it.

4. The only master branch is available in our case and we will create a pipeline for the master branch only:

Figure 9.5: Blue Ocean - Branches

NOTE

Identifying key metrics and tracking them is required to compare AS IS situation and later improvements.

5. **The activity** tab will show you all the pipeline **RUN** activities and their status:

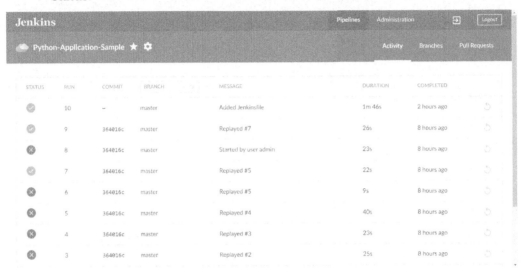

Figure 9.6: Pipeline RUN activities

6. Verify the pipeline execution and its steps:

Figure 9.7: Pipeline execution

7. Click on the **Changes** link to get details on the recent changes in the repository:

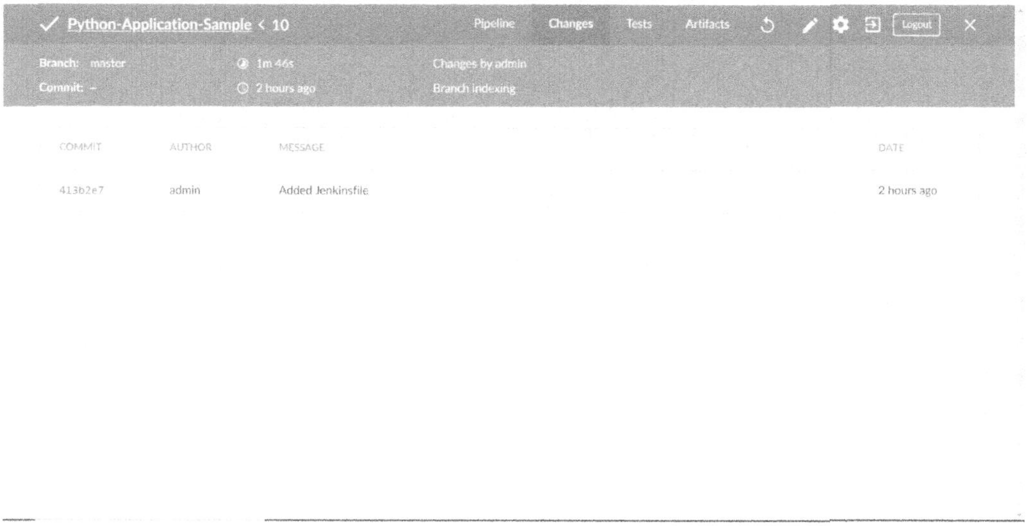

Figure 9.8: Changes

In the next section, we will see details about static code analysis using SonarQube.

Static code analysis using SonarQube

SonarQube has a default Python-related quality profile. We can make custom profiles as well.

> ### TIP
>
> Stash and unstash are designed to share files between stages and nodes.
>
> Archive artifacts help to store the output files such as WAR file, APK file or IPA file after we build the project. Users can download artifacts later. We can access archived artifacts from the Jenkins Dashboard/Project Dashboard. Artifacts are available until the build log is kept.
>
> **Example:** To build an Angular sample application, Docker is installed on a virtual machine that is available as an agent. We will stash the ZIP file of the distributions folder (`dist\\browser`) and unstash it on the agent where our dockerfile is available. We will run our Dockerfile and create an image and as the final step, we will create and run the container:
>
> ```
> 1.    stage('Continuous Integration') {
> 2.       steps {
> 3.      bat 'npm install'
> 4.      bat 'npm run lint > lint.txt'
> ```

```
5.    bat 'npm install karma-junit-reporter --save-dev &&npm run
      test'
6.   junit 'TESTS-*.xml'
7.      publishCoverage(adapters:      [coberturaAdapter('coverage\\
     cobertura-coverage.xml')],              sourceFileResolver:
     sourceFiles('NEVER_STORE'))
8.   bat 'npm run build:prod:en'
9.   zip(dir: 'dist\\browser', zipFile: 'browser.zip')
10.  stash(includes: 'browser.zip', name: 'dist')
11.    }
12.  }
13.  stage('Deploy to Dev') {
14.    agent {
15.      node {
16.        label 'centos'
17.      }
18.    }
19.    steps {
20.      sh 'docker version'
21.      unstash 'dist'
22.      sh 'chmod 755 browser.zip'
23.      unzip(dir: 'dist/browser', zipFile: 'browser.zip')
24.      sh 'docker build . -t test/angular-sample'
25.      sh 'docker run -p 8080:80 --detach test/angular-sample'
26.    }
27.  }
```

Let's verify console logs and SonarQube dashboard.

1. The following is an example of a successful static code analysis using SonarQube:

Figure 9.9: SonarQube step logs

2. Visit the URL given in logs or open SonarQube to get more details on static code analysis performed using SonarQube:

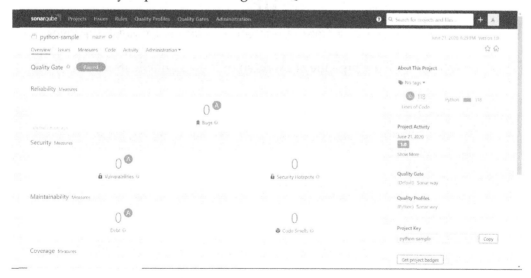

Figure 9.10: SonarQube Dashboard

3. Verify the Sonar way profile for Python and make changes as per your requirements:

Figure 9.11: *Python Quality Profile*

4. In the next section, we will cover details about unit test execution and code coverage.

TIP

In case Jenkins crash to a state where configurations cannot be recovered, then the Jenkinsfile can help us get up and running in no time as all the steps required to execute the pipeline are written in the Jenkinsfile itself.

Unit test execution and code coverage

Perform the following steps to execute Unit tests and calculate Code coverage:

1. Go to the Blue Ocean dashboard and Python pipeline. Click on the **Tests** tab to see all the results of the unit test execution:

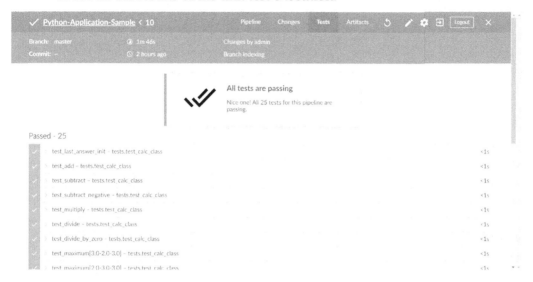

Figure 9.12: Blue Ocean Tests

NOTE

Goals: End-to-end Automation, Standardized Toolset and Processes, Communication and Collaboration tools, Effective usage of Cloud and Container resources, Common Goals and roadmap based on Maturity Model, Common Key performance indicators, Continuous Improvement, and Continuous Innovation

2.   Check logs for the unit test execution and code coverage in the tradition dashboard of Jenkins:

Figure 9.13: *Unit Tests and Code Coverage*

3.   Verify the status for a specific run of a pipeline:

Figure 9.14: *Pipeline status*

TIP

Set email or slack notification for each failure or important event so the pipeline is maintained in a healthy state.

4. In the branch status view, we can get charts for unit test reports and code coverage reports:

Figure 9.15: *Branch Status*

5. Click on the test results chart to get more details related to the unit test execution:

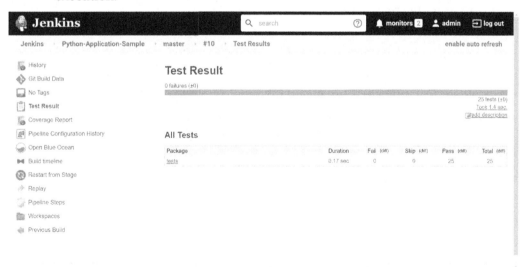

Figure 9.16: *Test Result*

6. Click on **Package** to get more details about a class-wise test for a sample application of Python:

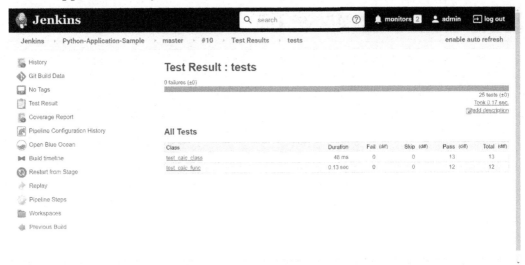

Figure 9.17: *All Tests – Class-wise*

TIP

How to quickly create a pipeline?

1. Learn Groovy.

2. Create a pipeline script in the Jenkinsfile.

3. Use the pipeline syntax section available in the Jenkins pipeline or Jenkins job or use Blue Ocean to create the pipeline syntax easily.

The efficient answer is to use the pipeline syntax section available in the Jenkins pipeline or Jenkins job or use Blue Ocean to create the pipeline syntax easily.

7. Click on a class to get all the individual unit tests:

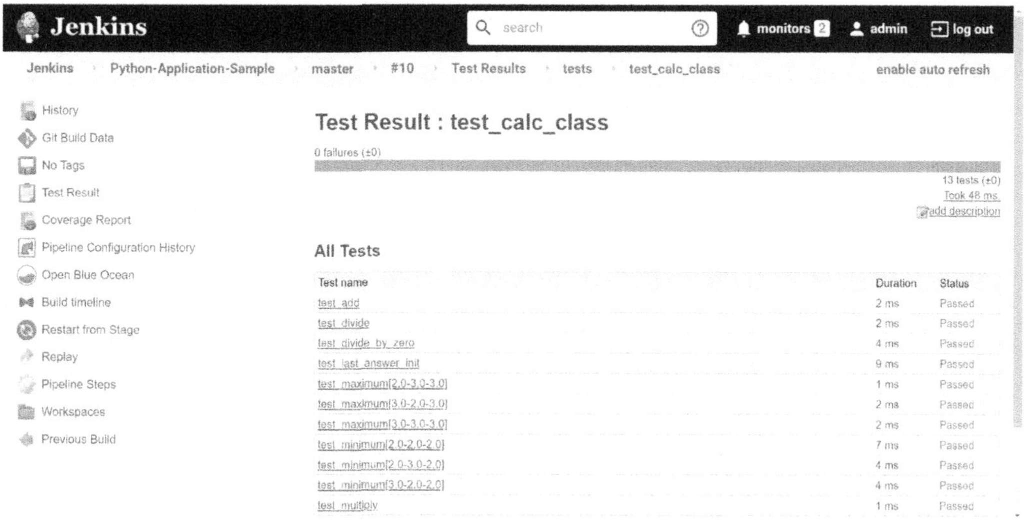

Figure 9.18: Individual unit tests

8. Click on the Code Coverage chart to get more details on Code coverage based on individual units:

Figure 9.19: Code Coverage breakdown

NOTE

Metrics: % decrease in bugs, vulnerabilities, and code smells, % increase in code coverage, % increase in test automation, % decrease in efforts of deployment, and % decrease in the overall release process.

9. Click on a specific package to get more details of coverage based on the file:

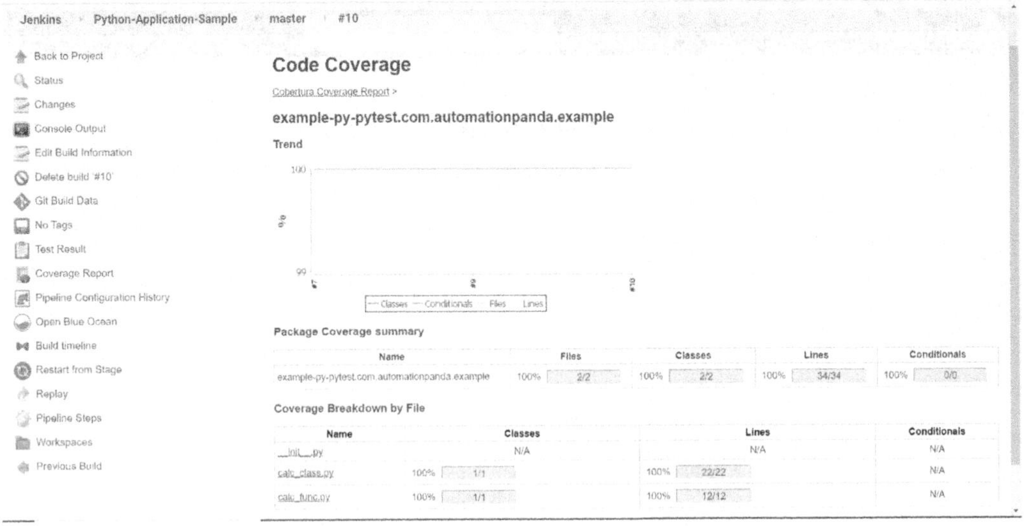

Figure 9.20: Coverage breakdown by file

TIP

Multi-branch pipelines help to create pipelines based on the Jenkinsfile available in the branch. How it is helpful? Consider the scenario when you want to have a different kind of configuration in different environments. In such cases, each branch specific to dev, test, staging, and prod branch can have different Jenkinsfile and each file can have a different configuration in the Jenkinsfile. While creating a pipeline in Blue Ocean, it will detect multiple branches with the Jenkinsfile and considering that all the agents are available, the pipeline will be executed:

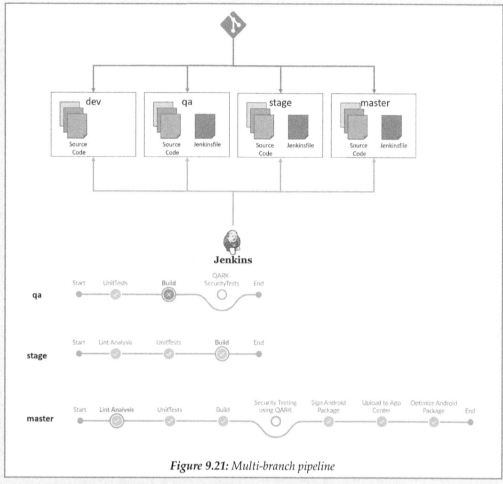

Figure 9.21: Multi-branch pipeline

It is useful when Jenkins crashes and you want to receiver all your pipelines. If the automation setup and agents are available, then all the pipelines can be restored as all the pipelines reside in a branch (version control system) in the form of Pipeline as Code.

Multi-branch pipelines inject `BRANCH_NAME` and `CHANGE_ID` information about the branch through the env global variable.

Example of Scan Multi-branch pipeline log:

```
1.   Checking branches...
2.      Checking branch sprint_cleanup
3.          'Jenkinsfile' not found
4.        Does not meet criteria
5.      Checking branch jenkins
6.          'Jenkinsfile' found
```

```
 7.      Met criteria
 8.   Changes detected: jenkins
       (899e3705ec381e81d4886af637f8a10d56a4bceb →
       33935c216079b9b9083dc10c8d24a24b019b41fa)
 9.   Scheduled build for branch: jenkins
10.     Checking branch master
11.         'Jenkinsfile' found
12.       Met criteria
13.     Checking branch param_rename
14.         'Jenkinsfile' not found
15.       Does not meet criteria
16.     Checking branch update_click
17.         'Jenkinsfile' not found
18.       Does not meet criteria
19.     Checking branch blog-55555
20.         'Jenkinsfile' not found
21.       Does not meet criteria
22.     Checking branch add_header
23.         'Jenkinsfile' not found
24.       Does not meet criteria
25.     Checking branch selection
26.         'Jenkinsfile' not found
27.       Does not meet criteria
28.     Checking branch rv-selection
29.         'Jenkinsfile' not found
30.       Does not meet criteria
31.     Checking branch transition
32.         'Jenkinsfile' not found
33.       Does not meet criteria
34.   Processed 10 branches
35.   [Mon May 18 14:02:01 IST 2020] Finished branch indexing. Indexing
       took 6.1 sec
36.   Finished: SUCCESS
```

In a multi-branch pipeline project, Jenkins automatically discovers, manages, and executes pipelines for all the branches which meet the criteria (Jenkinsfile in source control) considering the automation environment, including agents are available.

Build quality check

For build quality check, go to *Chapter 8: Building a CI/CD pipeline with Blue Ocean for a Hybrid Mobile Application* and refer to the section *Verify build quality*.

TIP

Which pipeline to use?
1. Build the pipeline plugin-based pipeline.
2. Scripted pipeline.
3. Declarative pipeline
    a.   Multi-branch pipeline
    b.   Blue Ocean

The efficient answer is the declarative pipeline as it is easy to understand and manage.

Continuous Delivery – Python application

We have already created a stage for Continuous Delivery. The CD part for Python is for an exercise. We have earlier covered how to create Azure App Service. Deployment is a part of the exercise:

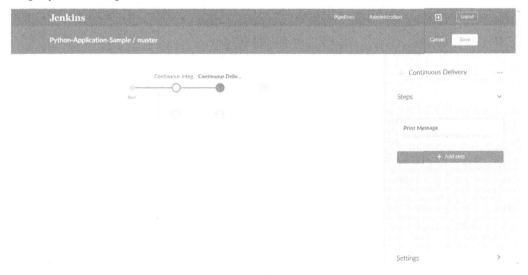

Figure 9.22: Continuous Delivery stage

Verify the **Full stage view** for the entire pipeline:

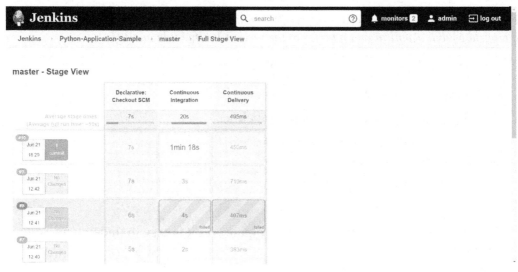

Figure 9.23: Full stage view

Done!

TIP

How to use when block?

```
1.   // Execute when parameters matches value
2.   stage('Security Testing using QARK') {
3.       when {
4.           expression {
5.   params.SecurityTesting == 'Yes'
6.           }
7.
8.       }
9.       steps {
10.          bat 'qark "app\\build\\outputs\\apk\\release\\app-debug.
     apk"'
11.      }
12.   }
```

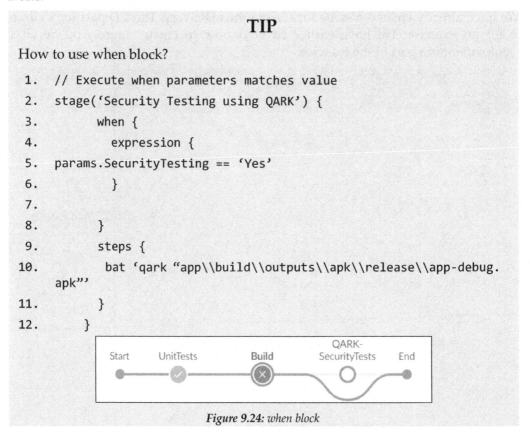

Figure 9.24: when block

```
1.   // skip a stage
2.   stage("Stage to Skip") {
3.     when {
4.       expression { false }
5.     }
6.     steps {
7.       echo 'This stage will never run'
8.     }
9.   }
10.  // Execute when branch = 'dev' and stage
11.
12.  stage("Security Testing") {
13.    when {
14.      branch 'dev'
15.    }
16.    steps {
17.      ...
18.    }
19.  }
20.  // Execute when with OR
21.  stage('RaceDay') {
22.    when {
23.      expression {
24.        params.Environment == 'Powai' || params.Environment ==
     'Women'
25.      }
26.    }
27.    steps {
28.      ...
29.    }
30.  }
31.  // Execute when with AND
32.  stage('RaceDay') {
33.    when {
34.      expression {
35.        params.Environment == 'Powai' &&params.Environment ==
```

```
      'Women'
36.       }
37.     }
38.     steps {
39.       ...
40.     }41. }
```

Conclusion

In this chapter, we created the CI pipeline for a sample application written in Python where we covered code analysis using SonarQube, unit test execution, code coverage calculation, and publishing results of unit tests and code coverage.

In the next chapter, we will cover DevOps practices implementation for .Net. We will configure CI/CD for .Net applications.

Multiple choice questions

1. **The code coverage tab provides the following details:**

   a. Covered Lines

   b. Uncovered Lines

   c. Line Coverage

   d. All of these

2. **State True or False: Python is an Object Oriented language:**

   a. True

   b. False

Answer

1. **d**

2. **a**

Questions

1. What is the difference between Python and other programming languages concerning the syntax?

2. Why Python is an Object Oriented language?

CHAPTER 10

Building CI/CD Pipeline for a DotNet Application

> "Don't compare yourself to others. Compare yourself to the person from yesterday."
>
> — *Anonymous*

A multinational FMCG organization decides to utilize DotNet-based applications for end users and the technical team suggests utilizing automation in application lifecycle management activities. Management wants to automate manual processes in the application lifecycle management and to increase productivity for frequent deployments. The need for the hour is to implement Continuous Integration and Continuous Delivery. In this chapter, we will cover the CI/CD implementation of DotNet applications with Jenkins. We will use the Pipeline as Code to create a CI/CD pipeline. Blue Ocean provides a simple way to create a pipeline using a simple user interface as well as a code editor to configure the **Continuous Integration (CI)** and **Continuous Delivery (CD)** pipeline for DotNet applications. We will distribute an application to the platform as a service provided by Microsoft Azure and that is Azure App Services. We will also utilize Octopus Deploy for easy deployment into Azure App Services and also direct deployment from the Jenkins pipeline. We will also provide some valuable "notes" related to DevOps, culture, challenges, market trends, and so on for a better understanding.

Structure

In this chapter, we will discuss the following topics:

- Introduction
- Multi-Stage pipeline for a DotNet app
  - o Create Azure App Services – Platform as a Service to host a DotNet web application
  - o Configure Octopus deploy
  - o Continuous Integration
    - Unit test Execution and Code coverage
    - Begin SonarQube analysis
    - Build a DotNet application
    - End Static code analysis using SonarQube
    - Upload build to Artifactory
  - o Continuous Delivery
    - Download build from Artifactory
    - Publish a DotNet application to Azure app service

Objectives

After studying this section, you should be able to:

- Understand how to perform static code analysis for a DotNet application
- Execute unit tests
- Calculate code coverage
- Verify build quality

Introduction

The organization has selected one application as a pilot while the other five early adopter DotNet applications are waiting in the queue. We have the responsibility to create a CI/CD pipeline using Pipeline as Code in Jenkins in the declarative syntax.

The following is the list of tools and deliverables that will be integrated into the pipeline:

Tools	
Version Control	Git
Code Analysis	SonarQube
Unit Tests	MSTest
Code Coverage	OpenCover
Build Script	MSBuild
Continuous Integration	Jenkins
Continuous Delivery	NuGet Package, Octopus Deploy, Azure App Services
Pipeline	Pipeline as Code. Jenkinsfile, Blue Ocean
Expected Deliverables or Features in an Automated pipeline	
<ul><li>Installation and configuration of Jenkins</li><li>Distributed Architecture/Master Agent Architecture (Covered in *Chapter 11: Best Practices*)</li><li>Role-based access (Covered in *Chapter 11: Best Practices*)</li><li>Configuration of a CI/CD pipeline using Pipeline as Code</li><li>Documentation<ul><li>o Documentation of defined processes and implementations</li><li>o Technical documentation – How to guides</li></ul></li><li>Best practices documentation for the usage of Jenkins/Blue Ocean (Covered in *Chapter 11: Best Practices*)</li></ul>	

Table 10.1: *Tools and deliverables*

In the next section, we will create a pipeline for a sample DotNet application using the Blue Ocean interface in a step-by-step manner.

TIP

The freestyle project is very important in Jenkins as it can be used in orchestration with the command execution such as batch or shell commands.

Below is a big picture of CI/CD implementation that we will cover in this chapter.

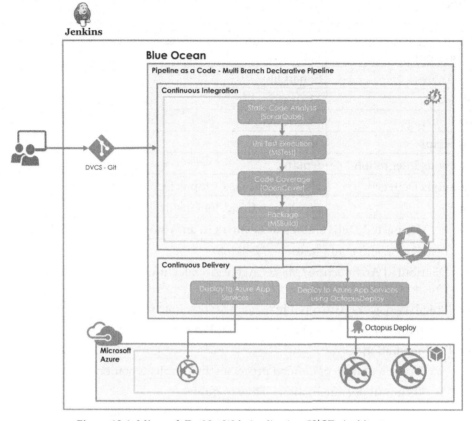

Figure 10.1: *Microsoft DotNet Web Application CI/CD Architecture*

Pre-requisites tools to be installed on the Build server:

- .Net Framework
- Nuget
- MSBuild
- MSTest
- OpenCover
- Sonarqube Scanner for MSBuild (Can be installed from project nugget packages)
- Octopus CLI tool

Let's create a pipeline for a sample DotNet application using Blue Ocean.

We will configure static code analysis using SonarQube, unit test execution using mstest, and code coverage calculation using OpenCover, and report for a sample DotNet application.

Multi-stage pipeline for a DotNet app using Blue Ocean

We will need the following plugins in Jenkins to create a CI/CD pipeline for a sample DotNet application:

- Azure App Service plugin
- Octopus Deploy plugin
- Code Coverage API plugin
- SonarQube Scanner for Jenkins

Create Azure App Service – Platform as a Service to host a DotNet web application

For the configuration of the entire Azure App Service configuration, refer to *Chapter 3: Building a CI/CD pipeline for a Java Web Application*.

The only difference is that was a Java web app and this is a Microsoft DotNet web application. Select the option **ASP .NET V4.7** instead of JAVA in **Runtime stack** when you create Azure App Service while referring to *Chapter 3: Building a CI/CD pipeline for a Java Web Application*.

Figure 10.2: *Azure App Service creation for DotNet Web App*

Add three slots to the app service you create:

1. DEV
2. TEST
3. Production (default)

We will deploy in the following ways:

1. Publish from Jenkins directly to the DEV slot of Azure App Service.

2. Push package to Octopus Deploy and from Octopus Deploy to TEST and the Production slot of Azure App service.

TIP

The pipeline template helps to orchestrate tasks that can be executed on multiple build agents.

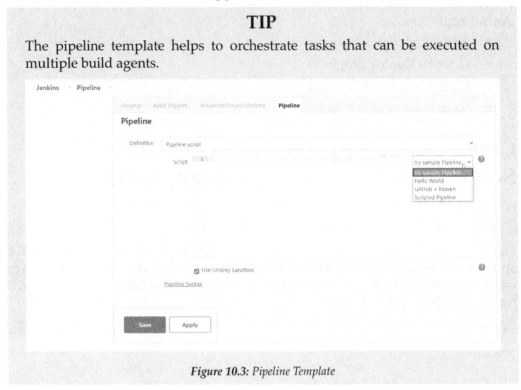

Figure 10.3: Pipeline Template

So, we will now first configure Octopus Deploy in the following steps to add Azure-related setup and to create a project in Octopus Deploy to perform the deployment process.

Configure Octopus Deploy for deployment to Azure App Service

Assuming that Octopus Deploy is installed and ready to use, we will start with the creation of Environments and Project in Octopus Code Deploy. Perform the following steps to create the entire application which can be used to deploy to different slots of Azure App Service. To get more details on Octopus Deploy, refer to https://octopus.com/docs/installation.

Create Environment in Infrastructure (Test and PROD)

This section is related to the creation of an infrastructure setting of the environment in Octopus Deploy. Let's create environment:

1. Go to Octopus `dashboard | Infrastructure` (from the top menu bar) | `Environments` (from the side menu bar):

Figure 10.4: *Create Infrastructure Environment - Octopus*

2. Click on the `Add Environment` button and enter the `New environment name` as shown in the following screenshot:

Figure 10.5: *Create Environment - Octopus*

3. Click on the `Save` button. On successful creation of the environment, you will be navigated to the screen as shown in the following screenshot:

Figure 10.6: *Create Environment - Octopus*

The environment is created successfully and now we need to add deployment targets to this environment.

Add Azure account to Octopus Deploy

Before adding Deployment targets, which are target present in Azure App Service, we first need to add Azure Subscription details by creating an account in Octopus Deploy. This account is the connectivity between Octopus Deploy and Azure services. Follow the given steps to add an account in Octopus Deploy.

> **Refer to** *Chapter 3: Building a CI/CD pipeline with Blue Ocean for a Java Web Application* **for Azure app creation and all the details required related to Azure Subscription.**

1. Navigate to **Octopus Deploy dashboard | Infrastructure** (from top menu bar) | **Accounts** (from the side menu bar):

Figure 10.7: Create an Azure Account - Octopus

2. Click on **Add Account**, and select **Azure Subscription**:

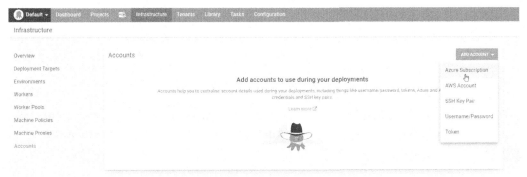

Figure 10.8: Create an Azure Account - Octopus

3. Enter all the required details related to Azure subscription, as shown in the following screenshot.

4. Details required from Azure will be **Subscription ID, Tenant ID, Application ID,** and **Application password**:

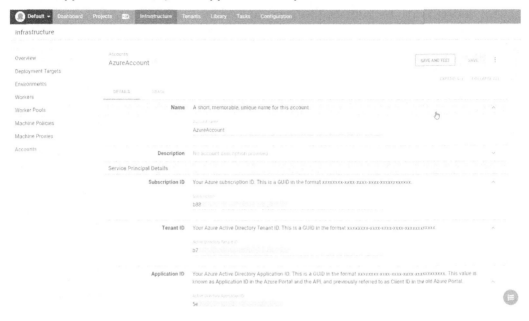

Figure 10.9: Create an Azure Account - Octopus

5. Click on the **Save and Test** button at top right corner of the screen:

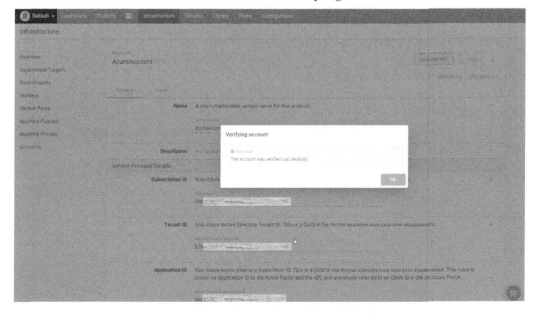

Figure 10.10: Test Azure Account Connection - Octopus

6. Click on **OK and Save** to save the Account details. Once the account is successfully created, you can see the Account in the list of the Azure Subscription account in Octopus code deploy as shown in the following screenshot:

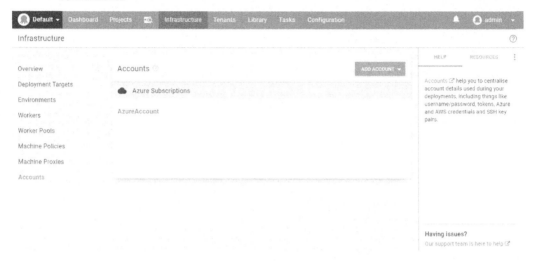

Figure 10.11: Create an Azure Account – Octopus

Now, we can add Deployment targets that are present in this particular Azure account subscription.

Create Deployment targets (Azure App Service) specific to the environment

You can add many deployment targets to a single Environment. We will show only the creation of the deployment target where the target environment is in the Azure App service-specific slot (TEST and Production).

1. Go to the Environment you created, click on the **Add Deployment Target** button to create a new environment:

Figure 10.12: Create a deployment target - Octopus

2. Select Azure as shown in the following screenshot. Once you select **Azure** from the following list, Azure-related options will be displayed as shown in the following screenshot. Select **Azure Web App** and click on the **Add** button to add the deployment target:

Figure 10.13: *Add the deployment target - Octopus*

3. Add the required details such as **Display name**, select the **Environment** you created from the drop-down menu, add **the Target Role** as shown in the following screenshot:

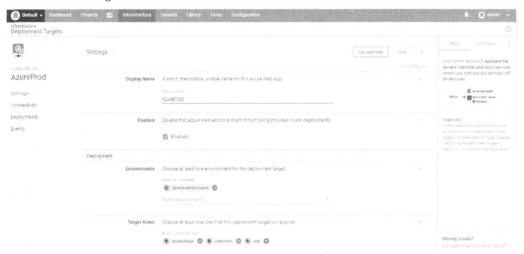

Figure 10.14: *Deployment Target details - Octopus*

4. Then, scroll down and select the **AzureAccount** you added to Octopus from the drop-down list:

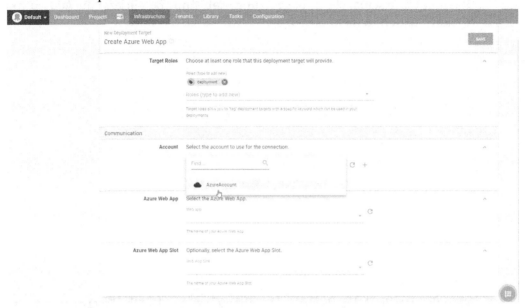

Figure 10.15: Deployment Target Azure Account - Octopus

5. Once you select the **AzureAccount**, a drop-down list will be populated with a list of all the Azure Web Apps. Select the **App** which you want to be the target App:

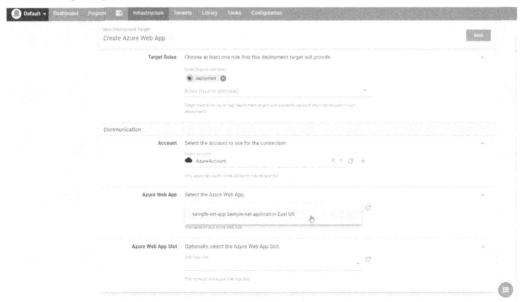

Figure 10.16: Deployment Target Azure Web App - Octopus

6. If you are creating the **Production** target, leave the **Azure Web App Slot** empty, or else select the slot name from the drop-down list as shown in the following screenshot:

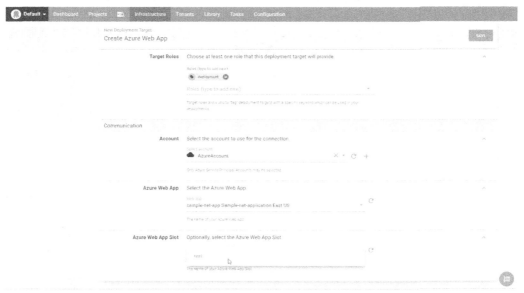

Figure 10.17: Deployment Target Azure Web App Slot - Octopus

7. That's it. We are done with all the details. Click on the **Save** button at the top-right corner of the screen. And when you save and go back to **Targets**, you will find the target you created in the list of **Healthy** targets as shown in the following screenshot:

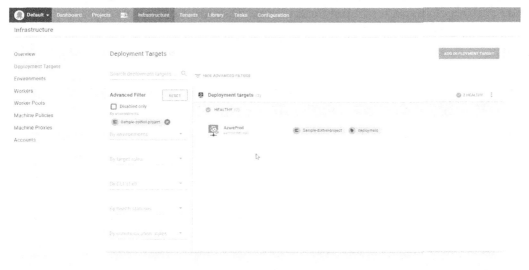

Figure 10.18: Deployment Target Health Checkup - Octopus

TIP

The External Job template helps to record the execution of a process executed outside Jenkins.

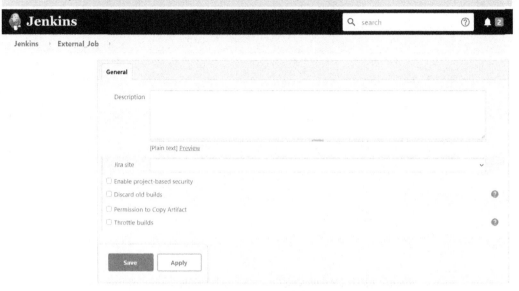

Figure 10.19: External Job template

Now, we have added one target. Add more targets to the different environments for the creation of the entire CI/CD in all the environments, including Test and Prod. We have added two environments for Test and Production, and each environment has one target, respectively pointing to slots Test and Production, as shown in the following screenshot:

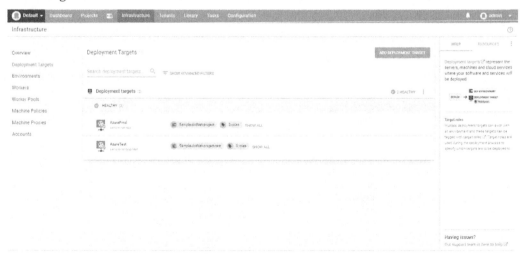

Figure 10.20: List of Deployment targets - Octopus

As we are ready with targets and environments, we can now create a project to deploy to Azure App but before that, we will create a lifecycle.

Create a lifecycle in Octopus Deploy

The Octopus lifecycle is the process in which the deployments to the various environments are ordered in a sequence in which they should be executed. So, we will now create the new lifecycle in Octopus Deploy by performing the following steps:

1. Navigate to **Octopus Deploy dashboard | Library** (from the top menu bar) **| Lifecycle** (from the side menu bar):

Figure 10.21: Create Lifecycle - Octopus

2. Click on the **Add Lifecycle** button. Enter **Lifecycle Name** and other details as shown in the following screenshot:

Figure 10.22: Create lifecycle - Octopus

3. After you enter all the details, **Add Phases** to the lifecycle as shown in the following screenshot:

Figure 10.23: Create lifecycle Phases - Octopus

4. Once the **Phases** for test and prod are added, save the lifecycle. You can preview the entire lifecycle as shown in the following screenshot on the same lifecycle page at the bottom of the screen:

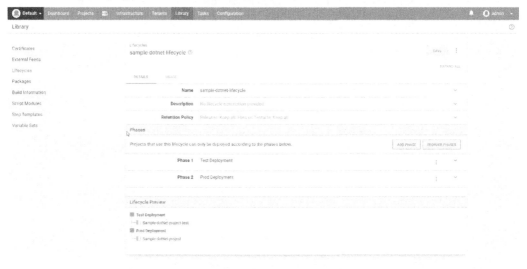

Figure 10.24: Create a lifecycle preview - Octopus

This is how the lifecycle of the project is configured. We can use this lifecycle in the project that we are going to create in the next step.

Create a project in Octopus Deploy

The Octopus Deploy project is nothing but a collection of steps for deployment to different targets. So first let us create a project in Octopus and then we will add steps to the Deployment process. The following are the steps to create a project in Octopus Deploy:

1. Navigate to the **Projects** tabs on the Octopus Deploy. You will be navigated to the following page:

Figure 10.25: Create Project - Octopus

2. Click on the **Add Project** button to create the project. Once you click on the button, you will be directed to the page as shown in the following screenshot. Enter the **Name, Details**, and select the lifecycle you created:

Figure 10.26: Create a project - Octopus

3. Click on the **Save** button. Once the project is saved, you will be navigated to the following page:

Figure 10.27: Create a project - Octopus

Now, in the next step, we will add the steps for deployment to the project in Octopus Deploy which you just created.

Create the Deployment process for Azure App Service in the project

In this section, we will discuss how to configure the deployment process for Azure App Services for deployment:

1. Click on the **Define Your Deployment Process** button on the project page as shown in the following screenshot:

Figure 10.28: Create Deployment process - Octopus

2. Click on the **Add step** button to create steps in the deployment process:

Figure 10.29: Add Step to Deployment Process - Octopus

3. Select **Azure** from the list populated by clicking on the **Add Step** button, as shown in the following screenshot:

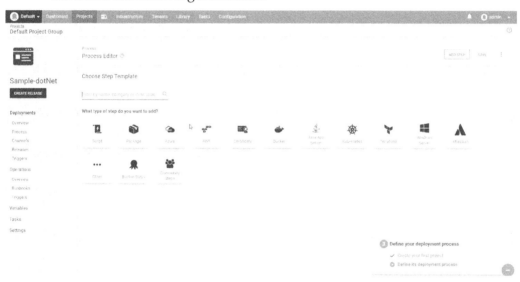

Figure 10.30: Azure Step in Deployment Process - Octopus

4. Then, on the selection of **Azure**, many options get populated on the same screen. Hover on **Deploy an Azure Web App** and click on the **Add** button as shown in the following screenshot:

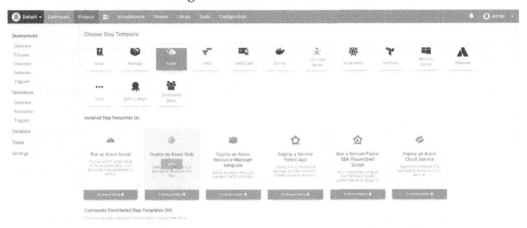

Figure 10.31: Deploy an Azure Web App Step - Octopus

5. Add the details related to steps such as step name, enabled, execution details, and so on:

Figure 10.32: Configure Step for Deployment - Octopus

6. Enter the package name in the package section as shown in the preceding screenshot.

7. Scroll down and enter the details related to **Deployment**:

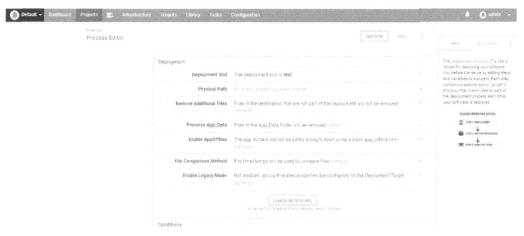

Figure 10.33: *Deployment details in the step of deploy process - Octopus*

8. Scroll more and configure conditions like the environment (I have selected the test environment as the first step and prod in the second step) for which you want to run this step and so on:

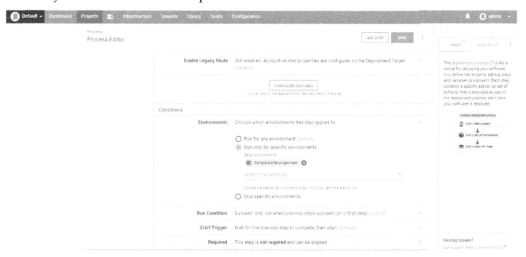

Figure 10.34: *Deployment process conditions - Octopus*

9. Save and add one more step to deploy to a production environment in the condition.

    The project configuration is completed in Octopus and it is now ready to get packages, release and deploy them to the Azure Web App.

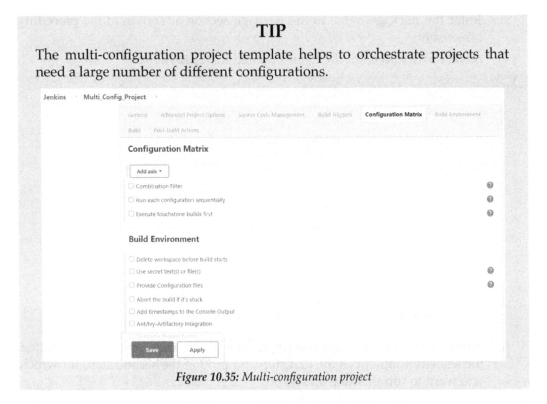

TIP

The multi-configuration project template helps to orchestrate projects that need a large number of different configurations.

Figure 10.35: Multi-configuration project

Integration of Jenkins and Octopus Deploy

Let's connect Octopus Deploy in Jenkins for pushing packages from Jenkins, create a release and trigger Octopus to the Azure web App deployment from Jenkins. For this first, we need to create an API key in Octopus. So, follow the given steps to connect Octopus Deploy to Jenkins.

Install the Jenkins plugin 'Octopus Deploy'.

1. Navigate to **Octopus Deploy dashboard | User** (at the top-right corner of the screen, click on the user where you are logged in) | **Profile**:

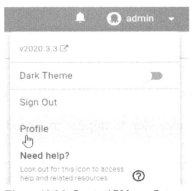

Figure 10.36: Create API key - Octopus

2. On the **Profile** page, go to the **My API keys** option from the left-hand side menu bar as shown in the following screenshot:

Default
Dashboard
Projects
Infrastructure
Tenants
Library
Tasks
Configuration
My Profile
My Profile
CHANGE PASSWORD
SAVE
Display Name
admin
Email Address
[redacted]@outlook.com
You can change your picture at
gravatar.com
My Profile
My Logins
My API Keys
My Recent Activity

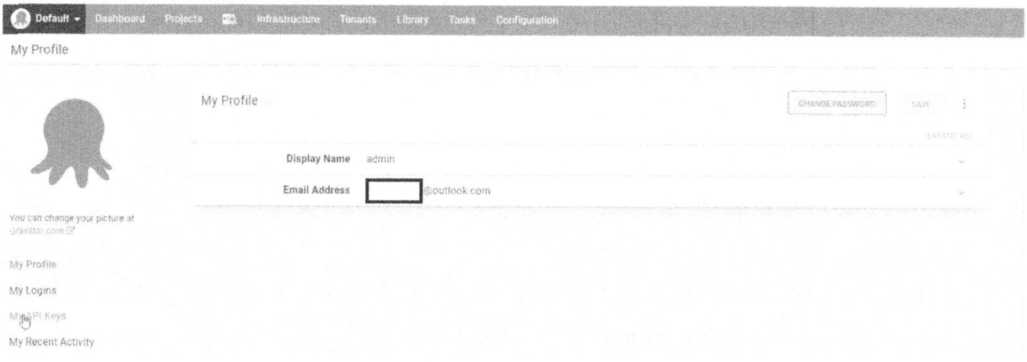

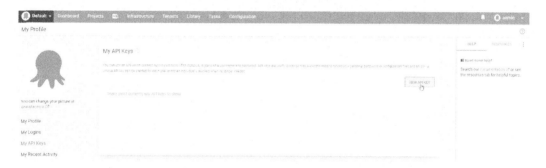

Figure 10.37: Create API keys - Octopus

3. Click on the **New API key** button on the page:

Default
Dashboard
Projects
Infrastructure
Tenants
Library
Tasks
Configuration
admin
My Profile
My API Keys
NEW API KEY
My Profile
My Logins
My API Keys
My Recent Activity

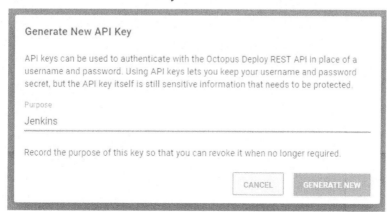

Figure 10.38: Create API keys - Octopus

4. Enter the name for the API key:

Generate New API Key
API keys can be used to authenticate with the Octopus Deploy REST API in place of a username and password. Using API keys lets you keep your username and password secret, but the API key itself is still sensitive information that needs to be protected.
Purpose
Jenkins
Record the purpose of this key so that you can revoke it when no longer required.
CANCEL
GENERATE NEW

Figure 10.39: Create API key - Octopus

5. Copy the API key generated as this is displayed only once:

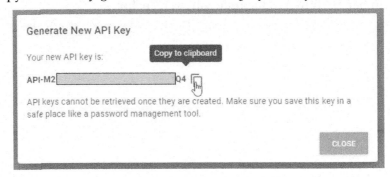

Figure 10.40: Copy API key generated - Octopus

6. Now, let's go and configure Jenkins to connect to Octopus. First, we need an Octopus CLI tool in **Global tool configuration** in the Jenkins setting as shown in the following screenshot:

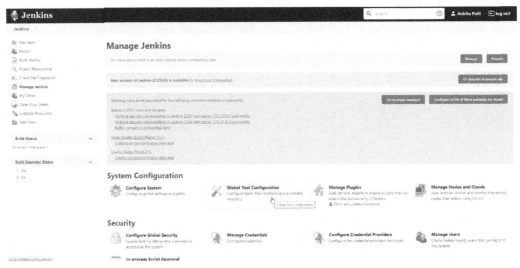

Figure 10.41: Global tool configuration – Octopus

Enter the Name and path to the Octopus CLI tool and click on **Save**:

Figure 10.42: Octopus Deploy CLI tool - Jenkins

7. Now, go to **Jenkins | Manage Jenkins | Configure System** and then search for the Octopus Deploy plugin. Enter the Server Id, URL, and API key which you copied in the configuration.

Figure 10.43: Add details to Octopus Deploy in System configuration - Jenkins

Now, the configuration for the connectivity between Octopus and Jenkins is configured and saved for further usage in the pipeline. By the end of this step, Octopus Deploy is ready for deployment from Jenkins.

Let us now start with the pipeline configuration in Jenkins starting with Continuous Integration.

TIP

The Bitbucket Team/Project scans a Bitbucket Cloud team (or Bitbucket Server Project) for all repositories matching some defined markers.

Figure 10.44: Bitbucket Team/Project

Continuous Integration – DotNet application

In this step, we will see the continuous integration steps required for a DotNet web application.

> **The CI process for the DotNet application is a bit different than other applications. Here, we need to build the application before unit testing and SonarQube analysis. Without getting the .dll file, we cannot test and analyze the application.**

Let us start with the CI step configuration in the Jenkins pipeline.

Restore NuGet packages

This step is required for updating the Nuget dependency packages as per the latest dependencies required to build the DotNet application.

As we already know how to create the pipeline in Jenkins from previous chapters, we will directly move on to add the steps in the pipeline.

Go to the pipeline, add the Stage **CI**, and a new step **windows batch script** as shown in the following screenshot. Paste the following command in the batch script step:

```
nuget restore <project-name>.sln
```

Add the command in the Blue Ocean pipeline editor:

Figure 10.45: *Nuget Restore – Jenkins*

In the next section, we will start the configuration of code analysis.

Begin SonarQube analysis

This step will be just about beginning the SonarQube analysis for analysis with a particular configuration like SonarQube server URL, SonarQube Scanner config, src directory, etc.

Install and configure SonarQube Server in Jenkins | Manage Jenkins | System Configuration | SonarQube Server. Just follow the steps in *Chapter 3: Building a CI/CD pipeline for a Java Web Application* **for configuration of the SonarQube server in Manage Jenkins. Also, do not forget to add SonarQube credentials in the Jenkins credentials. Also, refer to** *Chapter 3: Building a CI/CD pipeline for a Java Web Application* **for these configurations both in SonarQube and Jenkins.**

1. For the SonarQube Scanner for MSBuild, we don't need to install it in Jenkins/ System. This is handled by code. Include the following code in `packages. config` of the project present in the main project folder where the `.csproj` file is present:

```
1.  <package  id="MSBuild.SonarQube.Runner.Tool"  version="4.0.2"
    targetFramework="net45" />
```

2. The next step is to add **Begin Analysis** to the SonarQube CI pipeline. So, for this, add a new step called **Prepare SonarQube Scanner Environment** as shown in the following screenshot. Fill in the details of the SonarQube installation and SonarQube credentials configured in Jenkins.

3. Also, add a child step **Windows Batch Script** using the following command:

```
1.  packages\MSBuild.SonarQube.Runner.Tool.4.0.2\tools\
    SonarQube.Scanner.MSBuild.exe     begin     /k:"Sample-Net-
    Application"
```

4. Refer to the following screenshot for the SonarQube begin analysis config in this step:

Figure 10.46: SonarQube Scanner begin analysis - Jenkins

Now, we need to build the application before executing the 'SonarQube End Analysis' in the next section.

Build a DotNet application

To build any DotNet application, we require a build tool called MSBuild. This build tool should be of the same version as the version compatible with the Application development .Net framework. In this case, we will use the .Net framework 4.7 for a sample .Net web application.

To use the MSBuild command, MSBuild should be added in the PATH of the system of the build server or you can add it by creating an environment variable in Jenkins.

Now, let us add the step to execute the MSBuild command. Add the windows batch script step to the pipeline using the following command:

```
1.  "C:\Program Files (x86)\Microsoft Visual Studio\2017\
    Professional\MSBuild\15.0\Bin\msbuild.exe" <project-name>.sln
```

As shown in the following screenshot, follow the instructions to execute the preceding command:

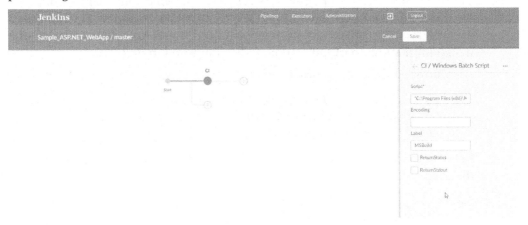

Figure 10.47: MSBuild .Net App script - Jenkins pipeline

Executing this step will compile and build the DotNet project files from the .cs to .dll format which are required to analyze the code and also to execute unit test cases, and run the application. In short, .dll is the build files of the DotNet application.

Unit test execution and code coverage

As we have the .dll file ready, we can directly execute the MSTest to unit test the application. In DotNet, the test result format is not readable or publishable in Jenkins so we will require an additional tool to get the code coverage and test result.

To perform unit testing using MSTest and code coverage using OpenCover, use the following command in the windows batch script step:

```
1.  "C:\Program Files (x86)\Jenkins\workspace\Sample_ASP.NET_
    WebApp_master\packages\OpenCover.4.7.922\tools\OpenCover.
    Console.exe" -target:"C:\Program Files (x86)\Microsoft
    Visual Studio\2017\Professional\Common7\IDE\MSTest.exe"
    -targetargs:"/testcontainer:\"AngularJSFormTests1\bin\Debug\
    AngularJSFormTests1.dll"""
```

Add the preceding command in the pipeline new step as shown in the following screenshot:

Figure 10.48: MSTest and Code Coverage using Open Cover

Now, we get the code coverage in the results.xml file which can be published and the **MSTest** result can be published which is in the .trx file. Let's publish code coverage results using the Publish Coverage plugin in the **Run Arbitrary pipeline script** step as shown in the following screenshot.

The publish code coverage script is as follows:

```
1.  publishCoverage adapters: [opencoverAdapter(mergeToOneReport: true,
    path:  'results.xml')],  sourceFileResolver:  sourceFiles('NEVER_
    STORE')
```

Figure 10.49: Publish Code Coverage - Jenkins pipeline

When the code coverage and unit testing is successfully executed, you will find the code coverage published on the Jenkins dashboard as shown in the following screenshot:

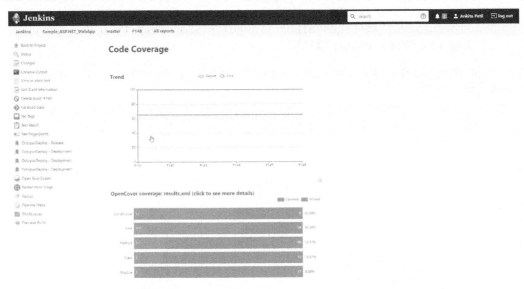

Figure 10.50: Code Coverage Report - Jenkins dashboard

Now, let us publish the Unit Test result by using the Publish MSTest result step, and provide the path to test the result file `.trx` file. Refer to the following screenshot for this configuration:

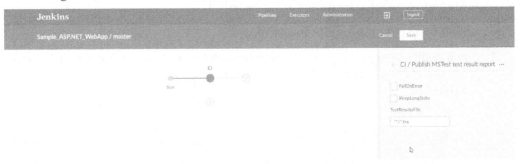

Figure 10.51: Publish MSTest result - Jenkins pipeline

On successfully execution, the test result will be published and the result looks like the following screenshot:

Figure 10.52: MSTest Result - Jenkins dashboard

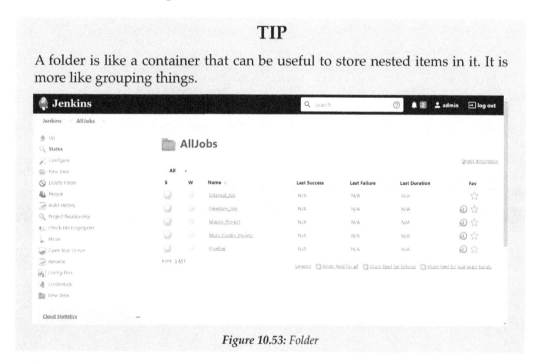

Figure 10.53: Folder

In the next section, we will configure how the static code analysis configuration should be completed.

End static code analysis using SonarQube

Now as we have the compile and build version of the code, we can start with SonarQube Scanner End analysis where the sonar runner starts analyzing the source code, and then uploads the analysis results to the SonarQube server set in the begin Analysis SonarQube Scanner environment.

To perform this end analysis, we need to add a new step **Prepare SonarQube Scanner Environment** to the pipeline, and then add the child step to run the following command for the end analysis:

```
1.  packages\MSBuild.SonarQube.Runner.Tool.4.0.2\tools\SonarQube.
    Scanner.MSBuild.exe end
```

The following screenshot shows the entire step configuration in the Jenkins pipeline:

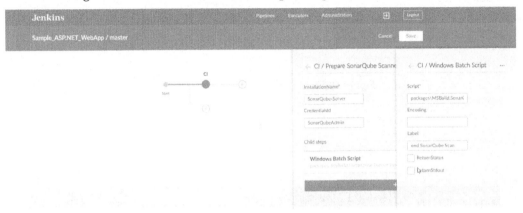

Figure 10.54: SonarQube End analysis - Jenkins pipeline

Once you run the analysis successfully, the result will be published on the SonarQube dashboard as shown in the following screenshot:

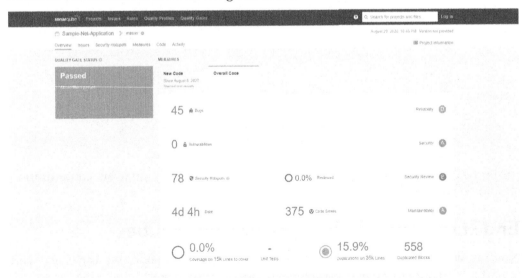

Figure 10.55: SonarQube Dashboard after analysis

Now, as we have checked the Code quality and if the quality gate meets defined criteria, we can proceed for the creation of a publishing directory.

Create Publish Directory

In a DotNet web application, there is a method called **Publish** to create a ready to deploy directory called the Publish **directory** which contains all compiled .dll (bin), content, scripts, views, and some configuration files.

This is the directory that is required if you want to deploy to the IIS server and the Azure Web App directly through the Jenkins pipeline. To create such a publish directory, you need to add the following lines to the .csproj file of the main web application:

```
1.  <Import Project=".."\packages\**\MSBuild.Microsoft.VisualStudio.
    Web.targets" />
2.  <Target Name="PublishToFileSystem"
    DependsOnTargets="PipelinePreDeployCopyAllFilesToOneFolder">
3.    <Error Condition="'$(PublishDestination)'==''" Text="The
    PublishDestination property must be set to the intended
    publishing destination." />
4.    <MakeDir Condition="!Exists($(PublishDestination))"
    Directories="$(PublishDestination)" />
5.    <ItemGroup>
6.      <PublishFiles Include="$(_PackageTempDir)\*\.*" />
7.    </ItemGroup>
8.    <Copy SourceFiles="@(PublishFiles)" DestinationFiles="@
    (PublishFiles->'$(PublishDestination)\%(RecursiveDir)%(Filename)%
    (Extension)')" SkipUnchangedFiles="True" />
9.  </Target>
```

Once this code is added to the .csproj file, we can build the project using **Publish** as an argument to the MSBuild command to create this publish directory so that we can directly deploy it to the Azure Web App. The following is the MSBuild command to publish the DotNet web app:

```
1.  "C:\Program Files (x86)\Microsoft Visual Studio\2017\
    Professional\MSBuild\15.0\Bin\msbuild.exe" "AngularJSForm/
    AngularJSForm. csproj" "/p:Platform=AnyCPU;Configuration=Release;
    PublishDestination =Publish" /t:PublishToFileSystem
```

In Jenkins, add a new step **Windows batch script** and add the preceding command to the step, as shown in the following screenshot:

Figure 10.56: Publish a DotNet Web App using MSBuild

The following screenshot will show the content of the publishing directory created after this step in the workspace:

Name	Date modified	Type	Size
bin	8/29/2020 10:50 PM	File folder	
Content	8/29/2020 10:50 PM	File folder	
ControllersNg	8/29/2020 10:50 PM	File folder	
fonts	8/29/2020 10:50 PM	File folder	
Models	8/29/2020 10:50 PM	File folder	
Scripts	8/29/2020 10:50 PM	File folder	
Views	8/29/2020 10:50 PM	File folder	
Global.asax	8/12/2020 8:30 PM	ASP.NET Server A...	1 KB
libman.json	8/12/2020 8:30 PM	JSON File	1 KB
packages.config	8/20/2020 11:49 PM	XML Configuratio...	2 KB
Web.config	8/29/2020 10:50 PM	XML Configuratio...	6 KB

Figure 10.57: Content of Publish directory

This is how Continuous Integration for a DotNet application can be configured using Jenkins. We will now see the Continuous Delivery in the next section.

TIP

The multi-branch pipeline template creates a set of pipelines based on detected branches having the Jenkinsfile in one repository.

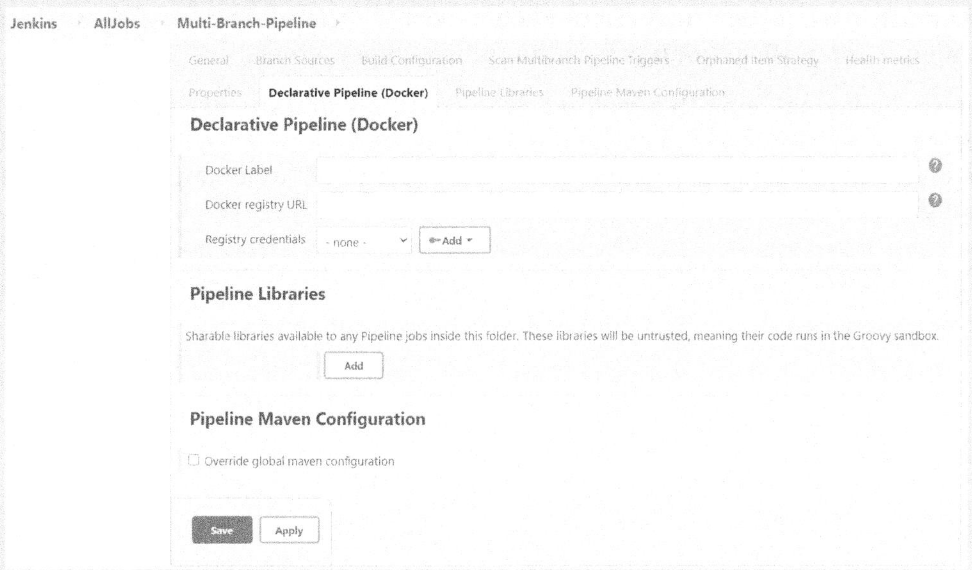

Figure 10.58: Multi-branch pipeline

Continuous Delivery - DotNet application

We will see the CD in two different ways to deploy to the Azure Web App. One using the Jenkins Azure App Service plugin and the second one is deploying through Octopus Deploy to the Azure Web App.

For two different methods, we need two different kinds of deployable as follows:

- Deployment through the Jenkins Azure App Service plugin requires the **Publish** directory which we created in the CI step. We will see this step to just deploy to the Dev target slot of Azure App Service.
- Deployment through Jenkins to Octopus Deploy and then to Azure App service requires the `.nupkg` package which can be created in two ways. One using the NuGet command and the other from the Octopus Deploy Jenkins plugin. Using this method, we will see the deployment to two different target environments (Test, Prod) which we created in Octopus Deploy at the start of this chapter.

Now that we know a brief about the two methods of deployment, let us start the deployment with the first method.

Publish the DotNet application to Azure App Service

This method of deployment will be suitable for applications which have only one or two servers for that particular environment. But if you have more servers, then the best practice would be to use a Deployment tool like Octopus Deploy so that you can configure different environments with multiple target servers.

Before deploying using this method, we need the **Publish directory** ready to deploy, as we have already created it in CI. Then, add a new stage called **CD** and add a step called **Publish an Azure Web App**. Refer to the following screenshot and configure the step:

Figure 10.59: Publish an Azure Web App

Save the step and run. The deployment should be successful in the Dev slot of Azure web application. Refer to the following console log screenshot for the successful deployment to the Azure Web App dev slot:

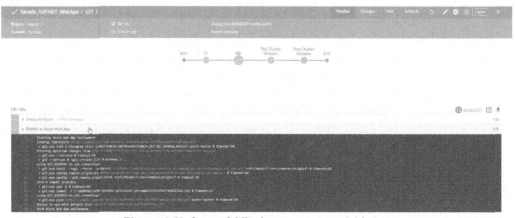

Figure 10.60: Successful Deployment to Azure Web App

In the next section, we will discuss how to deploy the DotNet application in Azure App Services using Octopus Deploy.

Deploy to Azure App Service using Octopus Code Deploy from the Jenkins pipeline

Now, let's start with the deployment of the DotNet App using Octopus Deploy as a deployment tool. As we already know that the deployment through Octopus deploy requires the .nupkg package.

To deploy the DotNet web app to Octopus Deploy, we need to follow the following four steps:

1. Package Application (nuget package in .nupkg format).
2. Push Package to Octopus Deploy.
3. Create Release in Octopus Deploy for the push package.
4. Deploy the Release from Octopus Deploy.

Before we start this pipeline, make sure that the **Octopus Deploy** Jenkins plugin is installed and configured. If this is configured, as shown at the start of this chapter, then we can start from the first step and implement the overall deployment form the Jenkins pipeline.

Package Application (nuget package in .nupkg format)

Add a new stage **Test** and add a new step called **Octopus Deploy: Package Application**. This step will create a .nupkg extension package which is a NuGet package:

Figure 10.61: Octopus Deploy: Package Application

Save the step and this package will be created in the target directory. If you want you can archive this package in Jenkins, but we are going to push this package to Octopus in the next step which acts as the artifacts version management also for the packages which we push to Octopus Deploy.

But to maintain the version, we need to tag the proper package version per build which is done using the `${BUILD_NUMBER` Jenkins build parameter, which will be used in all the steps.

As in this step, the package is ready to deploy, and we will see how to push this to Octopus deploy.

Push Package to Octopus Deploy

Add a new step **Octopus Deploy: Push Package**. Refer to the following screenshot to configure this step:

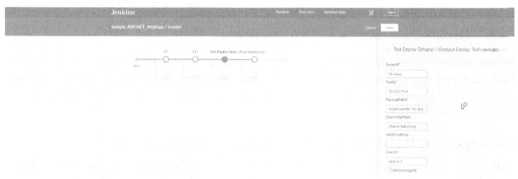

Figure 10.62: *Push Package to Octopus Deploy*

Once this step is configured and run successfully, you will find the package uploaded to Octopus deploy as shown in the following screenshot. To view the package in Octopus, go to **Library | Packages | sample-net-app:**

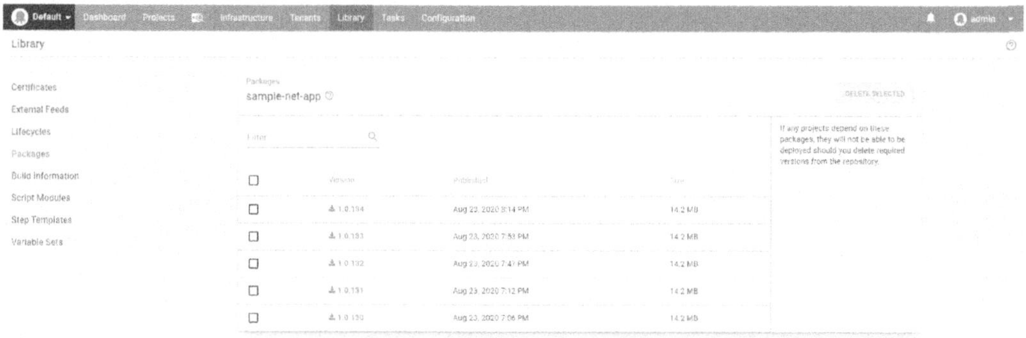

Figure 10.63: *Package library in Octopus Deploy*

This library contains all the versions of the package uploaded. In short, if we use Octopus Deploy, we don't need any artifactory to maintain the version of the application.

Now, once the package is pushed to Octopus, let us now create a release from Jenkins in Octopus Deploy in the following step.

Create Release in Octopus Deploy for the push package

Add a new step **Octopus Deploy: Create release**. Refer to the following screenshot to create a release in Octopus deploy from the Jenkins pipeline:

Figure 10.64: Create release to Octopus deploy

Once the release creation is triggered, you will see the release in the Octopus **deploy projects | Sample-dotNet | Releases**. Now, as a release is created in Octopus Deploy, we will configure the next step to deploy the release to the Azure Web App.

Deploy the release from Octopus Deploy

In the Jenkins pipeline, add a new step called **Octopus Deploy: Deploy Release**. Refer to the following screenshot to configure this step. This deploy step will trigger the deployment of the release to the **Test** target environment. Similarly, we will configure one more stage for production deployment of the same release. But first, refer to the following screenshot to configure the test environment deployment:

Figure 10.65: Deploy release to test environment

Once this deployment is done, the pipeline stage **Test** for deployment looks like the following screenshot:

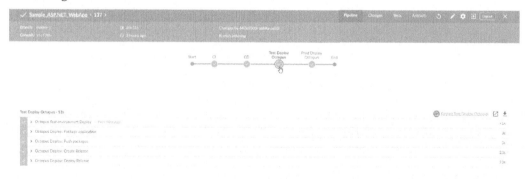

Figure 10.66: Test environment deployment stage

Now, we will configure the PROD deployment stage. Let us start with the promotion stage to get approval for the deployment to PROD once the test environment is tested and ready to deploy the same release to the production environment.

Add a new stage **Prod Deploy Octopus** and add a step **Wait for Interactive Input** as shown in the following screenshot:

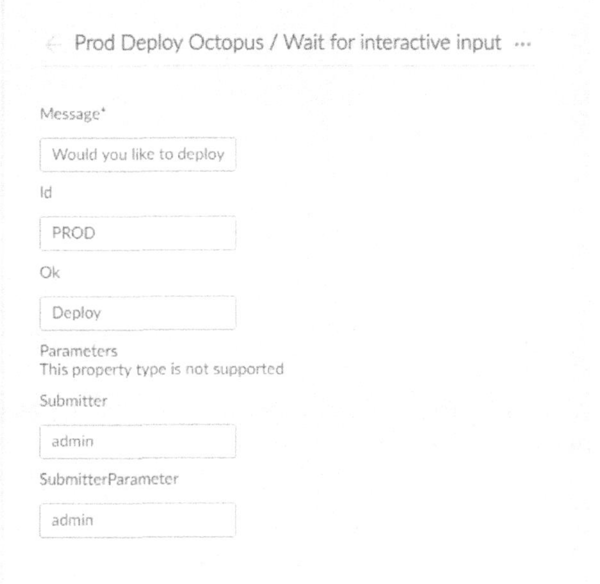

Figure 10.67: *Promotion to PROD stage*

Now, add one more step to deploy to the production target environment; refer to the following screenshot to configure the octopus deploy in a similar way we configured release in the previous stage:

Figure 10.68: *Deploy release to prod*

After this, save the steps and run the pipeline. The following screenshot displays the pipeline promotion step during the pipeline execution:

Figure 10.69: Promotion step for approval to deployment

On successful execution of the Jenkins pipeline, we can see the pipeline view as shown in the following screenshot:

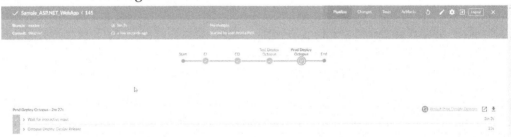

Figure 10.70: Pipeline Success

The final build dashboard in Jenkins should look like the following screenshot:

Figure 10.71: Successful build dashboard in Jenkins

Let us now see the release log and dashboard in Octopus deploy. First, let us see the deployment log in the Octopus deploy release as shown in the following screenshot:

Figure 10.72: Deployment logs in Octopus Deploy release

Successfully deployed release for both environments will look like the following screenshot:

Figure 10.73: Octopus deploy the release

The final deployment to the Azure Web App is successful and the website will be accessible as shown in the following screenshot:

Figure 10.74: *Azure Web App ready to use after deployment*

This is how the Jenkins pipeline can be configured to deploy to the Azure Web App and Octopus deploy. Refer to the following pipeline Jenkinsfile whole source code:

```
1.   pipeline {
2.     agent any
3.     stages {
4.       stage('CI') {
5.         steps {
6.           bat(script: 'nuget restore AngularJS.sln', label: 'Nuget
     Restore')
7.             withSonarQubeEnv(installationName: 'SonarQube-Server',
     credentialsId: 'SonarQubeAdmin') {
8.                 bat(script: 'packages\\MSBuild.SonarQube.Runner.
     Tool.4.0.2\\tools\\SonarQube.Scanner.MSBuild.exe        begin
     /k:"Sample-Net-Application"', label: 'Begin Analysis')
9.             }
10.
11.           bat(script: '"C:\\Program Files (x86)\\Microsoft Visual
     Studio\\2017\\Professional\\MSBuild\\15.0\\Bin\\msbuild.exe"
     AngularJS.sln', label: 'MSBuild')
12.             withSonarQubeEnv(installationName: 'SonarQube-Server',
     credentialsId: 'SonarQubeAdmin') {
13.                 bat(script: 'packages\\MSBuild.SonarQube.Runner.
     Tool.4.0.2\\tools\\SonarQube.Scanner.MSBuild.exe end', label:
     'end SonarQube Scan')
14.             }
15.
16.               bat(script: '"C:\\Program Files (x86)\\Microsoft
```

```
      Visual            Studio\\2017\\Professional\\MSBuild\\15.0\\
      Bin\\msbuild.exe"         "AngularJSForm/AngularJSForm.csproj"
      "/p:Platform=AnyCPU;Configura              tion=Release;Publish
      Destination=Publish" /t:PublishToFileSystem', label: 'MSBuild')
17.             bat(script: '"C:\\Program Files (x86)\\Jenkins\\
      workspace\\Sample_ASP.NET_WebApp_master\\packages\\
      OpenCover.4.7.922\\tools\\OpenCover.Console.exe" -target:"C:\\
      Program   Files   (x86)\\Microsoft  Visual   Studio\\2017\\
      Professional\\Common7\\IDE\\MSTest.exe"             -targetargs:"/
      testcontainer:\\"AngularJSFormTests1\\bin\\Debug\\
      AngularJSFormTests1.dll""', label: 'Code Coverage via MS Test')
18.         mstest(testResultsFile: '**/*.trx')
19.         script {
20.             publishCoverage adapters: [opencoverAdapter(mergeTo
      OneReport:  true,  path:  'results.xml')],  sourceFileResolver:
      sourceFiles('NEVER_STORE')
21.         }
22.
23.          bat(script: 'nuget spec && nuget pack AngularJSForm/
      Angular JSForm.csproj', label: 'Nuget package creation')
24.          archiveArtifacts(artifacts: '**/AngularJSForm*.nupkg',
      onlyIfSuccessful: true, fingerprint: true)
25.       }
26.     }
27.
28.     stage('CD') {
29.       steps {
30.         echo 'Deploy to Azure'
31.         azureWebAppPublish(azureCredentialsId: 'dotNET', appName:
      'sample-net-app',   resourceGroup:   'sample-net-application',
      deployOnlyIfSuccessful: true, slotName: 'dev', sourceDirectory:
      'AngularJSForm\\obj\\Release\\Package\\PackageTmp')
32.       }
33.     }
34.
35.     stage('Test Deploy Octopus') {
36.       steps {
37.         echo 'Octopus Test environment Deploy'
38.          octopusPack(toolId: 'OctoCLITool', packageId: 'sample-
```

```
       net-app', packageFormat: 'nuget', sourcePath: 'AngularJSForm',
       outputPath: 'target', packageVersion: '1.0.${BUILD_NUMBER}')
39.              octopusPushPackage(packagePaths: 'target/sample-
       net-app.1.0.${BUILD_NUMBER}.nupkg',            overwriteMode:
       'OverwriteExisting', serverId: 'Octopus', toolId: 'OctoCLITool',
       spaceId: 'Spaces-1')
40.              octopusCreateRelease(serverId: 'Octopus', toolId:
       'OctoCLITool', project: 'Sample-dotNet', releaseVersion:
       '1.0.${BUILD_NUMBER}', spaceId: 'Spaces-1', environment:
       'Sample-dotNet-project-test', waitForDeployment: true,
       jenkinsUrlLinkback: true, deployThisRelease: true, channel:
       'sample-dotnet-channel')
41.            octopusDeployRelease(toolId: 'OctoCLITool', serverId:
       'Octopus', spaceId: 'Spaces-1', releaseVersion: '1.0.${BUILD_
       NUMBER}', project: 'Sample-dotNet', environment: 'Sample-dotNet-
       project-test', waitForDeployment: true)
42.         }
43.       }
44.
45.     stage('Prod Deploy Octopus') {
46.       steps {
47.         input(message: 'Would you like to deploy to prod?', ok:
       'Deploy', id: 'PROD', submitter: 'admin', submitterParameter:
       'admin')
48.              octopusDeployRelease(serverId: 'Octopus', toolId:
       'OctoCLITool', spaceId: 'Spaces-1', project: 'Sample-dotNet',
       releaseVersion: '1.0.${BUILD_NUMBER}', environment: 'Sample-
       dotNet-project', waitForDeployment: true)
49.         }
50.       }
51.
52.     }
53.  }
```

Finally, we have successfully configured the Jenkins pipeline for the DotNet web application.

Conclusion

In this chapter, we configured the Octopus Deploy tool for deployment to the Azure Web App. We configured different web application target environments, different targets, projects and lifecycles in Octopus deploy.

Then, we configured the Jenkins CI for DotNet web applications using tools such as MSBuild, MSTest, SonarQube scanner, and OpenCover. We also configured the deploy stage for the Dev slot using the Jenkins Azure App Service plugin.

Finally, we configured deployment to the Azure Web App from Jenkins through Octopus Deploy. In the next chapter, we will discuss the best practices to manage Jenkins and pipelines.

Multiple choice questions

1. **Which tool have we used to calculate code coverage in this chapter?**

    a. SonarQube

    b. Jacoco

    c. OpenCover

2. **The Code Coverage tab provides the following details:**

    a. Covered Lines

    b. Uncovered Lines

    c. Line Coverage

    d. All of these

Answer

1. d

2. c

Questions

1. What is the difference between Azure App Services and Octopus Deploy?

2. How is static code analysis different in DotNet in comparison to other programming languages?

CHAPTER 11

Best Practices

> "If you always do what you've always done, you'll always be where you've always been."
>
> — *T.D. Jakes*

Jenkins is an open-source automation server that is written in Java. Jenkins has evolved a lot based on the evolution of technology and from a user experience perspective.

In this book, our main objective is to create Continuous Integration and Continuous Delivery pipelines using the Pipeline as Code. We created the CI/CD pipeline for programming languages such as Java, Android, iOS, Angular, NodeJS, Python, Ionic Cordova, Flutter, and DotNet. It is important to keep various reports such as Static Code Analysis, Unit tests execution results, and Code coverage in a similar format, irrespective of the programming language to bring uniformity on the table. We have tried to focus on the aspect of uniformity and ease of use across the chapters.

The following are some of the areas were Jenkins had evolved over the years with time:

1. Jenkins installation in the Docker Container
2. Jenkins in Azure Kubernetes Services
3. Scaling – Controller Agent architecture or Distributed builds

4. Dockerfile as Jenkins Agent

5. Security [(Authentication - Jenkins own Database, OpenLDAP, Azure Active Directory, Enterprise Directory), (Authorization - Project-based security, Matrix-based security, Access Control)]

6. Backup (Full backup, Incremental backup), Tools configuration

7. Environment variable configuration

8. Cloud configurations

In all such areas, Jenkins has improved not only its technical features but also its user experience or UI too. After Jenkins 2.0 release in 2016, the game has changed. Jenkins has become a popular choice for the DevOps community as an Automation server and not only a Continuous Integration server.

Over the years a lot of best practices have been documented and we will discuss some best practices in this chapter based on our experience.

Structure

In this chapter, we will discuss the following topics:

- Best practices
    - o Jenkins installation using Docker and Azure Kubernetes Services
    - o Controller Agent Architecture
        - ▪ Load balancing
    - o Dockerfile as Jenkins Agent
    - o Security
    - o Backup and Restore
    - o Monitoring
    - o Configuration

Objectives

After studying this unit, you should be able to configure and utilize Jenkins in an effective manner.

Best practices

In this chapter, we will discuss Jenkins best practices that make the life of a Jenkins engineer easier than usual.

This section describes Jenkins best practices to get a feel of what Jenkins can contribute throughout the Application Lifecycle Management activities. We will discuss best practices related to installation, distributed architecture, security, monitoring, backup and restore, and pipelines.

Easy installation with fault tolerance

Let's see how to install Jenkins using Docker and Kubernetes to get it quickly up and running.

Install Jenkins using Docker

How to install Jenkins using Docker containers and Blue Ocean? Let's install Jenkins using Docker container.

1. Use the following Docker image available at DockerHub: **https://hub.docker.com/r/jenkinsci/blueocean/**

2. Docker `pull` command: `docker pull jenkinsci/blueocean`

3. Execute the following command to create a container:

```
1.  sudo docker run -p 8080:8080 -p 50001:50001 -v /home/mitesh/
    Desktop/jenkins_home:/home/mitesh/jenkins_home  jenkinsci/
    blueocean
```

4. The admin password is available in the log. Open a browser on **http://localhost:8080**. Complete the initial setup wizard and visit **http://localhost:8080/blue**.

   Visit **https://www.jenkins.io/doc/book/installing/** for more details.

Install Jenkins on Azure Kubernetes Services (AKS)

We need to install the Azure CLI to perform this task. To get details on how to install the Azure CLI, refer to *Chapter 6: Building a CI/CD pipeline with Blue Ocean for an Angular Application (Section: Deploy Angular App to Azure Kubernetes)* Services (AKS). Once the Azure CLI is installed, follow the given steps:

1. We can execute the Azure CLI with the `az` command. Use the `az login` command to sign in. A successful login will open a browser window with a message in the Agent.

2. Create Resource Group in Azure Cloud using `az group create -l westus -n aks-jenkins`.

3. We can create the Azure Container Registry using the `az acr create -n sampleImages -g aks-jenkins --sku` basic command.

4. Verify the creation of the Container Registry using the `az acr list` command.

5. Before we push an image to the Container Registry, we must tag it with the fully qualified name of the ACR login server. The login server name is in the format `<registry-name>.azurecr.io` (all lowercase), for example, `sampleimages.azurecr.io` using `docker tag jenkinsci/blueocean sampleimages.azurecr.io/blueocean:v1` command.

6. Verify with the `docker images` command:

```
REPOSITORY                    TAG       IMAGE ID       CREATED         SIZE

jenkinsci/blueocean    latest       c4239db11ad3   34 hours ago      62MB

sampleimages.azurecr.io/blueocean      v1        c4239db11ad3   34
hours ago     562MB
```

7. Push the image to ACR using the `docker push sampleimages.azurecr.io/blueocean` command.

8. Verify ACR using the `az acr repository list --name sampleImages --output table` command:

```
Result

---------

Blueocean
```

9. The Docker image is available in ACR. The next task is to perform the Azure Kubernetes Services operation from the agent. Install the AKS CLI using the `az aks install-cli` command.

10. Create the Kubernetes cluster using the `az aks create` command: `az aks create -g aks-jenkins -n JenkinsCluster --generate-ssh-keys --attach-acr sampleimages`

11. Use `--generate-ssh-keys` to generate SSH key files '/home/mitesh/.ssh/id_rsa' and '/home/mitesh/.ssh/id_rsa.pub' under `~/.ssh` to allow SSH access to the VM.

12. Use `az aks get-credentials` to get access credentials for a managed Kubernetes cluster (Azure Kubernetes Services). Once the context is merged in the current context, we can operate `kubectl` commands directly from the terminal and get details on the AKS cluster:

```
az aks get-credentials --resource-group aks-jenkins --name
JenkinsCluster
```

13. The following is the YAML that we have used to deploy the Docker Image stored in ACR to AKS. We have used Deployment and Service "kind" for this deployment:

```
1.   apiVersion: apps/v1
2.   kind: Deployment
3.   metadata:
4.    name: blueocean-deployment
5.    labels:
6.       app: myapp
7.       type: front-end
8.   spec:
9.    template:
10.      metadata:
11.       name: blueocean-pod
12.       labels:
13.          app: blueocean
14.      spec:
15.       containers:
16.         - name: blueocean
17.           image: sampleimages.azurecr.io/blueocean:v1
18.           ports:
19.           - containerPort: 8080
20.           volumeMounts:
21.           - name: jenkins-home
22.             mountPath: /var/jenkins_home
23.       volumes:
24.         - name: jenkins-home
25.           emptyDir: {}
26.    replicas: 1
27.
28.    selector:
29.      matchLabels:
30.          app: blueocean
31.    ---
32.   apiVersion: v1
33.   kind: Service
34.   metadata:
35.    name: blueocean-service
36.    labels:
```

```
37.        app: blueocean
38.        type: front-end
39.  spec:
40.    selector:
41.        app: blueocean
42.    ports:
43.      - protocol: TCP
44.        port: 8080
45.        targetPort: 8080
46.    type: LoadBalancer
```

14. Execute **kubectl apply -f angular-deployment.yaml**.

15. The kubectl apply command is used to manage applications with the use of files. These files define Kubernetes resources. It helps to create and update resources in a Kubernetes cluster by running kubectl apply. This is one of the most used ways of managing Kubernetes applications in a production environment.

16. We have already merged the context so let's execute kubectl get services to get details on **Services** available in the cluster. In the preceding YAML, one deployment and one service are available:

```
1.  [root@localhost Desktop]# kubectl get nodes -o wide
2.  NAME                            STATUS  ROLES   AGE    VERSION
    INTERNAL-IP    EXTERNAL-IP    OS-IMAGE             KERNEL-
    VERSION        CONTAINER-RUNTIME
3.  aks-nodepool1-21399502-vmss000000    Ready    agent    17m
    v1.15.11    10.240.0.4    <none>       Ubuntu 16.04.6 LTS
    4.15.0-1089-azure    docker://3.0.10+azure
4.  aks-nodepool1-21399502-vmss000001    Ready    agent    17m
    v1.15.11    10.240.0.5    <none>       Ubuntu 16.04.6 LTS
    4.15.0-1089-azure    docker://3.0.10+azure
5.  aks-nodepool1-21399502-vmss000002    Ready    agent    17m
    v1.15.11    10.240.0.6    <none>       Ubuntu 16.04.6 LTS
    4.15.0-1089-azure    docker://3.0.10+azure
```

17. To get details on pods, execute the kubectl get pods command:

```
1.  [root@localhost Desktop]# kubectl get pods
2.  NAME                                    READY    STATUS
    RESTARTS    AGE
3.  blueocean-deployment-5bf949dc79-v9trt    1/1      Running    0
    4m49s
```

We need an admin password and to get that, execute `kubectl logs blueocean-deployment-5bf949dc79-v9trt`.

18. Configure Jenkins using the external IP address of Service. To get the external IP, use the `kubectl` get services command. Use the port number given in the deployment YAML.

19. Observe the `volumeMounts` block in YAML and explore other options for that block. Some useful resources for further exploration are as follows:

   • Persistent Volumes: **https://kubernetes.io/docs/concepts/storage/persistent-volumes/**

   • Jenkins on Kubernetes Engine: **https://cloud.google.com/solutions/jenkins-on-kubernetes-engine**

   • How to configure a manually provisioned Azure Managed Disk to use as a Kubernetes persistent volume? **https://stackoverflow.com/questions/48774021/how-to-configure-a-manually-provisioned-azure-managed-disk-to-use-as-a-kubernete**

   • Exploring Jenkins on Kubernetes with Azure Storage **https://www.cloudbees.com/blog/exploring-jenkins-kubernetes-azure-storage**

Done!

Controller Agent Architecture

Initially, a single Jenkins server can serve to build jobs but over time, application components increase, applications change, new projects come, and the scenario changes within a year. Jenkins is almost out of resources if all the projects and all the components are managed on a single server. It is bound to go down in such a situation.

The Controller-Agent architecture or Distributed architecture comes to the rescue in such a situation. Agents can be physical systems, virtual machines, Docker containers, cloud-based virtual machines such as Amazon EC2, Azure Virtual machines, and so on.

Jenkins Controller	Jenkins Agent
System on which Jenkins is installed.	A remote executable file in the form of a JNLP file is used to connect to the Jenkins Controller. No need to install Jenkins on the Agent.
Handles HTTP requests and manage the built environment.	Actual execution is delegated to Agents.
Delegates build Job or schedule it on the available agents.	Serves Jenkins build/pipeline execution request.

`JENKINS_HOME` contains all the data related to Jobs/Pipelines.	The remote root directory contains all the execution and other artifacts.
A more powerful yet important component.	Provides an execution environment so that the Jenkins Controller is not overloaded.
Can be in the form of a physical or virtual machine or container.	Can be in the form of a physical or virtual machine or container.
One controller can manage multiple agents. It can monitor the status of Agents and act accordingly.	Multiple agents can serve to the controller and hence, parallel execution is possible in the pipeline as multiple executors are also available.
The Jenkins controller can execute build on its own.	Multiple environments with different configurations can be made available to execute build requests.

Table 11.1: *Jenkins Controller vs. Jenkins Agent*

Let's check if the Agent can access the controller and vice versa with the ping command and IP address:

1. Go to Virtual box VM and ping the IP address of the system where Jenkins is installed:

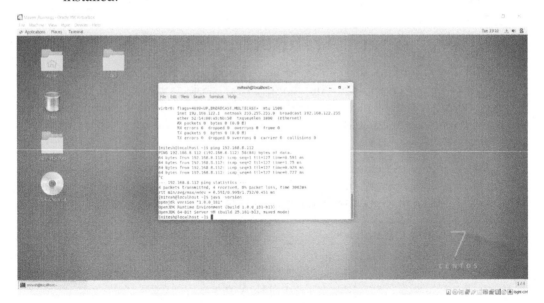

Figure 11.1: *Virtual machine as Jenkins Agent*

2. Go to **Manage Jenkins | Manage Nodes** and click on the **New Node**:

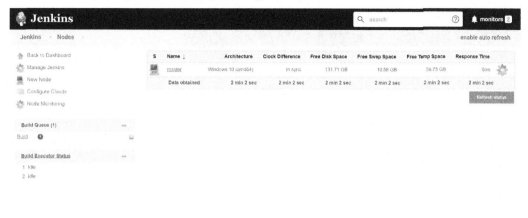

Figure 11.2: *Nodes in Jenkins*

3. Provide **Node name** and click on **OK**:

Figure 11.3: *New Node*

4. Configure `/home/mitesh/Desktop/JenkinsAgent` as the Remote root directory:

Figure 11.4: Node Configuration

5. An agent is not connected. Let's try to connect the Maven agent. Change the Jenkins URL if it is using the localhost. Use the IP address so Jenkins can be accessed outside the system where it is installed:

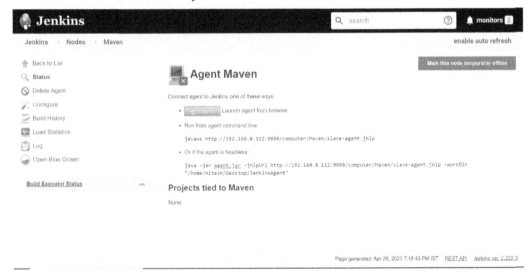

Figure 11.5: Disconnected Agent

6. Go to Virtualbox VM. Open the Jenkins URL and open Nodes. Click on `agent.jar` and download it in the local system. Similarly, execute `jnlpUrl` in the browser and it will ask you to save `slave-agent.jnlp`.

7. Keep both the files in the same folder. For example, Downloads.

8. Execute the following command: javaws **http://192.168.8.112:9999/computer/ Maven/slave-agent.jnlp**

Figure 11.6: Connect Agent with the controller using the command line

9. Verify if the Agent is connected on the Jenkins Dashboard:

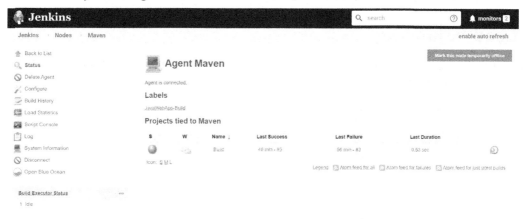

Figure 11.7: Connected Agent

10. Execute the job and verify the console output. Note the IP address and Java version:

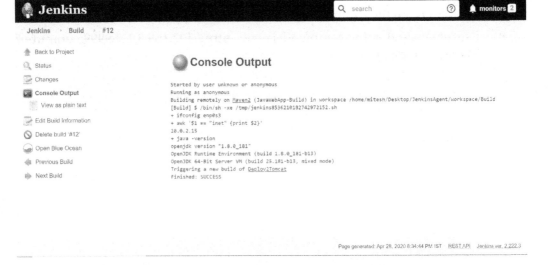

Figure 11.8: Build Execution on a specific Agent

This is how an agent can be connected and jobs can be delegated to agents for execution so the load on the controller is not much, and you don't need to set up the entire environment on the Jenkins controller.

NOTE

The happy team performs better. Appreciate team members and celebrate success to motivate teams.

Load balancing

Labels in Agent configuration helps to balance load or make agents available for execution. It is kind of a pool of agents available for service:

1. Provide the same label while configuring the Jenkins agent. Let's assume we want to have two VMS for the Java build execution. Make them Jenkins agents as we did in the earlier section and provide the same label to each one of them:

Figure 11.9: *Labels in Agent Configuration*

2. Click on the label link available on the Agent page and we can see how many agents have the same label attached to it:

Figure 11.10: *Nodes with the same Label*

3. While configuring any **Build Job or Pipeline,** provide **Label** as an
    agent and not the name:

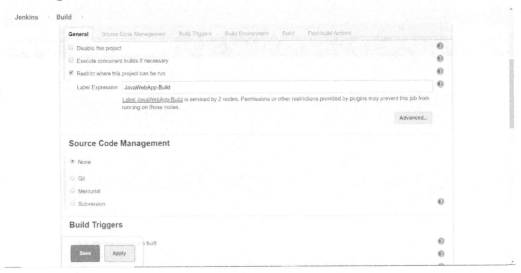

Figure 11.11: Label Name as Label Expression

4. Execute the build and verify the output. Note the IP address and agent
    (Maven2) in this case which executed the build:

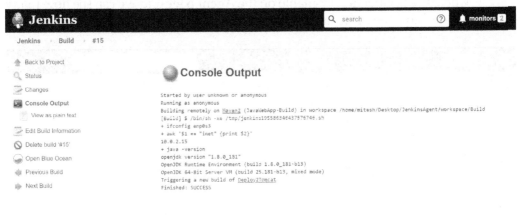

Figure 11.12: Build execution on Labeled node

5. To check whether both the agents are available for execution or not, make the agent offline. Hence, only one agent will be active to serve the build execution request:

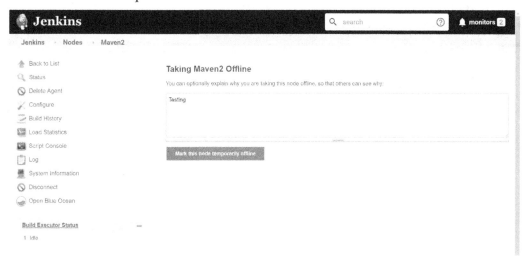

Figure 11.13: Make Agent offline

6. The **Maven2** agent on which the earlier job was executed is disconnected and not available for use:

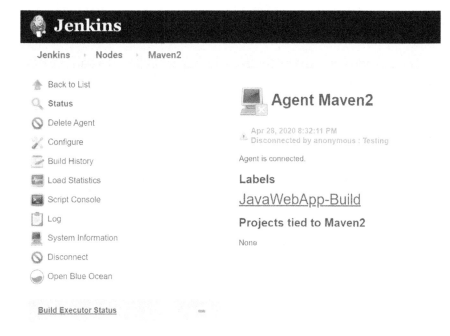

Figure 11.14: Disconnected Agent

7. Execute the build again. Now, verify the console output and you will find that the IP address is different from an agent that was having the same label that executed the build request as it was available to serve the build execution request:

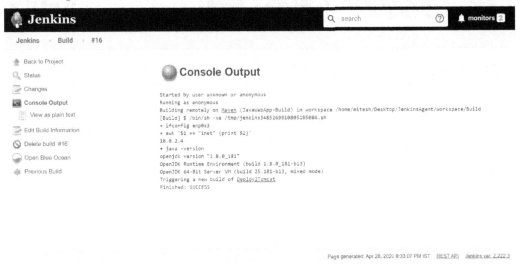

Figure 11.15: Build execution on another node

NOTE

Tools are enablers. Tools are important but culture is a critical factor in the DevOps transformation exercise.

In the next section, we will discuss the security aspect in Jenkins and see how we can make Jenkins safer to use.

Dockerfile agent in the declarative pipeline

Dockerfile agents can help to easily test and build the project and save resources. The following is a content of a Dockerfile that exists in our code:

```
1.   // download the code from the repository
2.   FROM alpine/git as clone
3.   WORKDIR /app
4.   RUN git clone <GIT_REPO_URL>
5.
6.   // Use maven image to copy the directory of application code from
     above
7.   FROM maven:3.6.3-jdk-8 as build
8.   WORKDIR /app
9.   COPY --from=clone /app/sample-java-app/app
```

The Jenkinsfile contains details about the agent and in this case, it is a dockerfile:

```
1.   pipeline {
2.       agent {
3.                       dockerfile true
4.       }
5.       stages {
6.           stage('Build') {
7.               steps {
8.                               // Execute Batch script if OS
     flavor is Windows
9.                             sh 'mvn clean package'
10.                            // Publish JUnit Report
11.                            junit '**/target/surefire-reports/
     TEST-*.xml'
12.                            archiveArtifacts(artifacts:
     'target/**/*.war', onlyIfSuccessful: true, fingerprint: true)
13.               }
14.           }
15.       }
16.  }
```

Let's observe some important logs from the Jenkins Console:

```
1.   Obtained Jenkinsfile from dfe1102804f5b906ba5b4b49cb966f10e960c1ab
2.   Running in Durability level: MAX_SURVIVABILITY
3.   [Pipeline] Start of Pipeline
4.   [Pipeline] node
5.   Running on Jenkins in /var/jenkins_home/workspace/java-sample-
     web_docker
6.   [Pipeline] {
7.   [Pipeline] stage
8.   [Pipeline] { (Declarative: Checkout SCM)
9.   [Pipeline] checkout
10.  using credential 06cddaf1-532c-4d90-a204-0dccfd54aba3
11.  Cloning the remote Git repository
12.  Cloning with configured refspecs honoured and without tags
13.  Cloning repository xxxxxxxxxxxxxxxxxxxxxxxxxxxxxxxxxxxx.git
14.   > git init /var/jenkins_home/workspace/java-sample-web_docker
```

```
      # timeout=10
15.   Fetching upstream changes from xxxxxxxxxxxxxxxxxxxxxxxxxxxxxxx.git
16.    > git --version # timeout=10
17.   using GIT_ASKPASS to set credentials
18.      >    git    fetch   --no-tags   --force  --progress   --
      xxxxxxxxxxxxxxxxxxxxxxxxxxxxxxx.git   +refs/heads/*:refs/remotes/
      origin/* # timeout=10
19.    > git config remote.origin.url xxxxxxxxxxxxxxxxxxxxxxxxxxxxxxx.git
      # timeout=10
20.    > git config --add remote.origin.fetch +refs/heads/*:refs/
      remotes/origin/* # timeout=10
21.    > git config remote.origin.url xxxxxxxxxxxxxxxxxxxxxxxxxxxxxxx.git
      # timeout=10
22.   Fetching without tags
23.   Fetching upstream changes from xxxxxxxxxxxxxxxxxxxxxxxxxxxxxxx.git
24.   using GIT_ASKPASS to set credentials
25.      >    git    fetch   --no-tags   --force  --progress   --
      xxxxxxxxxxxxxxxxxxxxxxxxxxxxxxx.git   +refs/heads/*:refs/remotes/
      origin/* # timeout=10
26.   Checking out Revision dfe1102804f5b906ba5b4b49cb966f10e960c1ab
      (docker)
27.    > git config core.sparsecheckout # timeout=10
28.    > git checkout -f dfe1102804f5b906ba5b4b49cb966f10e960c1ab #
      timeout=10
29.   Commit message: "Update Jenkinsfile"
30.   First time build. Skipping changelog.
31.    > git --version # timeout=10
32.   [Pipeline] }
33.   [Pipeline] // stage
34.   [Pipeline] withEnv
35.   [Pipeline] {
36.   [Pipeline] stage
37.   [Pipeline] { (Declarative: Agent Setup)
38.   [Pipeline] isUnix
39.   [Pipeline] readFile
40.   [Pipeline] sh
41.   + docker build -t 5dd3ddc4a1806600b5fc1cd2387e0eedff92b008 -f
      Dockerfile .
```

```
42.  Sending build context to Docker daemon  13.76MB
43.
44.  Step 1/6 : FROM alpine/git as clone
45.   ---> f54f496311fb
46.  Step 2/6 : WORKDIR /app
47.   ---> Running in c8ba2ced5cc0
48.  Removing intermediate container c8ba2ced5cc0
49.   ---> 921a0675126a
50.  Step 3/6 : RUN git clone xxxxxxxxxxxxxxxxxxxxxxxxxxxxxx.git
51.   ---> Running in e50c08d6a710
52.   [91mCloning into 'sample-java-app'...
53.   [0mRemoving intermediate container e50c08d6a710
54.   ---> 7cb7be0c3d5f
55.  Step 4/6 : FROM maven:3.6.3-jdk-8 as build
56.   ---> 97495355e4f9
57.  Step 5/6 : WORKDIR /app
58.   ---> Using cache
59.   ---> 18c34e2d0e6d
60.  Step 6/6 : COPY --from=clone /app/sample-java-app/app
61.   ---> 41edde9ae237
62.  Successfully built 41edde9ae237
63.  Successfully                                    tagged
     5dd3ddc4a1806600b5fc1cd2387e0eedff92b008:latest
64.  [Pipeline] }
65.  [Pipeline] // stage
66.  [Pipeline] isUnix
67.  [Pipeline] sh
68.  + docker inspect -f . 5dd3ddc4a1806600b5fc1cd2387e0eedff92b008
69.  .
70.  [Pipeline] withDockerContainer
71.  Jenkins      seems      to      be      running      inside
     container                    96770dd957b2e5ed4afb00a4886
     9ec33764965f29960bcf214269be26584e389
72.
73.  [Pipeline] {
74.  [Pipeline] stage
```

```
75.  [Pipeline] { (Build)

76.  [Pipeline] sh

77.  + mvn clean package

78.  [INFO] Scanning for projects...

79.  Downloading from central: https://repo.maven.apache.org/maven2/
     io/spring/platform/platform-bom/2.0.3.RELEASE/platform-bom-
     2.0.3.RELEASE.pom

80.  Progress (1): 2.7/40 kB

81.  Progress (1): 5.5/40 kB

82.

83.  Progress (1): 74/79 kB

84.  Progress (1): 78/79 kB

85.  Progress (1): 79 kB

86.

87.  Downloaded   from   central:   https://repo.maven.apache.org/
     maven2/org/apache/maven/surefire/surefire-junit4/2.13/surefire-
     junit4-2.13.jar (79 kB at 122 kB/s)

88.

89.  ---------------------------------------------------------

90.   T E S T S

91.  ---------------------------------------------------------

92.  Running     org.springframework.samples.sample-java-app.model.
     ValidatorTests

93.  INFO  Version - HV000001: Hibernate Validator 5.2.4.Final

94.  Tests run: 1, Failures: 0, Errors: 0, Skipped: 0, Time elapsed:
     5.103 sec

95.

96.  INFO    EhCacheManagerFactoryBean  -  Shutting  down  EhCache
     CacheManager

97.  INFO    LocalContainerEntityManagerFactoryBean  -  Closing  JPA
     EntityManagerFactory for persistence unit 'sample-java-app'

98.

99.  Results :

100.

101. Tests run: 59, Failures: 0, Errors: 0, Skipped: 0

102.

103. [INFO]

104. [INFO] --- maven-war-plugin:2.3:war (default-war) @ sample-java-
     app ---
```

```
105.
106.  [INFO] Packaging webapp
107.  [INFO] Assembling webapp [sample-java-app] in [/var/jenkins_
      home/workspace/java-sample-web_docker/target/sample-java-app-
      4.2.5-SNAPSHOT]
108.  [INFO] Processing war project
109.  [INFO] Copying webapp resources [/var/jenkins_home/workspace/
      java-sample-web_docker/src/main/webapp]
110.  [INFO] Webapp assembled in [3014 msecs]
111.  [INFO] Building war: /var/jenkins_home/workspace/java-sample-
      web_docker/target/sample-java-app.war
112.  [INFO] ------------------------------------------------------------
      ----------
113.  [INFO] BUILD SUCCESS
114.  [INFO] ------------------------------------------------------------
      ----------
115.  [INFO] Total time:  08:48 min
116.  [INFO] Finished at: 2020-07-07T06:48:30Z
117.  [INFO] ------------------------------------------------------------
      ----------
118.  [Pipeline] junit
119.  Recording test results
120.  [Pipeline] archiveArtifacts
121.  Archiving artifacts
122.  Recording fingerprints
123.  [Pipeline] }
124.  [Pipeline] // stage
125.  [Pipeline] }
126.  $  docker  stop  --time=1  82184fd356a0aa403d6c1ad3cb8f8b651
      797624a354230f7ee87b743e38fde2a
127.  $  docker  rm  -f  82184fd356a0aa403d6c1ad3cb8f8b651797624a
      354230f7ee87b743e38fde2a
128.  [Pipeline] // withDockerContainer
129.  [Pipeline] }
130.  [Pipeline] // withEnv
131.  [Pipeline] }
132.  [Pipeline] // node
133.  [Pipeline] End of Pipeline
134.  Finished: SUCCESS
```

TIP

Create an image to run as an agent that has JDK and Maven installed in it from scratch:

```
1.   FROM openjdk:8-jdk-alpine
2.   LABEL Mitesh Soni <XXXXXXXXXXXXXXXX@gmail.com>
3.   RUN apk add --no-cache curl tar bash procps
4.
5.   # Downloading and installing Maven
6.
7.   #1- Define a constant with the working directory
8.   ARG USER_HOME_DIR="/root"
9.
10.  #2 - Define the URL where maven can be downloaded from
11.  ARG        MVN_DOWNLOAD_URL=http://apachemirror.wuchna.com/maven/
     maven-3/3.6.3/binaries/apache-maven-3.6.3-bin.tar.gz
12.
13.  #3- Define the SHA key to validate the maven download: https://
     downloads.apache.org/maven/maven-3/3.6.3/binaries/apache-
     maven-3.6.3-bin.tar.gz.sha512
14.  ARG SHA=c35a1803a6e70a126e80b2b3ae33eed961f83ed74d18fc
     d16909b2d44d7d ada3203f1ffe726c17ef8dcca2
     dcaa9fca676987befeadc9b9f 759967a8cb77181c0
15.
16.  #4- Create the directories, download maven, validate the download,
     install it, remove the downloaded file and set links
17.  RUN mkdir -p /usr/share/maven /usr/share/maven/ref \
18.      && echo "Downlaoding apache-maven-3.6.3" \
19.      && curl -fsSL -o /tmp/apache-maven.tar.gz ${MVN_DOWNLOAD_URL}
     \
20.      \
21.      && echo "Checking download hash" \
22.      && echo "${SHA}  /tmp/apache-maven.tar.gz" | sha512sum -c - \
23.      \
24.      && echo "Unziping maven" \
25.       && tar -xzf /tmp/apache-maven.tar.gz -C /usr/share/maven
     --strip-components=1 \
26.      \
27.      && echo "Cleaning and setting links" \
28.      && rm -f /tmp/apache-maven.tar.gz \
```

29.   && ln -s /usr/share/maven/bin/mvn /usr/bin/mvn
30.
31.   #5- Define environmental variables required by Maven, like Maven_
        Home directory and where the maven repo is located
32.   ENV MAVEN_HOME /usr/share/maven
33.   ENV MAVEN_CONFIG "$USER_HOME_DIR/.m2"
34.
35.   CMD [""]

Execute sudo docker build. -t jdk/maven to create an image. Verify images using Docker images:

```
REPOSITORY        TAG            IMAGE ID          CREATED            SIZE

jdk/maven         latest         346639f08caf      41 seconds ago     122MB

jenkinsci/blueocean latest       c4239db11ad3      9 hours ago        562MB
```

Create a container from the image using the following command:

```
docker container run -d -t jdk/maven bash

9552b99ca6d7f81f5c91299e308de2583c3888807a311440d79ede0810eb3846

#####################
```

Get the container ID using the docker ps -a command:

```
CONTAINER ID    IMAGE        COMMAND     CREATED        STATUS         PORTS
9552b99ca6d7    jdk/maven    "bash"      About a minute ago    Up
About a minute

9de0daae3a38            jenkinsci/blueocean    "/sbin/tini -- /usr/…"
4 hours ago             Up 4 hours             0.0.0.0:8080->8080/tcp,
0.0.0.0:50000->50000/tcp
```

Execute the command in the container using the docker exec -it 9552b99ca6d7 bash command:

```
bash-4.4# mvn -version
Apache Maven 3.6.3 (cecedd343002696d0abb50b32b541b8a6ba2883f)
Maven home: /usr/share/maven
Java version: 1.8.0_212, vendor: IcedTea, runtime: /usr/lib/jvm/
java-1.8-openjdk/jre
Default locale: en_US, platform encoding: UTF-8
OS name: "linux", version: "3.10.0-1127.10.1.el7.x86_64", arch:
"amd64", family: "unix"
```

In the next section, we will discuss security.

Always secure Jenkins

This best practice is about authentication and authorization of users and enforcing access control. Security is an integral part of DevOps practices. In Jenkins, there are multiple ways available to configure Jenkins securely. We can configure authentication and authorization using multiple tools such as Azure AD, OpenLDAP, etc. We can configure authorization at a global level as well as the project level as well.

In the upcoming section, we will configure authentication, authorization, and other options to secure the Jenkins setup.

Jenkins integration with Azure Active Directory (Azure AD)

What if you want to authenticate Jenkins using Azure Active Directory to manage users effectively and maintain control and governance? The Azure AD plugin provides features to set up authentication and authorization via Microsoft Azure Active Directory. Let's integrate Jenkins and Azure AD:

1. Go to **Manage Jenkins | Manage Plugins | Available | Search Azure AD** and click on install without a restart:

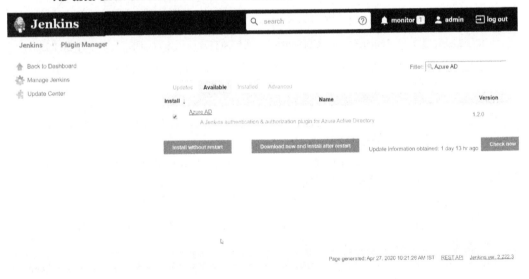

Figure 11.16: Azure AD Plugin

2. Next, set up Azure AD so we can integrate details in Jenkins so that both can communicate.

3. Go to the Microsoft Azure Portal that is available at **http://portal.azure.com/**. Search Azure Active Directory and click on **App registrations**, then click on **New registration**:

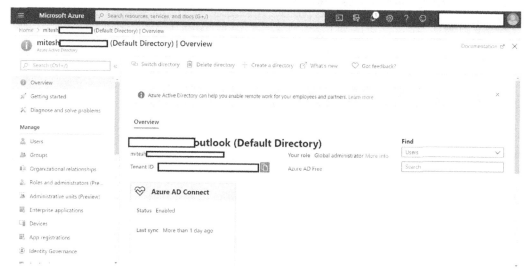

Figure 11.17: Azure AD

4. Click on **New Registration**.
5. Give a user-facing display name.
6. Select **Accounts** in this organizational directory only (xxxxxxxxxxoutlook **(Default Directory)** only - Single-tenant).
7. Click on **Register**.

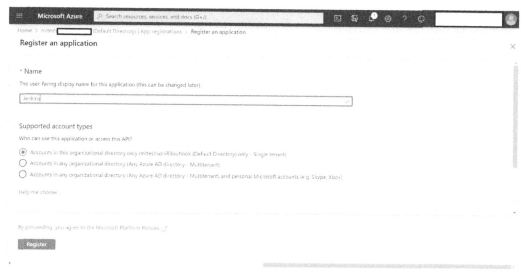

Figure 11.18: Register an application

8. Note down the Application/Client ID and Directory/Tenant ID. These values will be useful in Jenkins to configure Azure AD related details in the **Global Security Configuration** settings.

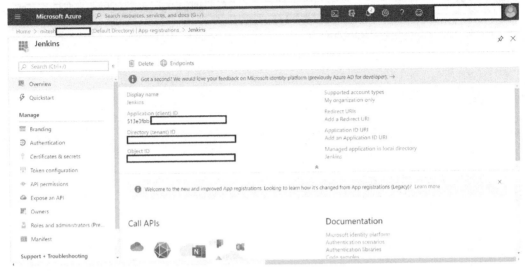

Figure 11.19: Tenant and Client ID

9. Go to **Certificates & secrets** in the application that we created in Azure AD.

10. Create a **New client secret** to configure it in Jenkins so that the identity of the application can be proven.

11. Click on **New client secret**:

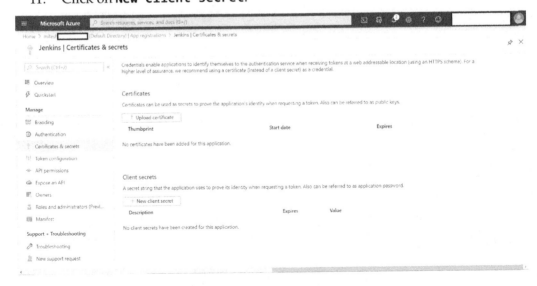

Figure 11.20: Certificates & secrets

12. Provide a name and duration and click on **Add**:

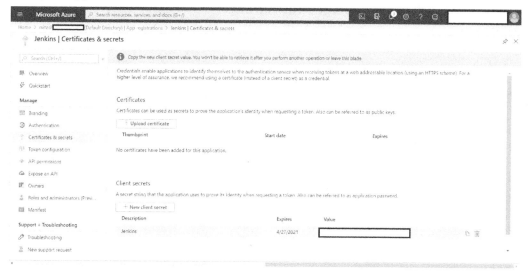

Figure 11.21: *Add a Client secret*

13. Copy the client secret value. It won't be available for access the next time.

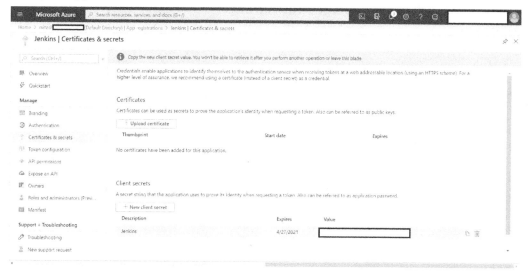

Figure 11.22: *New client secret*

14. Go to **Authentication** and click on **Add Platform**.

15. We are trying to access the web application so click on **Web**:

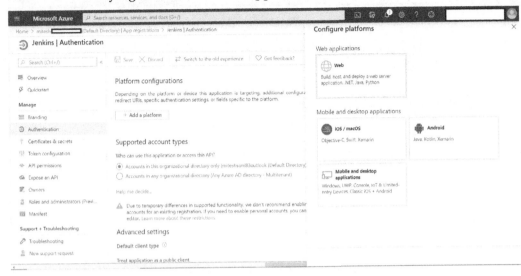

Figure 11.23: Web Platform

16. Provide **Redirect URI** and click on **Save**:

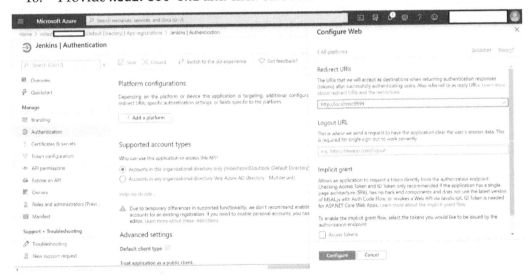

Figure 11.24: Redirect URIs in Web Platform

17. Verify the Redirect URIs:

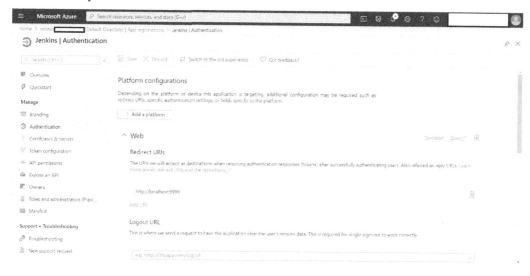

Figure 11.25: Platform configuration

18. Go to API permissions, and add the following permissions:

1. `Microsoft Graph: Directory.Read.All / Delegated`
2. `Microsoft Graph: Directory.Read.All / Application`
3. `Microsoft Graph: User.Read / Delegated`

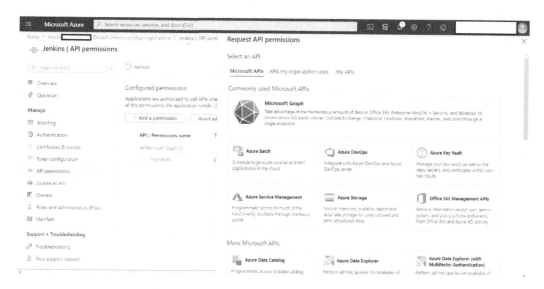

Figure 11.26: API Permissions - Microsoft Graph

19. Go to API permissions, and add the following permissions:

```
1.  Azure Active Directory Graph: Directory.Read.All / Delegated
2.  Azure Active Directory Graph: Directory.Read.All / Application
3.  Azure Active Directory Graph: User.Read / Delegated
```

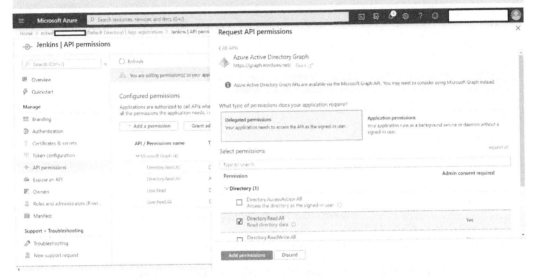

Figure 11.27: API Permissions - Azure AD Graph

20. Verify all the permissions:

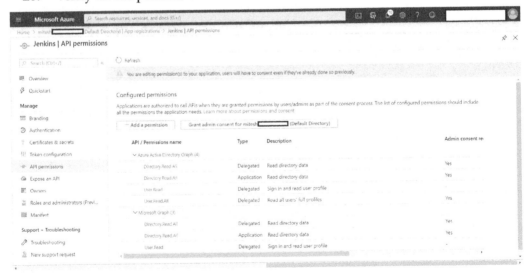

Figure 11.28: Configured Permissions

21. Grant Permissions to accounts:

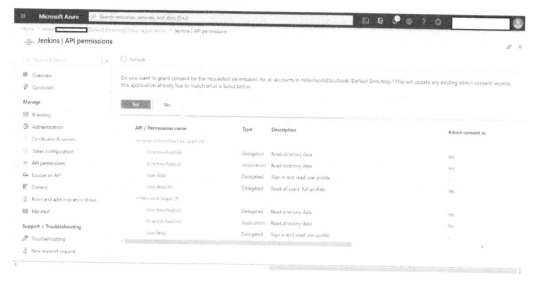

Figure 11.29: API Permissions

22. Permission is granted successfully:

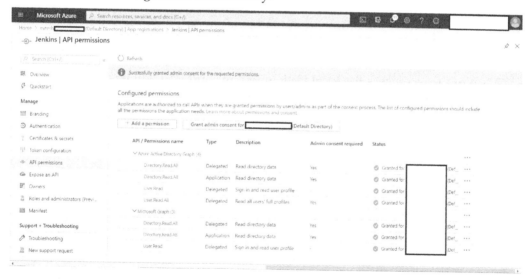

Figure 11.30: Admin Consent

23. Once we have all the configuration and information available, go to **Manage Jenkins | Global Security Configuration | Security Realm**. Click on **Azure Active Directory**.

24. Configure values for **Client ID, Tenant ID**, and **Client secret** that we noted earlier.

NOTE

Opportunity in test automation: Unit test automation, function test automation, performance test automation, and security test automation.

25. Click on verify the application.

26. Click on **Save**:

Figure 11.31: Global Security Configuration

27. Now, try to access the local URL of Jenkins and you will be redirected to the Azure login page where you can try to log in with the existing user available in Azure AD of your subscription:

Figure 11.32: Microsoft Azure Login

28. In the first attempt to log in, you may be asked to change the password:

Figure 11.33: Password

29. Oops! It is not working. The URL specified in **Redirect URI** is not valid it seems.

Figure 11.34: Signing issues

30. Modify the existing URI with **http://localhost:9999/securityRealm/finishLogin**.

31. Click on **Save**:

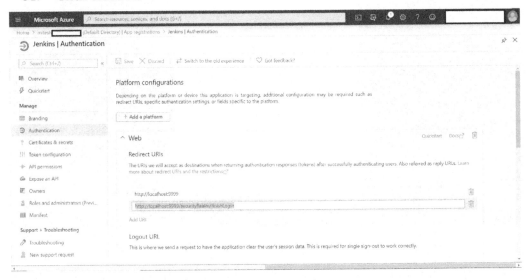

Figure 11.35: Redirect URIs

32. Try to log in again and now you will be redirected to the Jenkins page but now you will get **Access Denied**:

Figure 11.36: Jenkins Access Issues

33. Disable the login in Jenkins by making a change in the tag `<useSecurity>true</useSecurity>` to `<useSecurity> </useSecurity>` false in config.xml in Jenkins home.

34. Start Jenkins again, go to **Authorization** in **Global Security Configuration** in **Manage Jenkins**, and add the user and provide access rights:

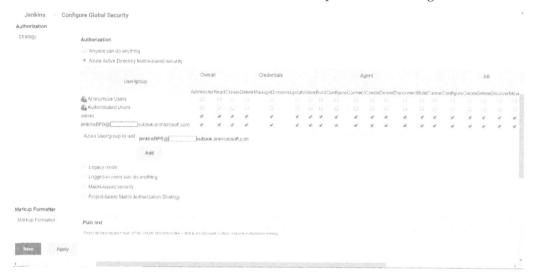

Figure 11.37: Authorization

35. Try to log in again:

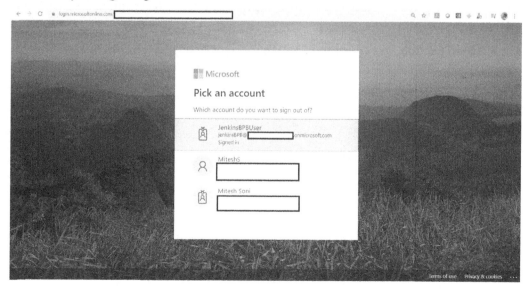

Figure 11.38: Login

Bingo! Now, you can log in using Azure AD credentials in Jenkins and manage users directly in Azure AD and not at the Jenkins' level:

Figure 11.39: Successful Login using Azure AD

In the next section, we will configure the project-based security.

Project-based security

Jenkins authentication and authorization are good but what if we want to provide security at the project or job level? How to provide access to certain users in specific jobs or pipelines only?

Go to **Specific job** and check the **Enable project-based security** checkbox:

Figure 11.40: Project-based security

NOTE

DevOps helps to gain competitive advantage, high-quality outcome, and faster time to market that result in happy customers and happy employees.

Jenkins also publishes security advisories. Visit **https://www.jenkins.io/security/ advisories/**.

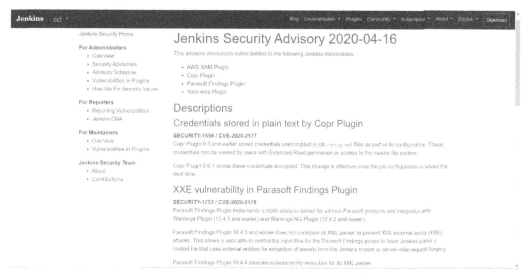

Figure 11.41: Security advisories

In the next section, we will discuss the *Backup and Restore* plugin available in Jenkins.

Backup and restore

Backup and restore is an important activity in Jenkins management and maintenance. Consider a scenario where you need to migrate to the Jenkins setup from one system to another system due to a lack of resources in the existing system. One way is to copy the entire Jenkins Home directory and keep the backup for multiple days and perform manually or using a script.

Another way is to use the ThinBackup plugin.

Let's see how the ThinBackup plugin works:

1. Install **Plugins** from the **Manage Plugins** section available in **Manage Jenkins**:

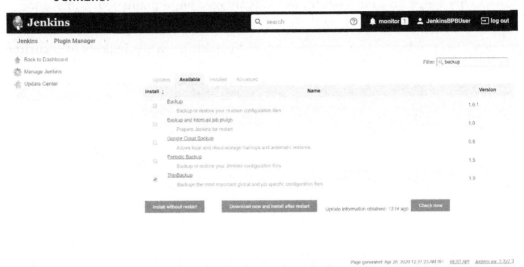

Figure 11.42: Thin Backup Plugin

2. Go to **Manage Jenkins | ThinBackup**. Click on **Settings**:

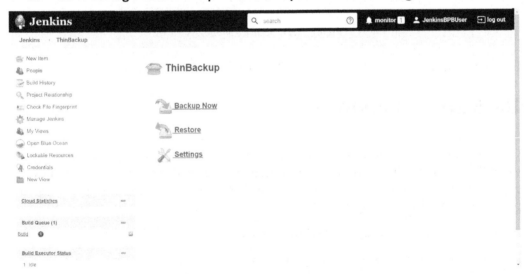

Figure 11.43: Thin Backup

3. Configure the backup directory, backup schedule for full and incremental backup as per your needs:

Figure 11.44: Thin Backup configuration

4. Click on **Backup Now**.

5. Go to restore and verify multiple list items based on a number of times you have taken the backup:

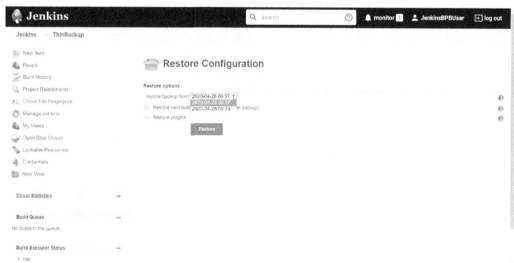

Figure 11.45: Restore configuration

6. To check whether the backup and restore works as expected, change the JENKINS_HOME directory in **Environment variables** and restart Jenkins.

7. This means a fresh setup. Skip all plugin installations and go to the Jenkins Dashboard.

8. Go to **Manage Jenkins | Manage Plugins | Available** and install the **ThinBackup** plugin only:

Figure 11.46: New Jenkins setup - plugins

9. After successful installation, go to **Manage Jenkins | ThinBackup**. Click on **Settings**.

10. Configure **Backup Directory** which was configured earlier.

11. Go to **Restore** and verify if the same Backup list is available.

12. Click on **Restore**:

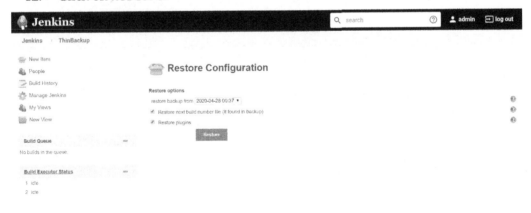

Figure 11.47: Restore Configuration

TIP

The following are some important tips while taking the backup:

1. Don't upgrade any incompatible Plugin. It might break the setup.

2. In the production support, upgrade plugins one by one and verify before proceeding ahead.

3. Take the backup of JENKINS_HOME manually as well at a certain interval.

4. The server snapshot can be helpful if there is no point of return.

5. Simulate failure and practice the backup and restore process multiple times.

13. The restoration activity will take time. Make sure that you are connected to the internet so that plugins are also installed based on the backup.

14. Verify the following console log in Jenkins:

1. .

2. .

3. .

4. .

5. ```
2020-04-27 19:42:59.700+0000 [id=108]   INFO   h.model.
UpdateCenter$DownloadJob#run: Starting the installation of
branch-api on behalf of admin
```

6. ```
2020-04-27   19:42:59.700+0000   [id=108]              INFO
h.m.UpdateCenter$InstallationJob#_run: Skipping duplicate
install of: Branch API@2.5.6
```

7. ```
2020-04-27 19:42:59.700+0000 [id=108]   INFO   h.model.
UpdateCenter$DownloadJob#run: Installation   successful:
branch-api
```

8. ```
2020-04-27 19:42:59.700+0000 [id=108]    INFO    h.model.
UpdateCenter$DownloadJob#run: Starting the installation of
workflow-api on behalf of admin
```

9. ```
2020-04-27   19:42:59.700+0000   [id=108]   INFO
h.m.UpdateCenter$InstallationJob#_run: Skipping duplicate
install of: pipeline: API@2.40
```

10. ```
2020-04-27 19:42:59.708+0000 [id=108]    INFO    h.model.
UpdateCenter$DownloadJob#run:    Installation    successful:
workflow-api
```

11. ```
2020-04-27 19:42:59.718+0000 [id=108]   INFO   h.model.
UpdateCenter$DownloadJob#run: Starting the installation of
pubsub-light on behalf of admin
```
```

```
12.  2020-04-27    19:42:59.719+0000    [id=108]              INFO
     h.m.UpdateCenter$InstallationJob#_run: Skipping duplicate
     install of: Pub-Sub "light" Bus@1.13
13.  2020-04-27 19:42:59.720+0000 [id=108]    INFO    h.model.
     UpdateCenter$DownloadJob#run:    Installation    successful:
     pubsub-light
14.  2020-04-27    19:42:59.838+0000    [id=18]               INFO
     o.j.h.p.t.ThinBackupMgmtLink#doRestore: Restore finished.
```

pipeline

Once the Restore activity is finished, verify if all plugins and jobs are available as it was earlier in the original JENKINS_HOME directory.

Figure 11.48: Jenkins Dashboard

In the next section, we will discuss Monitoring.

Monitoring

On the Jenkins Dashboard, there are three notifications. Let's verify and fix them:

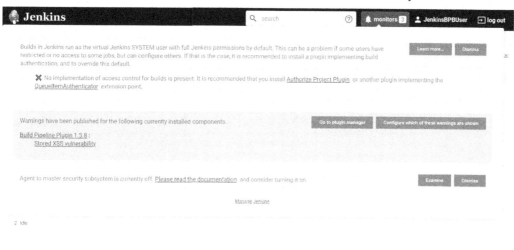

Figure 11.49: Jenkins Monitoring

1. Go to **Manage Jenkins** and verify the messages available at the top. We have enabled the project-based security in the **Security** section in this chapter. The access control is still not configured:

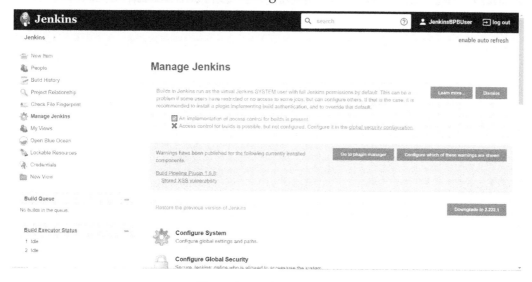

Figure 11.50: Manage Jenkins

2. To configure **Agent Controller security**, go to **Manage Jenkins | Global Security Configuration**.

3. Configure **Random as TCP Port** for an inbound agent.

4. Enable **Agent Controller Access Control**:

Figure 11.51: Agent Controller Security

5. Go to **Manage Jenkins | Manage Plugins | Available** and install the **Authorize Project** plugin:

Figure 11.52: Authorize Project Plugins

6. Go to **Manage Jenkins | Global Security Configuration**.

7. A new section called **Access Control for Builds** is available.

8. Configure the **Strategy** and click on **Save**.

Figure 11.53: *Access Controls for Builds*

In the next section, we will discuss the Jenkins configuration-related practices.

Tools configuration

It is important to understand how to configure tools in Jenkins so we can utilize tools effectively without any changes in the existing pipelines.

Configure tools in the **Global Tools Configuration** section available in the **Manage Jenkins** section. If there is more than one version of the same tools, then configure tools based on the version with a generic name.

For example, to configure Java:

*   JDK 1.8
*   JDK 11
*   JDK 12

Don't configure the individual tool version based on the agent at a global level. But utilize the tools location section available in the Agent configuration. It will keep names common across agents and also manage different tools and their locations. A common mistake is to declare all tools from controllers and agents at a global level and that is not required.

Environment variables

Don't configure environment variables based on the agent at a global level. But utilize the environment variables section available in the Agent configuration. A common mistake is to declare all environment variables from controllers and agents at a global level and that is not required.

Pipeline

The following are some of the best practices while creating a pipeline or orchestration:

- Use Blue Ocean to create the Jenkinsfile and a multi-branch pipeline for its efficient usage.

- If the domain-specific language construct is not available, then use a script in the DSL to make the automation work.

- Combine commands in a single step or use a script file for multiple command execution.

- Avoid using a scripted pipeline as it has its learning curve and is not easy to understand.

- Use Blue Ocean and Snippet generator to generate the Jenkinsfile for the declarative pipeline quickly.

- Use the controller agent architecture in the pipeline and use multiple agents for execution so parallel execution is possible.

Conclusion

Jenkins best practices have evolved and it will continue to evolve in the future based on technical aspects as well as user experience is concerned. The controller agent architecture helps to improve the overall build execution performance as well as it helps to manage and maintain the automation infrastructure with ease. We covered authentication and authorization concerning security in this chapter. Backup and restore is critically important the moment your Jenkins controller crashes and there is no backup available. Best practices help to increase the usage of Jenkins or any automation server to transform the existing culture of an organization and this is a continuous process.

Points to remember

- Agents can be physical systems, virtual machines, Docker containers, cloud-based virtual machines such as Amazon EC2, Azure Virtual machines, and so on.

- Multiple agents can serve to the controller and hence parallel execution is possible in the pipeline as multiple executors are also available.

- Labels in the Agent configuration help to balance load or make agents available for execution. It is a kind of a pool of agents available for service.

- The Azure AD plugin provides features to set up authentication and authorization via Microsoft Azure Active Directory.

- Jenkins Redirect URI for the web platform is URI with **http://localhost:9999/securityRealm/finishLogin**.

Multiple choice questions

1. **For load balancing, labels can be used in Jenkins while configuring the Controller Agent Architecture. State true or false.**

   a. True

   b. False

2. **It is compulsory to have an App Registration to integrate Jenkins with Azure AD. State true or false.**

   a. True

   b. False

3. **The client secret is not needed to configure in Jenkins to integrate Jenkins with Azure AD. State true or false.**

   a. True

   b. False

4. **The web platform configuration is a must to integrate Jenkins with Azure AD. State true or false.**

   a. True

   b. False

5. **Which is the correct Redirect URI of Jenkins that needs to be configured in Azure Active Directory?**

   a. **http://localhost:9999**

   b. **http://localhost:9999/securityRealm/finishLogin**

6. **The following permissions are required to integrate Jenkins with Azure AD. State true or false.**

   ```
   1.  Microsoft Graph: Directory.Read.All / Delegated
   2.  Microsoft Graph: Directory.Read.All / Application
   ```

```
3.  Microsoft Graph: User.Read / Delegated
4.  Azure Active Directory Graph: Directory.Read.All / Delegated
5.  Azure Active Directory Graph: Directory.Read.All / Application
6.  Azure Active Directory Graph: User.Read / Delegated
```

   a. True

   b. False

7. **Client ID, Tenant ID, and Client secret are three values from Microsoft Azure that need to be configured in Jenkins. State true or false.**

   a. True

   b. False

8. **To disable the login in Jenkins, change <useSecurity>true</useSecurity> to <useSecurity> </useSecurity> false in config.xml. State true or false.**

   a. True

   b. False

Answers

1. a
2. a
3. b
4. a
5. b
6. a
7. a
8. a

Questions

1. What is Azure Active Directory?

2. What is authentication?

3. What is authorization?

4. What is the distributed architecture?

Index

Ziyad
and
Akil.

Iniya
and
Akil

Made in the USA
Middletown, DE
01 October 2021